Marx's *Grundrisse*

BLOOMSBURY READER'S GUIDES

Titles available in this series

Aristotle's 'Politics': A Reader's Guide, Judith A. Swanson
Badiou's 'Being and Event': A Reader's Guide, Christopher Norris
Berkeley's 'Principles of Human Knowledge': A Reader's Guide, Alasdair Richmond
Deleuze's 'Difference and Repetition': A Reader's Guide, Joe Hughes
Deleuze and Guattari's 'A Thousand Plateaus': A Reader's Guide, Eugene W. Holland
Deleuze and Guattari's 'What is Philosophy': A Reader's Guide, Rex Butler
Descartes' 'Meditations': A Reader's Guide, Richard Francks
Hegel's 'Phenomenology of Spirit': A Reader's Guide, Stephen Houlgate
Heidegger's 'Being and Time': A Reader's Guide, William Blattner
Hobbes's 'Leviathan': A Reader's Guide, Laurie M. Johnson Bagby
Kant's 'Critique of Aesthetic Judgement': A Reader's Guide, Fiona Hughes
Kierkegaard's 'Fear and Trembling': A Reader's Guide, Clare Carlisle
Levinas' 'Totality and Infinity': A Reader's Guide, William Large
Locke's 'Second Treatise of Government': A Reader's Guide, Paul Kelly
Marx and Engels' 'Communist Manifesto': A Reader's Guide, Peter Lamb
Nietzsche's 'Beyond Good and Evil': A Reader's Guide, Christa Davis Acampora and Keith Ansell Pearson
Nietzsche's 'Thus Spoke Zarathustra': A Reader's Guide, Clancy Martin
Rousseau's 'The Social Contract': A Reader's Guide, Christopher Wraight
Spinoza's 'Ethics': A Reader's Guide, J. Thomas Cook
Wittgenstein's 'Philosophical Investigations': A Reader's Guide, Arif Ahmed
Wittgenstein's 'Tractatus Logico-Philosophicus': A Reader's Guide, Roger M. White

Forthcoming from Bloomsbury

Kant's 'Critique of Practical Reason': A Reader's Guide, Courtney D. Fugate

BLOOMSBURY READER'S GUIDES

Marx's *Grundrisse*

SIMON CHOAT

Bloomsbury Academic
An imprint of Bloomsbury Publishing Plc
B L O O M S B U R Y
LONDON • OXFORD • NEW YORK • NEW DELHI • SYDNEY

Bloomsbury Academic
An imprint of Bloomsbury Publishing Plc

50 Bedford Square	1385 Broadway
London	New York
WC1B 3DP	NY 10018
UK	USA

www.bloomsbury.com

BLOOMSBURY and the Diana logo are trademarks of Bloomsbury Publishing Plc

First published 2016

British Library Cataloguing-in-Publication Data
A catalogue record for this book is available from the British Library.

ISBN: HB: 9781472531902
PB: 9781472526748
ePDF: 9781472523112
ePub: 9781472534002

Library of Congress Cataloging-in-Publication Data
A catalog record for this book is available from the Library of Congress.

Series: Reader's Guides

Typeset by Fakenham Prepress Solutions, Fakenham, Norfolk NR21 8NN

For Liz.

CONTENTS

ACKNOWLEDGEMENTS

Several people have aided the writing of this book, either by reading and commenting on draft versions of the chapters or by discussing the *Grundrisse* with me. In particular, I would like to thank: John Grant, Julian Wells, Dave Tinham, John Spiers, Steve Keen, Judith Ryser, Daniel Fitzpatrick, Sam Halvorsen, Rick Saull, Bryan Mabee, and Jeff Webber. Only I am responsible for any errors in what follows.

Above all, I must thank Elizabeth Evans and, despite the fact that he actively hindered the completion of this book, William Choat.

ABBREVIATIONS

CW: Karl Marx and Frederick Engels (1975–2005) *Collected Works*, 50 vols. London: Lawrence & Wishart.

C1: Karl Marx (1976) *Capital: A Critique of Political Economy*, vol. 1, trans. Ben Fowkes. Harmondsworth: Penguin.

C2: Karl Marx (1978) *Capital: A Critique of Political Economy*, vol. 2, trans. David Fernbach. Harmondsworth: Penguin.

C3: Karl Marx (1981) *Capital: A Critique of Political Economy*, vol. 3, trans. David Fernbach. Harmondsworth: Penguin

PREFACE

This book is a guide in the sense that a map is a guide to a particular territory. In the same way that you would not sit and home and look at a map instead of going for a walk, it is not my intention that you read this book *instead* of Marx's *Grundrisse*: it should be read alongside the *Grundrisse* to help you get your bearings or should be consulted at times when you are feeling lost. As with any map (especially for a territory as large as the *Grundrisse*), not everything can be covered: the aim is not to reconstruct the *Grundrisse* but rather to guide you through its central concepts, claims and arguments.

The numbers in brackets in the text refer to page numbers in the Penguin edition of the *Grundrisse*:

> Karl Marx (1973) *Grundrisse: Foundations of the Critique of Political Economy (Rough Draft)*, trans. Martin Nicolaus. London: Penguin.

This edition has been used because it is the most widely read and also because it is available for free on the Marxists Internet Archive. I am grateful to Martin Nicolaus for permission to quote from his translation. Occasionally, I have modified the translation and this is marked by '*tm*'. My own insertions into quotations are marked 'SC' in text.

CHAPTER ONE

Context

The *Grundrisse* is the name given to the notebooks that Karl Marx wrote in London in 1857–8. Its full title in German is *Grundrisse der Kritik der Politischen Ökonomie (Rohentwurf)*, which is translated into English as *Foundations* (or *Outlines*) *of the Critique of Political Economy (Rough Draft)*. Written for purposes of self-clarification rather than publication, these dense and elliptical notebooks provide us with insights not only into Marx's theories, but also into his working method. For this reason they have been referred to as Marx's 'laboratory'.[1] It would be just as accurate, however, to call them a labyrinth: while logical and systematic, they also contain many dead ends, circular repetitions and confusing detours, and once you enter them you may regret having done so. In a letter of May 1858 to Friedrich Engels, Marx himself claimed that the manuscript on which he was working was 'a real hotch-potch' (*CW40*: 318). The *Grundrisse* is nonetheless one of Marx's most important and influential writings, and a knowledge of it is vital for an understanding of his work as a whole. To begin guiding ourselves through this labyrinth, it will be helpful to place the text in its biographical, intellectual, and political and economic context.

Biographical background

Marx was born in Trier, Prussia, in 1818. In 1835, he went to study Law at the University of Bonn and after one year transferred to the University of Berlin. It was here that Marx developed an interest in the philosophy of G. W. F. Hegel: as he wrote to his father in 1837, he 'got to know Hegel from beginning to end, together with most of his disciples' (*CW1*: 19). He also associated with and befriended some of those disciples, the so-called Young or Left Hegelians, who sought to develop Hegel's philosophy for progressive or radical ends. Marx finished his studies in 1841, submitting a thesis to the University of Jena, which earned him a doctorate. Thwarted in his ambition to become a university teacher, he became a writer and editor for various short-lived journals, while continuing to write and publish more philosophical works. It was at those journals that Marx first began to investigate economic questions. As he later put it: 'In the year 1842–43, as editor of the *Rheinische Zeitung*, I first found myself in the embarrassing position of having to discuss what is known as material interests' (*CW29*: 261–2). His writings of the early and mid-1840s show his political development from a Hegelian-inflected radical liberalism to revolutionary communism.

The *Rheinische Zeitung* was eventually suppressed and, in 1843, a recently married Marx moved to Paris to work for another journal; here he became friends with Engels. Increasingly involved in radical politics, in 1847 both men joined the Communist League, for whom they wrote the *Communist Manifesto*, published in 1848 while revolutions swept across Europe. Ultimately those revolutions failed and Europe faced a counter-revolutionary wave of violent oppression. Marx was expelled from several European cities until, in 1849, he settled in London, where he lived with his wife and children until his death in 1883.

Intellectual context

Lenin famously claimed that Marxism was 'the legitimate successor' to three currents of thought: 'German philosophy, English political economy and French socialism'.[2] The influence of each of these currents can be seen very clearly in the *Grundrisse*.

Hegel and dialectics

The German philosopher who most influenced Marx was undoubtedly Hegel. The nature and extent of Hegel's influence is, however, a continuing source of debate. It is agreed that Marx's early works draw heavily on Hegel, but it has been argued – most famously by Louis Althusser – that the mature Marx abandoned or rejected Hegel.[3] The *Grundrisse* must play an important role in this debate: clearly not an 'early' work, it is nonetheless saturated with Hegelian terminology. Precisely what it is that Marx takes from Hegel remains a matter of dispute, but it is evident from comments in both correspondence and published works that the mature Marx valued Hegel's dialectic, while nonetheless viewing it as deficient. In January 1858, while writing the *Grundrisse*, Marx wrote to Engels: 'If ever the time comes when such work is again possible, I should very much like to write 2 or 3 sheets making accessible to the common reader the *rational* aspect of the method which Hegel not only discovered but also mystified' (*CW40*: 249).

Some commentators think that we cannot really understand the *Grundrisse* without first understanding Hegel, especially his *Science of Logic*. I have some sympathy with that point of view, but it also raises problems: Hegel is a notoriously difficult philosopher, and fully understanding his *Logic* in particular could take several years of study. As such, if we insist that readers must understand Hegel before starting the *Grundrisse*, then it is going to severely restrict readership of the latter.

Nonetheless, it certainly helps to have an initial and basic knowledge of Hegel's dialectical method before we begin the *Grundrisse*. In contrast to analytical approaches, dialectics insists that nothing can be understood in itself or only in terms of its differences from other things: everything is part of a wider whole, and that whole must itself be understood as a *process*. The movement of this process can be viewed as a series of stages, with each stage understood in terms of its own limits or contradictions: each is in tension with itself, and in this sense it negates itself. As Marx puts in the 1873 Afterword to *Capital I*, the dialectic 'includes in its positive understanding of what exists a simultaneous recognition of its negation, its inevitable destruction' (*C1*: 103). While every state of affairs negates itself, this is a 'determinate negation', however: the result of the negation is not nothing, but a new stage which transcends the old stage while preserving some of its features. This simultaneous overcoming and conservation is termed by Hegel (and following him Marx) '*aufheben*'. As Hegel puts it in the *Science of Logic*, '*aufheben*', or 'to sublate', 'equally means "*to keep*," "to 'preserve'," and "to cause to cease," "*to put an end to*" [...] That which is sublated is thus something at the same time preserved'.[4] To this extent, Marx's own engagement with Hegel is itself dialectical, simultaneously negating and preserving aspects of Hegel's work.

When Hegel claims that the dialectic must be understood as 'grasping opposites in their unity, or the positive in the negative', therefore, we should understand those 'opposites' as mutually constitutive and productive contradictions.[5] In identifying contradictions, the dialectician presents himself as the demystifier of appearances, and to that extent dialectics necessarily involves a distinction between appearance and essence, or form and content. As Marx states in *Capital III*, 'all science would be superfluous if the form of appearance of things directly coincided with their essence' (*C3*: 956). But the job of dialectics is not to demolish that which is merely apparent in order to reveal some essential core. This is because, first, the forms of appearance themselves are necessary and real, so the aim is to show why an essence assumes a certain form of appearance. Second, the essences that we are interested in are not unchanging things but the relations that make up a whole.

This necessarily abbreviated and simplified summary of the dialectical method is likely to seem highly abstract (as indeed it is in Hegel's work). One of the many merits of Marx's work is that it shows how these abstract claims and concepts can be put to work. We will see that in the *Grundrisse* Marx presents capital as a process that can only be understood by moving beyond the appearances of exchange relations to reach the relations of production. Capital is a unity of opposites, full of contradictions – between, for instance, production and circulation – that drive the capitalist mode of production towards its dissolution or sublation.

Marx himself emphasized the differences between his dialectic and that of Hegel: whereas he was a materialist, Hegel was an idealist (*CW42*: 544). Where Hegel (according, at least, to Marx) understands history as the movement of ideas or forms of consciousness, Marx sees it as the movement of forms of material production: ideas are a product and reflection of the material conditions from which they emerge. Hence his claim in the 1873 Afterword to *Capital I* that with Hegel the dialectic 'is standing on its head. It must be inverted, in order to discover the rational kernel within the mystical shell' (*C1*: 103). As Marx put it in 1859: 'It is not the consciousness of men that determines their existence, but their social existence that determines their consciousness' (*CW29*: 263). In order to investigate the forms of our social existence, Marx had to engage with political economy, in particular the works of Adam Smith and David Ricardo.

Political economy

While its roots can be traced back to ancient Greece, the study of political economy really began in the seventeenth century, as an attempt to explain the growth of wealth that occurred as feudalism declined and trade and commerce increased. Adam Smith saw this emerging 'commercial society' as both productive of and based upon individual freedom: in *The Wealth of Nations* (1776), he argued that the market was a natural development ruled by 'an invisible hand' and which should, as far as possible, be freed from the artificial restrictions imposed by government.[6] Marx thus saw political economists such as Smith as apologists for capitalism.[7] Nevertheless, he respected their work, though he always distinguished between classical political economy – beginning with William Petty and reaching a high point with Smith and, especially, Ricardo – from the post-Ricardian 'vulgar economists' whom he viewed as little more than spokesmen for bourgeois society (*C1*: 174–5n.).

Marx's first real engagement with political economy began in Paris in 1844.[8] He undertook an immanent critique of political economy, undermining it from within by turning its premises against its own conclusions. He argued that the problem with political economy is that 'it takes for granted what it is supposed to explain'. In particular, it assumes that capitalism is natural and eternal: for example, it 'starts with the fact of private property; it does not explain it to us' (*CW3*: 271, 270).

It was not really until 1845, however, with *The German Ideology*, that Marx began to formulate his own economic categories.[9] The target of *The German Ideology* is the Young Hegelians rather than the political economists, but in criticizing the idealism of the former Marx develops what is called (though not by Marx himself) 'the materialist conception of history' or 'historical materialism'. Marx is a materialist because he argues that if we are to understand human history we must start not (as do

Hegel and his followers) with forms of consciousness or the ideas that we have about ourselves, but with the ways in which humans produce and reproduce their conditions of life. He is a *historical* materialist because he further argues that our 'mode of production' changes through history (for example, from slavery to feudalism to capitalism). Each mode of production has its own distinctive forces of production (the activity of production and its tools and technology) and social relations. For most of human history, the latter have been class relations: each society is dominated by a ruling class which owns and controls the means of production. In *The German Ideology* the emphasis is firmly on the forces of production as the motor of historical change: as those forces develop they come into conflict with the social relations, leading to a period of social revolution that ushers in new relations.

Broadly speaking, this historical-materialist approach is retained and used by Marx for the rest of his working life. Its central arguments are reiterated in abbreviated form, for instance, in the 'Preface' to *A Contribution to the Critique of Political Economy*, a volume published in 1859 and based upon sections of the *Grundrisse*. What is missing in *The German Ideology*, however, is any serious consideration of *value*, which is perhaps the central concept of the *Grundrisse* and all of Marx's subsequent economic works. His theory of value was developed through a careful critical reading of the classical political economists.

Early political economy had been dominated by the doctrines of mercantilism, which identified wealth with money (primarily gold). A vociferous critic of mercantilism, Smith argued that 'wealth does not consist in money, or in gold and silver; but in what money purchases'.[10] Money simply facilitates the exchange of commodities. But what then determines the value of the commodities exchanged? In a distinction later adopted and modified by Marx, Smith distinguishes between 'value in use' – the utility that an object has for us – and 'value in exchange' – the power it has for purchasing other commodities. For example, nothing is more useful than water, but it has little value in exchange, whereas a diamond is of little use but has enormous value in exchange. So what determines value in exchange? At first Smith seems unequivocally committed to a *labour theory of value*: labour 'is alone the ultimate and real standard by which the value of all commodities can at all times and places be estimated and compared'.[11] In Smith's example: if it takes twice as long to hunt and kill a beaver than a deer, then one beaver has the value of two deer. Labour thus determines the value or 'natural price' of a commodity, while its market price (the actual price for which it is sold) will vary according to supply and demand.

Later in *The Wealth of Nations*, however, Smith argued that labour determines value only in early societies. In civilized society, in which stock has been accumulated and land appropriated, the natural price for which a commodity is exchanged must pay not only the wages of the labourer, but also the profits of the owner of stock and the rent of the landlord – so the value of the commodity is determined by these three factors.[12]

But, *pace* Smith, just because profits and rent as well as wages have to be paid out of the price of the commodity, this does not mean that profits and rent must determine that price. As Marx puts it in a critique of Smith: 'The relation between the labour time contained in commodities A and B is in no way affected by how the labour time contained in A and B is appropriated by various persons' (*CW30*: 380–1). The confusions in Smith's account of value were highlighted by David Ricardo, who in contrast consistently affirmed the labour theory of value and its applicability in all societies: 'The value of a commodity, or the quantity of any other commodity for which it will exchange, depends on the relative quantity of labour which is necessary for its production.'[13] So, whereas for Smith a rise in wages would entail a rise in the price of commodities – because the price of commodities is for Smith determined by the wages of the labourer and the 'wages' of the capitalist and landlord – for Ricardo '[n]o alteration in the wages of labour could produce any alteration in the relative value of [...] commodities': only an increased quantity of labour could cause the value of a commodity to rise.[14] Ricardo does agree with Smith that profits and wages must be paid for out of the price of commodities – but given that rising wages will not increase the value of the commodity, they must instead be paid for by a fall in profits. Hence for Ricardo '[t]here can be no rise in the value of labour without a fall of profits'.[15]

This is what Marx appreciates about Ricardo in particular: as well as consistently affirming the labour theory of value, Ricardo shifts the focus of political economy from the *causes* of wealth to its *distribution*.[16] Given that he posits an inverse relationship between wages and profits, in Marx's terms Ricardo 'exposes and describes the economic antagonism of classes' (*CW31*: 392). As we will see in Chapters 2 and 3, however, Marx does not simply adopt Ricardo's theory of value, and he finds numerous confusions and contradictions in his work. Marx undertakes a *critique* of political economy, at least in part by applying to it the insights of dialectics: for Marx, capitalism is a historically specific and contradictory mode of production, whose contradictions will lead ultimately to its destruction. In contrast, 'Ricardo regards bourgeois, or more precisely, capitalist production as the *absolute form* of production' (*CW32*: 247). As such, and as we will see in Chapter 3, when Ricardo finds limits to production he must characterize them as 'natural' limits rather than recognizing them as the limits of *capitalist* production (see in particular 'Falling rate of profit' in Chapter 3).

Marx nonetheless found much to praise in Ricardo's work, as did other nineteenth-century socialist critics of capitalism, whose work forms a third influence on Marx.

Socialism

Ricardo affirmed labour as the ultimate source of value. But if labour is the source of value, then why is it that the labourer himself does not receive the full value of the product that he makes, with some of that value instead going to the capitalist and the landlord? This was the question asked in the 1820s and 1830s by several radical British economists, often grouped together under the label 'the Ricardian socialists'. Viewing the extraction of profits as a form of exploitation, the Ricardian socialists sought to remedy this injustice done to the worker: though the details of their specific proposals varied, ultimately they all argued for a fair system of exchange in which the immediate producers of commodities would exchange commodities of equal value.

Marx found various confusions in the works of the Ricardian socialists, but his basic objection was that they did not understand that 'the form of exchange of products corresponds to the form of production': the 'fair' exchange relations that they desired could only be implemented on the basis of entirely different relations of production (relations which would not require individual exchange at all!) (*CW6*: 143). We will see Marx make this point repeatedly in the *Grundrisse*: the root of capitalist exploitation is not an unequal exchange between capital and labour, but rather the relations of production which underlie exchange relations. As Engels later put it, socialism before Marx 'certainly criticised the existing capitalistic mode of production and its consequences. But it could not explain them, and, therefore, could not get the mastery of them. It could only simply reject them as bad' (*CW24*: 305).

Marx nonetheless respected the Ricardian socialists: there are favourable references to their work in the *Grundrisse*, and he may even have been influenced by their ideas.[17] Despite this, the explicit references to socialism in the *Grundrisse* are relentlessly hostile. Yet Marx's real target is not the Ricardian socialists but the French socialist Jean-Pierre Proudhon. The young Marx had admired Proudhon, but he broke with him in *The Poverty of Philosophy* (1847), a polemic with a title that is a play on Proudhon's *The Philosophy of Poverty* (1846). In *The Poverty of Philosophy*, the three currents of thought that we have been discussing come together: Marx first uses Ricardo to attack Proudhon's socialism, and then mocks Proudhon for his use of Hegel. According to Marx, Proudhon reduces the Hegelian dialectic to 'the most paltry proportions', using it to try to account for the movement or development of economic categories and ideas without understanding that the '[e]conomic categories are only the theoretical expressions, the abstractions of the social relations of production' (*CW6*: 165).

In 1847, however, Marx's own ideas were still relatively undeveloped: for example, he makes almost no criticisms of Ricardo in *The Poverty of Philosophy*. It is not until the 1850s, with the writing of the *Grundrisse*, that his mature economic theory emerges.

Political and economic context

The 1850s were not an easy time for Marx, personally or politically. While living in London, he suffered from poverty and ill health and as a political refugee he found himself under surveillance by police spies. Radical politics had been in retreat all across Europe in the wake of 1848, and in 1852 the Communist League was dissolved. Marx became convinced that a '*new revolution is possible only in consequence of a new* [economic – SC] *crisis*' and he retreated to the reading room of the British Museum to study the political economists (*CW10*: 135). The main outlet for his political activity in the 1850s was journalism, predominantly for the *New York Tribune*, one of the largest newspapers in the USA at the time. This was work which Marx did not always enjoy: in 1853, he wrote to a correspondent that 'I find perpetual hackwork for the newspapers tiresome. It is time-consuming, distracting and, in the end, amounts to very little' (*CW39*: 367).

In 1857, Marx's revolutionary hopes were reignited. A banking crisis, which began in New York City in the summer of 1857, triggered a severe economic crisis that quickly spread across the world and which Marx saw as the best opportunity for revolutionary agitation since 1848. Ultimately his hopes were unfulfilled – by early 1858 it was clear that the global economy was in recovery – but the crisis inspired an exceptionally productive burst of intellectual activity. In December 1857, he wrote to Engels: 'I am working like mad all night and every night collating my economic studies so that I at least get the outlines ['*Grundrisse*' – SC] clear before the *déluge*' (*CW40*: 217). In letters to both Engels and their acquaintance Ferdinand Lassalle, Marx declared that he was working on two projects (*CW40*: 224, 226). First, 'something on the present crisis', at that time consisting of newspaper articles, mainly for the *New York Tribune*, and notebooks full of related reports and statistics, potentially to be formed into a pamphlet (which never actually appeared).[18] Second, he was '[e]laborating the outlines of political economy'. The latter, of course, were the manuscripts that were posthumously published as the *Grundrisse*.

The *Grundrisse* and the critique of political economy

Although it certainly acted as encouragement and impetus, the economic crisis alone cannot explain why Marx began to write the *Grundrisse* in 1857.[19] The crisis coincided with something of a breakthrough in Marx's intellectual labours. As he wrote to Lassalle in February 1858, 'I am at last ready to set to work after 15 years of study' (*CW40*: 271). Instead of viewing the *Grundrisse* as the culmination or finale of those fifteen years of study, however, we must see it as the inauguration of an ambitious new project on political economy.[20] In the same letter to Lassalle, Marx sketched out a plan for a three-volume work, which was to contain: a critique of economic categories; a critique and history of political economy and socialism; and a historical outline of the development of economic categories and relations (*CW*40: 270). The first volume was to be divided into six books:

1. Capital
2. Landed property
3. Wage labour
4. The state
5. International trade
6. The world market

Over the next decade, this plan went through various permutations (some of which can be found in the *Grundrisse* itself: see 'Method of political economy' in Chapter 3). Marx himself confirmed a significant shift in 1865: in July of that year, he wrote to Engels indicating that the three-volume work had mutated into a four-book work (*CW*42: 173). A letter of October 1866 details this new plan (*CW*42: 328):

Book I. Process of Production of Capital
Book II. Process of Circulation of Capital
Book III. Structure of the Process as a Whole
Book IV. History of the Theory

What happened to the final five books of the first volume from the original plan (i.e. from landed property to the world market) is a matter of debate. It could be that Marx decided they were unnecessary or that he was unable to finish them or that they were absorbed in some way into the new plan.[21] Whichever way, this new plan anticipates the four volumes of *Capital* that were eventually published (that is, *Capital I-III* plus *Theories of Surplus-Value*, known as the fourth volume of *Capital*). Yet only *Capital I* was published during Marx's lifetime (in 1867, followed by revised editions). The other three volumes were only published after Marx's death and were compiled from various manuscripts written by Marx in the 1860s and 1870s.

In other words, the works that Marx published in his own lifetime – and even those that were edited and published after his death – may have formed only a tiny fraction of his intended output, though even that is hard to judge, given that those intentions seemed to keep changing.

So, where does the *Grundrisse* fit into all of this? Given that the project beginning in 1857 ultimately culminates in *Capital*, the *Grundrisse* can be seen as the first draft of *Capital*. As such, it can be useful to read the former from the perspective of the latter and doing so can help clear up many confusions and errors in the *Grundrisse*. As we will see, this approach echoes Marx's own approach to understanding history: starting with more developed forms can illuminate the earlier forms from which they have developed (see 'Method of political economy' in Chapter 3).[22] Yet we should be careful to avoid teleology: the *Grundrisse* is not simply the seed from which *Capital* will flower. There are many themes and ideas in the *Grundrisse* that cannot be found in later works, and it is in its own right a valuable resource, in many ways broader in scope than *Capital*. It may be reasonable to assume that if arguments or formulations present in the *Grundrisse* are changed or discarded by the time that Marx reaches *Capital*, this is because the earlier versions were inadequate and can safely be ignored. But, first, we should always remember that *Capital* itself was unfinished: even Marx's published writings were only ever works-in-progress. Second, we should not necessarily think that Marx was the best reader or interpreter of his own work. Third, even if there are inadequacies or mistakes in the *Grundrisse*, they nevertheless offer us valuable insights into the development of Marx's thought. Equally, however, we should not treat the *Grundrisse* – or any other of Marx's texts – as if it gives us the key to understanding Marx's work: there is no 'true' Marx, and ultimately how you read the *Grundrisse* will depend upon why you are reading it and what you want from it.

CHAPTER TWO

Overview of Themes

This chapter will survey some of the *Grundrisse*'s central concepts and arguments, explain the object and aims of Marx's analysis, and outline the structure of the text.

Central concepts and arguments

There are two main reasons for reading the *Grundrisse*. The first is that it aids our understanding of the development of Marx's thought. It is in the *Grundrisse* that we find the first elaboration of some of the key ideas of Marx's mature economic theory, including: the theory of surplus value and the distinction between absolute and relative surplus value; the claim that what the capitalist purchases is labour-*power* rather than simply labour; the division of capital into variable and constant capital and circulating and fixed capital; the distinction between surplus value and profit and the notions of the average rate of profit and the falling rate of profit. Although some of these ideas had appeared in germinal form in earlier works, their formulation is far more advanced in the *Grundrisse*.

Because they are still being worked out, however, these ideas are often not very clearly delineated in the *Grundrisse*: concepts are put to use without being defined or are defined only in confused terms. For example, in places Marx seems to be juggling with different (and conflicting) definitions of circulating and fixed capital and he continues to write about 'labour' when he actually means 'labour-power'. Perhaps most importantly, the distinction between abstract and concrete labour – which Marx identified as one of the most important and novel features of *Capital I* – is only touched upon in the *Grundrisse* (see in particular 'Exchange between capital and labour' in Chapter 3) (*CW42*: 407, 514). Yet, while these confusions can make the *Grundrisse* a difficult read, they are also what make it valuable: they let us see how Marx develops his concepts and to what problems he is responding when he does so. As Marxist historian Eric Hobsbawm puts it, the *Grundrisse* allows us to 'follow Marx *while he is actually thinking*'.[1]

The second main reason for reading the *Grundrisse* is that it contains themes and arguments that cannot be found elsewhere in Marx's writings. Three sections in particular stand out: the 'Introduction', which contains Marx's most detailed and explicit discussion of methodology anywhere in his work; 'Forms which precede capitalist production', which analyses pre-capitalist modes of production; and the so-called 'Fragment on machines', which has been extremely influential in debates within Marxism and beyond. We shall look at the influence of these sections further in Chapter 4.

There are also several themes which, although they appear in other writings by Marx, are developed in an unusual or distinctive way in the *Grundrisse*, often reflecting the special significance of the text as a kind of halfway point between Marx's early and mature writings. For example, the concept of alienation is vital to his early work: in the *1844 Manuscripts* the worker is described as being alienated from the product and activity of his labour, other workers and his 'species-being', or his uniquely human capacity to labour freely and consciously (*CW3*: 270–82). Alienation remains an important category in the *Grundrisse*, but in a change of emphasis it is conceived not as estrangement from our human nature but rather in terms of the separation of the labourer from the conditions of labour: under capitalism 'social wealth confronts labour [...] as an alien and dominant power', and the development of the productive powers of labour 'appears as a process of dispossession from the standpoint of labour or as appropriation of alien labour from the standpoint of capital' (831). Because capitalist production is privately organized, and not under communal control, productive activity is alienated:

> The social character of activity, as well as the social form of the product, and the share of individuals in production here appear

> as something alien to and existing outside the individuals, not as their relation to one another, but as their subordination to relations which subsist independently of them and which arise out of collisions between mutually indifferent individuals [....] Individuals are subsumed under social production [...] but social production is not subsumed under individuals, manageable by them as their common wealth. (157–8, *tm*)

The other side of this alienation is what Marx refers to repeatedly as capital's civilizing or universalizing influence (e.g. 287, 409, 542, 634). In its pursuit of profit, capital 'strives towards the universal development of the forces of production', 'tearing down all the barriers' in its way and developing a world market that 'drives beyond national barriers and prejudices' (540, 410). Capital not only revolutionizes production, enabling the production of more wealth with less labour time, it also transforms the individual, expanding our needs and creating 'the material elements for the development of the rich individuality which is as all-sided in its production as in its consumption' (325). Thus, it lays the foundations for the arrival of post-capitalist society and the 'social individual' whose activity is 'immediately general or *social* activity' (832).

Capital is thus 'the moving contradiction', at once alienating and civilizing, exploitative and progressive, producing 'not only the alienation of the individual from himself and from others, but also for the first time the general and universal nature of his relationships and capacities' (706, 162, *tm*). This progressive side of capital is given far more attention and emphasis in the *Grundrisse* than in any other of Marx's writings, with the possible exception of the *Manifesto*. It is not a coincidence that both texts were written during periods of political or economic turmoil, when Marx perhaps felt that he could celebrate the merits of a mode of production which he thought and hoped was about to collapse.

The interconnected and wide-ranging discussions of labour, time, machinery, nature, alienation and communism that we find in the *Grundrisse* arguably make it broader and richer than any other text Marx ever wrote. At the same time, however, there are certain themes or concepts which are conspicuously absent. There is almost no discussion of gender or women, despite these featuring relatively prominently elsewhere in Marx's work.[2] Furthermore, from the perspective of Marx's later works, the 1857–8 manuscripts can seem underdeveloped: compared to *Capital I*, there is little on wages or the struggle over the working day (indeed, there is arguably little discussion in general of the working class as an agent of political action); the famous parts of *Capital II* on simple and expanded reproduction are introduced in the *Grundrisse*, but no more than introduced; and the important division of surplus value into commercial profit, interest and rent that we find in *Capital III* is largely missing. Some of these themes have been purposely excluded from the *Grundrisse* because they fall outside the scope of what Marx calls 'capital in general', a concept that we must now examine.

Capital in general and value

We saw in Chapter 1 that the *Grundrisse* was the start of what was originally intended to be a three-volume work, with the first volume divided into six books, the first of which would be on 'Capital'. In April 1858, as he was coming to the end of his work on the *Grundrisse*, Marx explained to Engels that this first book on 'Capital' would itself be divided into four sections: capital in general; competition; credit; and share capital (*CW40*: 298). Although the *Grundrisse* is wide-ranging, it seems as if Marx intended it to cover only the first section on 'capital in general': throughout the text, he repeatedly states that he is dealing with capital in general and when he approaches a topic that he thinks relates to competition he tends to abort the discussion, stating that it does not yet belong here (e.g. 402–3, 762).

Why exactly Marx begins with capital – instead of, for example, with the earliest forms of production and then gradually moving towards production based on capital – is something that we will examine later (see especially 'Method of political economy' in Chapter 3). For now we will think about the distinction between capital in general and competition: why does Marx begin with the former rather than the latter? On the face of it, this is a strange decision: after all, isn't competition the essential feature of capitalism?

From the perspective of political economy, competition is indeed the distinguishing attribute of capitalism, as well as its central virtue: the classical political economists celebrated the arrival of a competitive market economy as an emancipation from the restrictions of feudalism, promoting competition between self-interested individuals as 'the ultimate development of human freedom' (652). In many ways the ideologists of present-day neoliberal capitalism go even further, elevating competition into a kind of ontological absolute (such that competition is the central principle and regulator of all human and non-human life).

For Marx, however, focusing on competition is deceptive: 'not a single category of the bourgeois economy, not even the most basic [...] becomes real through free competition alone' (651). Competition is not the essence of capitalism but rather the form of appearance of the inner laws of capital: it is 'the form of appearance in which their necessity realizes itself [...] Competition therefore does not *explain* these laws; rather, it lets them be *seen*, but does not produce them' (552). Remember that from Marx's dialectical perspective to call something a form of appearance is not to dismiss it as nothing: competition does not invent the laws of capital – whose nature we will examine in Chapter 3 – but it is through competition that those laws are realized and executed:

> Competition merely *expresses* as real, posits as an external necessity, that which lies within the nature of capital; competition is nothing more than the way in which the many capitals force the inherent determinants of capital upon one another and upon themselves. (651)

Given that competition executes rather than establishes the laws of capital, in order to investigate those laws we need to abstract from competition: instead of analysing many capitals in competition with each other, we analyse *capital in general*.[3] This means that we examine 'the aspects common to every capital as such', allowing us to grasp 'the specific characteristics which distinguish capital from all other forms of wealth' (449). Capital in general is an abstraction because in reality '[c]apital exists and can only exist as many capitals' (414). In reality, not only are there many individual capitalist firms competing against each other, there are also particular types of capital: for example, as well as the industrial capital that produces commodities, there is also the commercial capital that sells those commodities. It is from these that we must abstract: when we analyse capital in general we are 'concerned neither with a *particular* form of capital, nor with an *individual* capital as distinct from other individual capitals etc.' (310). This is why there is so little on commercial profit, interest and rent in the *Grundrisse*.

So abstracting from competition does not mean that we consider an individual capital in isolation, as somehow representative of capital in general: to examine capital in general is to examine 'the capital of the whole society' (346). Once we have established the laws of capital through the analysis of capital in general, *then* we can bring in competition: 'The relation of the *many* will [...] be explained after what they all have in common, the quality of being capital, has been examined' (517).

After about 1863, there is no mention of 'capital in general' in Marx's writings. Some argue that although the term disappears, the concept is retained, but it seems more plausible (as others have argued) that Marx comes to realize that in order to explain capital in general he also and simultaneously needs to examine many capitals and competition, thus rendering the former concept redundant.[4] Either way, we need to understand that while writing the *Grundrisse*, Marx thinks it is useful to examine capital in general or 'the specific distinguishing characteristics of capital as such' (661).

What are those distinguishing characteristics? Marx tells us that 'the aspects being developed here are those which make value in general into capital': those 'qualities which distinguish value as capital from value as pure value or as money' (661, 310). What exactly this means will become more clear in Chapter 3, but at this point it is worth making some initial comments about Marx's understanding of value.

It is sometimes thought that Marx simply adopted the labour theory of value from the classical political economists, albeit using it to reach very different conclusions (rather like the Ricardian socialists). But rather than challenging the conclusions of the political economists, Marx questions their assumptions. They asked what determines the value of commodities and their answer was labour time. But there is a prior question that they did not ask: why are products produced as commodities at all? A commodity is a specific kind of product – one that is produced in order to exchange it. If I bake a cake and eat it myself or give it away as a gift, I have produced a product; if I bake a cake and sell it at the market, I have produced a commodity. For Marx, it is only under capitalism that the commodity becomes the '*general form of the product*': only in capitalism are most products produced as commodities (*C1*: 950). Commodities can only be exchanged with each other because they are 'bearers of value', and hence it is only in capitalism that 'labour is expressed in value' (*C1*: 174). In other words – greatly simplifying and anticipating the analysis to come – value is not a transhistorical category, a product of human labour in general, but is unique to capitalism. As Marx put it in his April 1858 letter to Engels, value 'is simply bourgeois wealth in its most abstract form' (*CW40*: 298). Thus in the *Grundrisse* we read: 'The economic concept of value does not occur in antiquity [...] The concept of value is entirely peculiar to the most modern economy, since it is the most abstract expression of capital itself and of the production resting on it' (776).

To analyse value, therefore, is not just to establish the proportions in which commodities exchange with each other, but to examine capitalism as that mode of production in which wealth takes the form of value. In addition, it is to analyse the different forms that value takes – as exchange value, money, capital, and the different forms of capital. It is this analysis of value that structures the *Grundrisse*.[5]

Structure of the text

Never meant for publication, the manuscripts that make up the *Grundrisse* are a mess. In chronological order, they consist of:

- An essay on the vulgar political economists Bastiat and Carey, written in July 1857
- An 'Introduction', found in 'Notebook M' and written in August and September 1857
- Seven notebooks numbered I–VII; the precise dates of their composition are unknown, but they seem to have been written between October 1857 and May 1858

The seven notebooks are divided into two chapters, on money and capital, with the latter divided into three main sections: the production process of capital; the circulation process of capital; and capital as fructiferous (on the transformation of surplus value into profit). Broadly speaking, these three sections correspond to volumes I–III of *Capital*, respectively.

Marx was an exceptional prose stylist – such that even his notebooks are more elegant and entertaining than the completed works of most philosophers – but the unfinished nature of the *Grundrisse* does not make it an easy read: like an especially difficult modernist novel, it is characterized by very long paragraphs, few headings and numerous digressions. In reviewing his notebooks, Marx himself attempted to impose some order on them, drawing up an index and a summary of their contents.[6] Because Marx's own headings and divisions are not always evenly spaced, intuitive, or even especially useful, in Chapter 3 I have divided the text up in my own way, drawing upon but also sometimes departing from Marx's own suggestions. In the same chapter, we will also work through the details of Marx's argument: what follows is an initial synopsis of the text, divided into its main sections.

Introduction

Marx opens by telling us that our object of study is material production, before discussing how that object should be studied. Through a critique of the individualistic and ahistorical methodology of the political economists, he argues that we can speak of 'production in general' only as a rational abstraction that allows us better to distinguish between historically specific forms of production. Adopting the categories of production, distribution, exchange and consumption from political economy, he shows that they make up a totality of which production is the predominant moment, before discussing the order in which the economic categories should be investigated, arguing that we must ascend from the abstract to the concrete. This section ends with some notes on possible topics for research, including a brief meditation on art.

Chapter on Money

After the methodological reflections of the 'Introduction', the analysis begins with money, specifically with a critique of socialist proposals for monetary reform. Attacking the socialists for failing to recognize the priority of production over circulation and the distinction between price and value, Marx uses this critique as the springboard for a dialectical investigation of value. He shows that the contradictions between the use value and the exchange value of a commodity give rise to money. The analysis is somewhat confused (and confusing) because at this stage Marx does not always adequately distinguish value from exchange value and, as he himself admits, his presentation is highly idealist, as if he is describing the logical progression of concepts rather than real social relations. He nonetheless introduces historical reflections upon capitalism as a society resting upon exchange value and for which money forms the social bond. Examining the three functions of money – as measure of value, as medium of circulation and as end in itself – Marx shows that money brings with it further contradictions that can only be overcome by capital.

Chapter on Capital

Money is a form of value, but in itself it cannot create further value: money can be used to buy commodities, which can be sold for money, but doing so does not make any money. Capital, on the other hand, is self-expanding value: value that can increase itself. How it does this is what Marx examines in the 'Chapter on Capital'.

Section One: The Production Process of Capital

Marx shows that capital increases itself by purchasing the one commodity that can create value, namely labour-power. The exchange between capital and labour takes place according to the law of value: labour-power – the worker's capacity to perform labour – is purchased at its value. But during the production process the labourer can produce products of a greater value than the value of her own labour-power: she creates a *surplus* value, which is appropriated by capital. Surplus value can be increased by lengthening the working day (absolute surplus value) or by reducing the value of labour-power (relative surplus value) and from the perspective of capital the only labour that is 'productive' is that labour which produces surplus value. Hence, Marx begins with the production process because it is only here that surplus value is created. In showing that the source of value is labour, and not the means of production, Marx also begins to develop his theory of profit (developed in more detail in 'Section Three'), showing that different ratios of constant capital (laid out on means of production) to variable capital (laid out on wages) produce different rates of profit. Overall, Marx has defined capital not as a thing but as a social relation in which labour is exploited.

Section Two: The Circulation Process of Capital

Once surplus value has been created in the production process, it must be realized in the circulation process: the product containing surplus value must be sold as a commodity. Some of the surplus value realized must be posited as surplus capital and used to buy the conditions of further production. Thus capital posits its own presuppositions (producing as a result what it needs to begin its process again), which can be distinguished from the *historic* presuppositions that capital itself does not produce but which it requires in order to begin: primarily, capital needs living labour capacity separated from the means of production. Investigating its historic presuppositions, Marx differentiates capital from earlier social forms and discusses the dissolution of those pre-capitalist forms of production. He then looks at the circulation process and turnover times, with a digression on surplus population. Distinguishing between circulating and fixed capital, he ends the section by analysing machinery as the most adequate form of fixed capital.

Section Three: Capital as Fructiferous

The unity of production and circulation is the realization of surplus value as profit. This is a relatively short section, partly because Marx seems unsure whether some of its topics should be examined under the category of capital in general. Marx defines profit as the form of appearance of surplus value and establishes that there is an average or general rate of profit, which disguises the origins of profit in surplus labour, and a falling rate of profit, which Marx thinks will lead to crises and even the dissolution of capitalism itself.

CHAPTER THREE

Reading the Text

This chapter will lead you through the *Grundrisse*, using the headings outlined in Chapter 2. Given the unfinished and disorganized nature of Marx's notebooks, this cannot be a simple page-by-page or chapter-by-chapter guide. Nonetheless, as far as possible, I have followed the order of the Penguin edition. This means that rather than beginning with the essay on Bastiat and Carey we will instead begin with the so-called 'Introduction' (often called the '1857 Introduction'). Thematically, it makes sense to begin with the 'Introduction', as it is here that Marx lays out his methodology.

Introduction

The 'Introduction' is one of the best-known and most frequently cited sections of the *Grundrisse*. Its relation to the other notebooks, however, and its place within Marx's work as a whole are ambiguous. For various reasons, it stands almost as a separate work from the rest of the *Grundrisse*. More explicitly addressed to methodological questions than any of the other notebooks, it was the first part of the *Grundrisse* to be published.[1] Although clearly not ready for publication, the 'Introduction' is more polished and more obviously nearer completion than the notebooks that follow it. Despite this, it appears that it was later rejected – or at least put on hold – by Marx, who in the '1859 Preface' to *A Contribution to the Critique of Political Economy* stated:

> A general introduction, which I had drafted, is omitted, since on further consideration it seems to me confusing to anticipate

> results which still have to be substantiated, and the reader who really wishes to follow me will have to decide to advance from the particular to the general. (*CW29*: 261)

From our perspective, however, it is precisely the 'general' methodological claims of the 'Introduction' that make it so valuable. Marx rarely made explicit his methodology: either his method has to be inferred or reconstructed from his arguments (as in the case of *Capital I*) or his comments on method are so brief and schematic that they lend themselves to caricature and so tend to lead to distorting simplifications (as in the case of the '1859 Preface'). So although there is debate over whether the methodological principles presented in the 'Introduction' are actually those which Marx followed elsewhere (or possibly even in the *Grundrisse* itself), the 'Introduction' is nevertheless a goldmine of insights and repays repeated reading.

Production

The first line of the 'Introduction' states: 'The object before us, to begin with, *material production*' (83). Without material production, there would be no human life, so we start there. But how are we to analyse or comprehend material production? The forms and relations of production have been expressed in thought through the categories of political economy. So we proceed by undertaking a *critique* of those categories, which is exactly where Marx begins.

The problem with Smith and Ricardo, he claims, is that they are 'Robinsonades': in order to think about production, their model or starting point is the isolated individual who labours alone, like the titular hero of Daniel Defoe's *Robinson Crusoe*. For Marx, this is absurd: this isolated individual does not and cannot exist, because the individual is always dependent on a greater social whole. Even Robinson Crusoe (who, anyway, is not exactly a typical case) was isolated on his desert island only after he had developed his skills and knowledge within society. There can be no production by individuals alone and so our 'point of departure' must be '[i]ndividuals producing in society' or 'production by social individuals' (83, 85).

Marx does not attribute the errors of the classical political economists simply to faulty reasoning or defective logic. Rather, the categories of political economy are reflective of real social relations. The 'isolated individual' of the economic imagination was not simply an illusion, but reflected the development of bourgeois society in the eighteenth century. Whereas in pre-capitalist societies each individual was bound to a particular community – they belonged 'to a greater whole' – with the development of capitalism these bonds were loosened: each individual came to see his ties to others as voluntary, as 'external necessity', with social relations as 'mere means towards his private purposes' (84). So a process of individualization did take place in reality, but it was the product and phenomenal form of a deeper historical process, namely an increasingly developed and complex set of social relations in which people were becoming more and more interconnected. Hence classical political economy erred not in identifying individualization as a feature of contemporary society but in failing to recognize it as a product of real, historical development, instead transforming it into an ahistorical universal, 'an ideal, whose existence they project into the past' (83). The argument made here is repeated throughout the *Grundrisse* and forms the essence of Marx's critique of classical political economy: the latter has naturalized what is historical, taking as its point of departure what is in need of explanation.

The accuracy and fairness of Marx's assessment of classical political economy at this specific point can seem questionable: Smith, at least, was in a tradition of eighteenth-century thought that paid close attention to the historical development of societies (to the extent that some commentators have claimed that his work anticipates Marx's own materialist conception of history).[2] Yet at the same time Smith also clearly 'project[ed] into the past' elements of his own society, most obviously by locating a 'propensity to truck, barter, and exchange' in human nature.[3] More broadly, it was in the eighteenth century with Smith and others that the individual became both the basic unit of analysis and a normative ideal: society was presented as merely an aggregate of the actions of self-interested individuals and the best societies were claimed to be those that protected and advanced individual freedom. In addition, Marx's real target here is not so much the thinkers of the eighteenth and early nineteenth centuries – whose work he, for the most part, respected – but his own, mid-nineteenth-century contemporaries.

Marx now takes his argument against political economy – that its claims reflect (a certain aspect of) bourgeois society – and applies it specifically to the category of production. He argues that political economists such as John Stuart Mill present production 'as encased in eternal natural laws independent of history, at which opportunity *bourgeois* relations are then quietly smuggled in as the inviolable natural laws on which society in the abstract is founded' (87). For example: they claim that all production requires the existence of property, by which they understand *private* property. For Marx, this attempt to identify the general preconditions of production is flawed. If property means 'appropriation' then of course all production requires property, because production is precisely the 'appropriation of nature on the part of an individual within and through a specific form of society': this is a condition so general as to be tautological (87). If property refers to *private* property, then the claim is illegitimate: private property is a relatively late development and was predated by other forms of property (an argument to which Marx returns later: see 'Forms which precede capitalist production' below).

Marx's broad point here is that rather than looking at 'production in general', we need to examine historically specific forms or modes of production. In particular, the task is to examine the capitalist mode of production, by interrogating the categories of political economy that are the expression of this mode. This does raise a problem or question, however: granted that our aim is to focus on historically specific modes of production, if the concept of 'production' is to have any coherence then there must surely be some features that are common to all forms of production. Marx states that 'there is no production in general' or 'general production' (86). Yet isn't it necessary to define 'production in general' before we can examine its specific historical expressions? Marx himself claims that 'all epochs of production have certain common traits, common characteristics' (85). Later in the *Grundrisse*, he states that his critique of political economy should open with a chapter on production in general (which presumably would have been some version of the 'Introduction' itself) (320, 362). In other words, there is apparently a tension in Marx's analysis between his desire for *historical* specificity (above all, to distinguish what is unique about the capitalist mode of production) and his necessary reliance on *transhistorical* categories (such as 'production', or even 'production in general').

One way to resolve, or at least relieve, this tension is by making a distinction between thought and reality or history (a distinction which, as we will see shortly, is crucial to Marx's method). Historically speaking, there is no production in general: production always takes specific forms at different stages of social development. However, we can use the category of 'production in general' as a logical or 'rational abstraction' that can help us to analyse these specific forms. Our aim in doing so is not to identify what is essential to all forms of production as they have existed, but to establish the specific determinations of production in its various historical modes, such that 'their essential difference is not forgotten' (85). In contrast, political economy, in empiricist fashion, views 'production in general' not as a rational abstraction but as a set of general historical conditions that are common to all forms of production. For Marx, if we identify what is general to all production, it is only so that we can better understand what is unique to a specific mode of production.

Production, distribution, exchange and consumption

The political economists, of course, could not be entirely blind to historical distinctions. They could hardly have denied that there are clear differences between different historical eras: slavery is obviously not the same as serfdom. Their way of accounting for these historical differences is to distinguish production from distribution, exchange and consumption. According to 'the obvious, trite notion' upheld by political economy, production and consumption are essentially unchanging: production creates objects to satisfy given human needs and consumption is the 'terminal point' at which the objects are used to fulfil those needs (88, 89). From this perspective, therefore, both are governed by nature insofar as it is nature that determines our needs and so both are outside history. Only distribution and exchange, which connect production and consumption, can vary historically: distribution divides the objects of production according to social laws and exchange divides them according to individual demand. As Marx puts it, from the perspective of political economy 'production, distribution, exchange and consumption form a regular syllogism; production is the generality, distribution and exchange the particularity, and consumption the singularity in which the whole is joined together' (89).

The language of 'syllogism' is Hegelian, so the fact that Marx uses this term when criticizing the 'trite' and 'shallow' notions of political economy might seem to indicate a hostility towards Hegel (88, 89).[4] However, Marx's attitude towards and use of Hegel is more subtle and ambivalent. In what follows, he sets out to examine for himself the relations between production, distribution, exchange and consumption, demonstrating that they form a unity. This unity is neither that of political economy nor straightforwardly that of Hegel, but Marx nonetheless undertakes his demonstration using explicitly Hegelian language. Beginning with the relation between production and consumption, he locates three 'identities', or forms of relation, which are taken straight from Hegel's division of logic into immediacy, reflection and mediation, and return into itself.[5]

In the first place, it might be said that there is an 'immediate identity' between production and consumption. Production is immediately consumption because in the production process there is also consumption – of the instruments of production (e.g. machinery becomes worn out), of raw materials (coal, timber, etc.) and of the powers and capacities of the individual worker. On the other hand, consumption is immediately production, because consumption is always productive: when an individual consumes food, for example, she produces her own body and its powers.

Marx does not reject the existence of this immediate identity, but he thinks it does not get us very far. The 'immediate identity' between production and consumption 'leaves their immediate duality intact', and hence does not take us to the unity we are looking for (91). So Marx locates a second identity relation, which is the mutual dependence or mediation of production and consumption. Production mediates consumption by providing the object of consumption: there has to be something to consume (even if this 'something' is not a material object). Consumption mediates production in two ways. First, the former provides the purpose of the latter: 'a product only becomes a real product only by being consumed', e.g. clothes that are not worn are not really clothes. Second, consumption provides a motive and need for new production (91). Hence as well as an immediate identity between production and consumption – in the sense that there is consumption within production and vice versa – there are also these mediations between them, in the sense that each serves as a means for the other.

Marx finally distinguishes a third identity relation: each 'creates the other in completing itself, and creates itself as the other' (93). Consumption is the act in which the product becomes the product and the producer becomes a producer. For its part, production determines the manner of consumption: in Marx's example, '[h]unger is hunger, but the hunger gratified by cooked meat eaten with a knife and fork is a different hunger from that which bolts down raw meat with the aid of hand, nail and tooth'. Production also creates new needs that feed consumption. This last point is an important one and one which Marx will repeat throughout the *Grundrisse*. As he puts it: 'Production not only supplies a material for the need, but it also supplies a need for the material [...] Production thus not only creates an object for the subject, but also a subject for the object' (92). There is no human subject with eternal and static needs given by nature and who is the cause of production, because production itself creates new needs – and in this sense it also creates new subjects. Hence, *pace* humanist and anti-consumerist critiques, the problem with capitalism is not that it denies our natural needs or creates 'artificial' needs (by fooling us all into thinking that we need the latest mobile phone or whatever). To the contrary, it is capitalism's achievement that it creates so many new needs![6]

Partly because of the lack of clarity in Marx's presentation, it can be hard to distinguish this third relation between production and consumption from the second relation. One way to think about it is that whereas in mediation (i.e. the second relation) production and consumption are presented as separate but mutually dependent, in the third relation they are presented more clearly as 'moments of one process'. Moreover, this is a process that repeats itself. Consumption establishes the 'need for repetition' of the act of production: '[t]he individual produces an object and, by consuming it, returns to himself, but returns as a productive and self-reproducing individual' (93, 94). In other words, here we are talking about production that is simultaneously *re*production, both of the individual and of his society.

The conclusion of Marx's investigation of production and consumption is not that they are the same thing: they are distinct

– if they were not then it would be impossible to discuss the relations between them – but they are also part of a whole. Is this whole a Hegelian unity? That depends on how we interpret Hegel, but two points can be made. First, Marx's whole is not a harmonious unity. Production and consumption are distinct moments of the whole and as such they may not be in harmony or equilibrium: supply may outstrip demand, for example, leading to overproduction (see 'Realization of surplus value' below). This is a whole that contains tensions, breaks and disharmony. Second, one moment of the unity predominates over the other: production is the 'predominant moment' (*'übergreifende Moment'*: comprehensive, all-embracing, or transcending moment could be alternative translations). Production 'is the real point of departure': 'The process always returns to production to begin anew' (94, 99). What does Marx mean when he emphasizes the predominance of production? Is this a logical or conceptual claim that we must *think* production first, or (what is a different matter) that in the presentation of the results of our investigation we must begin with production? A historical claim that production predominates in capitalist society? Or an ontological or anthropological claim that production predominates in all human societies? At this point in the text it is hard to say, so we will return to this question once we have looked at Marx's discussions of the relation of production to distribution and exchange. His aim, as before, is to demonstrate that these are interconnected but not identical moments of a unity in which production predominates.

Distribution refers to the manner in which wealth or resources are distributed within a particular society. The usual starting point for political economy was to look at three forms of distribution: ground rent, wages and profit, which were supposed to rest on three different sources of value, respectively land, labour and capital. But, as Marx points out, these particular forms of distribution presuppose particular forms of production. Wages do not merely presuppose labour, but *wage-labour*, i.e. labour which takes place under specific relations of production; profits presuppose not merely 'capital' in the sense of the means of production (tools, machinery, etc.) but capital as a specific social relation; ground rent presupposes not merely land but 'large-scale landed property'. In other words, '[d]istribution is itself a product of production', not only in the sense that it is the products of production that are being distributed, but also in the sense that the form of production determines the form of distribution (e.g. it is wage–labour – and not simply labour – that gives us wages) (95).

But, granted that this form of distribution – of wages, profits and rent – can be considered secondary to production, is there not another kind of distribution that we have to consider? Isn't the form of production itself determined by a specific *distribution* both of the means of production (who owns machinery, land, etc. and who has access to them) and of the members of society among different kinds of production? In other words, it appears that we can actually only think of production itself in terms of this 'production-determining distribution' (97). In addition, the examples of history seem to demonstrate that distribution determines production: specific systems of laws, revolutionary upheavals and invading conquerors will all impose on a society a certain distribution that seems to structure production.

In response to these arguments for the predominance of distribution over production, Marx offers a logical argument and a historical argument. It is in some sense true that the 'distribution' of the means of production determines the form of production. But, Marx argues, given that production cannot be understood at all without examining the distribution of its different elements, logically speaking this form of 'distribution' must belong to production: it has no meaning outside of production. Hence, when we speak of the 'distribution' of the means of production and of classes, we are really talking about production. As he puts it in Notebook VII: 'These modes of distribution are the relations of production themselves' (832).

Historically speaking, it is also in some sense true that distribution structures production: for example, an invading nation will impose its own distribution of resources on a country, thereby restructuring its form of production. But that form of distribution is itself a product of the mode of production used by the invading nation. The case of law – where a system of law imposes a certain distribution of resources that seems to structure production – is perhaps more complex and ambiguous. A common criticism of Marxism in general is that its focus on forces and relations of production, and its consequent relegation of law and politics to the 'superstructure', is incoherent, because the relations of production are themselves necessarily legal relations: whether or not I own a factory is something that is established by law and hence the legal relations establishing the distribution of resources are logically prior to and determine relations of production.[7] Marx's answer in the 'Introduction' is that laws – which are anyway a relatively late development in human societies – merely 'perpetuate' or 'stabilize' a particular distribution and, as we have seen, distribution is ultimately determined by production. Whether or not this is a compelling argument is a matter of debate and Marx himself concedes that the influence of law must 'be determined in each specific instance' (98).

Finally, Marx reaches exchange. Under this category he includes circulation, given that the latter is 'merely a specific moment of exchange, or [it is] also exchange regarded in its totality' (98). Here the predominance of production is easier to establish. Many exchanges take place within the production process or are obviously and directly connected to it: when a worker exchanges her labour-power in return for a wage, for example, or when one capitalist buys machinery from another capitalist. But even simple exchanges that apparently lie outside the production process are determined by production. If, for example, I buy an apple from someone, then my purchase depends upon an entire mode of production that determines the nature and even the possibility of that exchange: the growing of the apple, its transportation to market, my ability to make the purchase and so on, all depend on a particular mode of production. This argument will be important later in the *Grundrisse*, when Marx will argue that simple exchange is only a formal and phenomenal aspect of capitalist relations of production.

Marx ends the second section of the 'Introduction' by noting: 'The conclusion that we reach is not that production, distribution, exchange and consumption are identical, but that they all form the members of a totality, distinctions within a unity' (99). As we have seen, within this totality production predominates, though we have also seen that this claim is a little obscure. It is at least in part clearly an epistemological claim: our investigation must start with production rather than with distribution, exchange or consumption. It is also a political claim, meaning that it has consequences (explicitly developed in the 'Chapter on Money') for political action: if production is predominant, then in order to effect radical social and political change we must transform production – ultimately by overthrowing capitalism – rather than merely introducing 'fairer' systems of distribution or exchange (still less fighting for the 'rights' of consumers!). Beyond this, it has been argued that Marx's assertion of the predominance of production is a kind of onto-anthropological claim. In this sense, it must be seen as a reiteration of Marx and Engels' arguments in *The German Ideology* that humans 'begin to distinguish themselves from animals as soon as they begin to *produce* their means of subsistence' (*CW5*: 31).[8] If this is Marx's argument, however, it is open to a strong objection, namely that while in capitalist societies production may predominate, the same cannot be said of pre-capitalist societies in which other social logics – such as the logic of symbolic exchange – predominate.[9] Hence others have argued that Marx's insistence on the predominance of production is not a transhistorical claim but instead refers to the imperative under capitalism to produce surplus value.[10] Yet at this point in the text such an interpretation hardly seems warranted: not only has Marx so far made no mention of surplus value, he has been discussing production in general and in demonstrating the predominance of production his examples have been taken from pre-capitalist as well as capitalist societies.

Ultimately, the best way to understand and assess the methodological claims that Marx puts forward in the 'Introduction' may be to see how they operate in practice, in his analyses of historical or existing modes of production. Such an approach is complicated – because it can be hard to tell whether the concrete analyses that Marx undertakes, in the *Grundrisse* or elsewhere, actually put into practice the method outlined in the 'Introduction' – but it makes sense because Marx is clear that any discussion of 'production in general' is of use only insofar as it helps us understand specific forms of production. 'Whenever we speak of production, [...] what is meant is always production at a definite stage of social development' (85). Does this mean that in order to investigate those definite stages of production we must start with the earliest and move through history until we reach capitalism? The short answer is No, for reasons that are explained in the third section of the 'Introduction'.

Method of political economy

How can we begin to understand a mode of production? Intuitively, it seems to make sense to start our investigation from 'the real and the concrete': that which we can observe and measure and seems given to us. For example, if we are to investigate the economy of a nation, then it seems to make sense to begin with its population. But this category of population is merely 'a chaotic conception' if we do not break it down further, for example by acknowledging that the population is composed of different classes. Yet we cannot understand these classes without the further concepts of wage labour and capital; and those concepts are in turn meaningless without a further knowledge of the concepts of value, exchange, division of labour and so on. In other words, if we started from an apparently 'concrete' category like population, then in order to understand it we would be led to work our way back through ever simpler and more abstract concepts, until we arrived at division of labour, value, etc. This analytical method – breaking down the concrete into ever more abstract concepts – was used by the early 'economists of the seventeenth century' (100). The 'scientifically correct method', in contrast, is synthetic rather than analytic: it starts with simple, abstract relations and determinations and from there ascends to more concrete categories such as population, state, nation, world market, etc. (101). Thus, we arrive back at population (for example), but this time as 'a rich totality of many determinations and relations' rather than as a chaotic conception (100). This is the method used by Marx and, he claims, by the later economists of the eighteenth and nineteenth centuries. Smith, for example, begins *The Wealth of Nations* with the abstract category of the division of labour and only in Book V reaches the state. Nonetheless, in Marx's hands the method is also used to criticize political economy and its assumptions: we have already seen Marx demonstrate that the starting points of political economy – the isolated individual, production in general – are in fact not simply given but are the results of prior determinations and can only be understood by examining the abstract relations that these categories presuppose.

In Marx's method, therefore, there is a distinction between two different meanings of 'concrete'. There is the real, historical concrete – actually existing or historical social relations – that is 'the point of departure in reality and hence also the point of departure for observation and conception'. But if we stopped there then we would not get beyond a crude, commonsense empiricism. Our aim must be to grasp and comprehend these real phenomena through the use of abstractions: 'the abstract determinations lead towards a reproduction of the concrete by way of thought' (101). If we do not use abstractions – in the sense of simple, *abstract* concepts like value and exchange – then we will end up with far worse abstractions – in the sense that we will be left only with empty, *abstract* categories (such as a category of population that does not take into account classes). By working our way up from abstract concepts, we will eventually arrive at a new 'concrete' as the 'rich totality of many determinations and relations'. *This* 'concrete is concrete because it is the concentration of many determinations, hence unity of the diverse. It appears in the process of thinking, therefore, as a process of concentration, as a result, not as a point of departure' (101).

So the first concrete – the concrete in reality or history – is the precondition of thought and ultimately it is from there that the abstract categories are derived. But our aim is the second concrete: the concrete in thought that is the product of the ascent from abstract to concrete.[11] Hence we can also make a distinction between the object of study and the method or mode of presentation or exposition. For example, the 'Introduction' began by telling us that 'the point of departure' is 'socially determined individual production'. But this is the point of departure in the sense that it is '[t]he object before us', i.e. our object of study as a real concrete (83). When it comes to the method of exposition, in order to comprehend production as a concrete in thought we must start with abstract concepts like value, labour and so on, which is what Marx does in the *Grundrisse*.

The understanding and use of abstraction in the 'Introduction' is thus very different from that found in earlier works such as *The German Ideology*, in which the aim was to overcome the abstractions of idealism (such as God or Man) and return to 'real premises' which can be 'verified in a purely empirical way' (albeit by relating those abstractions to actual social relations rather than simply denouncing them) (*CW5*: 31). Whereas in *The German Ideology* Marx was distancing himself from other Young Hegelians, in his discussions of the concrete in the 'Introduction', he draws heavily upon Hegel, who had claimed that 'every determination, anything concrete, every concept, is essentially a unity of distinguished and distinguishable elements'.[12] However, as ever with Marx, he makes a *critical* use of Hegel. According to Marx, the problem with Hegel is that he fails to make the crucial distinction between the real concrete and the concrete in thought. As such, Hegel thinks that the real is itself a product of thought, 'unfolding itself out of itself', as if 'the conceptual world as such is [...] the only reality'. But, for Marx, the ascent from the abstract to the concrete does not produce the real concrete: it 'is only the way in which thought appropriates the concrete, reproduces it as the concrete in the mind'. The real concrete – the object of study which we are trying to comprehend by reproducing as a concrete in thought – 'retains its autonomous existence outside the head just as before' (101). Indeed, it will remain untouched and inaccessible if we remain 'merely speculative, merely theoretical' (102). So while Marx is not an empiricist, nor does he think that theory or philosophy alone are adequate: to reach the concrete, thought must also rely on 'the working-up of observation [of the real concrete – SC] and conception into concepts', i.e. we need to draw upon empirical and statistical data and existing attempts at categorization (101). (Whether or not Marx follows this principle in the *Grundrisse* is open to question, given that in those notebooks – especially when compared with *Capital* – there is very little use of empirical data.)

We can also distinguish between the concrete in thought and the real concrete in terms of their genesis or development. Marx tells us that the process by which the concrete is reproduced in thought 'is by no means the process by which the concrete itself comes into being' (101). In other words, we should not necessarily expect the development of thought (leading to the concrete in thought) to reflect or correspond to the actual, historical development of the object of thought (the real concrete). There *may* sometimes be a correspondence, but this is something that must be assessed on a case-by-case basis. Take the example of money. This is a simple, abstract category which as both a category and a real historical entity existed before the more complex and concrete categories of wage labour, capital, banks, etc. 'To that extent the path of abstract thought, rising from the simple to the combined, would correspond to the real historical process' (102). For earlier, simple modes of production, only a simple conception of money is required, even though in those earlier modes of production money may have played a dominant role. With a more complex and concrete mode of production such as capitalism, money plays a subordinate role (in the sense that it is subordinate to capital) but we need a more concrete and developed conception of money (which can take account of its relations with wage labour, capital, banks, etc.). On the other hand, however, we can also find societies – Marx's example is Peru – which do not have money but which do have complex and developed economic forms such as cooperation and a developed division of labour (102). In this case, the path of history has not followed the path of logic or thought, because more complex forms preceded simpler forms.

There is no one, single path of development that all societies follow, then, and the relationship between the categories of thought and the development of history is complex. Simple forms may exist in both 'simple' and more 'developed' societies, but they do not do so in the same way. Money, for example, may exist in simple societies, but it 'makes a historic appearance in its full intensity only in the most developed conditions of society': it is only under capitalism that money permeates all relations, develops as world money, etc. 'Thus, although the simpler category may have existed historically before the more concrete, it can achieve its full (intensive and extensive) development precisely in a combined form of society' (103). We must take account, therefore, not only of the specific historical development of economic forms, but also the specific role that those forms play in different modes of production. Money may have existed in ancient Rome as it does in present-day Britain, but it existed in a very different way within very different social relations.

So far we have distinguished between the real concrete and the concrete in thought and have seen that their development does not always correspond: the order in which categories appear in the reproduction of the concrete in thought does not necessarily mirror the order in which the forms and relations that those categories express appear in history. Now Marx begins to think about the origins and genesis of the categories themselves, rather than simply the order in which they appear in thought. He does so using the example of labour.

'Labour seems quite a simple category' and it seems to be a transhistorical universal: prehistoric hunters labour just as computer programmers do (103). However, as the example of money has already shown us, the most simple category 'can achieve its full (intensive and extensive) development' only in the most advanced and complex societies (103). 'As a rule, the most general abstractions arise only in the midst of the richest possible concrete development' (104).[13] So it is with labour, which is why it is not until Smith, reflecting on bourgeois society, that the category of labour achieves its fullest abstraction and generality. The mercantilists located wealth in money: commerce and manufacturing were seen as productive of wealth, but only insofar as they produced money. The physiocrats of the mid-eighteenth century made an advance by locating the source of wealth in labour, yet they thought that only one type of labour – agricultural labour – created wealth. It was Smith who first claimed that it is labour in general that produces wealth.[14] With this category of labour we reach 'the abstract universality of wealth-creating activity', not tied to any one particular activity (104). Marx's argument is that this abstract category of general labour could only be developed within bourgeois society because it was only there that labour had in reality become general: in bourgeois society, no one form of labour predominates, such that 'individuals can with ease transfer from one labour to another, and where the specific kind [of labour – SC] is a matter of chance for them, hence of indifference' (104). Marx does not seem to be referring here to the deskilling of labour, but rather an 'indifference to particular forms of labour', about which he is more ambivalent or even enthusiastic (105). The contrast is with pre-capitalist societies, in particular feudalism, in which not only did agricultural labour predominate, but also labourers would have been tied – by birth, apprenticeship, tradition – to one particular type of labour.

Hence under capitalism 'the abstraction of the category "labour", "labour as such", labour pure and simple, becomes true in practice', because it becomes abstract in reality (105). The abstract category of labour is thus based on what later Marxist thinkers called a 'real abstraction': an abstraction that is located in material practices and actions rather than in our minds and which is then reflected in the categories of thought.[15] Having become general and abstract in reality – not tied to any one skill or activity – the concept of general or abstract labour could then be used retrospectively to examine previous societies.

Marx here seems to be developing the concept of 'abstract labour' which is so important to *Capital I*, where it is defined as labour 'in so far as it finds its expression in value', distinct from *concrete* useful labour that creates use values (*C1*: 132). But here in the 'Introduction' it is not clear whether Marx is discussing value-creating abstract labour or simply concrete labour in general, i.e. labour as the source of use values in general. The latter could exist at any time in history, whereas the former (value-creating abstract labour) is unique to capitalism (because it is only in capitalism that wealth takes the form of value). We will return to abstract labour later (see 'Exchange between capital and labour' below.)

Marx summarizes his analysis of labour as follows:

> This example of labour shows strikingly how even the most abstract categories, despite their validity – precisely because of their abstractness – for all epochs, are nevertheless, in the specific character of this abstraction, themselves likewise a product of historic relations, and possess their full validity only for and within these relations. (105)

It is for this reason that the categories that have been developed to express the relations of bourgeois society – 'the most developed and the most complex historic organization of production' – can be used to illuminate all previous social forms. Marx makes this point using an analogy:

> Human anatomy contains a key to the anatomy of the ape. The intimations of higher development among the subordinate animal species, however, can be understood only after the higher development is already known. The bourgeois economy thus supplies the key to the ancient etc.. (105)

At first glance, this looks like a teleological argument, as if bourgeois society provides the key to earlier societies because the former must necessarily develop into the latter. But the analogy is exact and does not rely on teleology. If human anatomy can tell us about the anatomy of the ape, it is because humans have developed from apes, not because apes were destined to become humans or because humans have realized the immanent tendencies of apes. Likewise, if capitalism is the key to understanding pre-capitalist societies, this is not because capitalism is their inevitable outcome but because it has developed out of those societies. Its categories therefore offer 'insights into the structure and the relations of production of all the vanished social formations out of whose elements it has built itself up, whose partly still unconquered remnants are carried along within it' (105).

Nonetheless, we must be careful (Marx even says that his claim 'that the categories of bourgeois economics possess a truth for all other forms of society' must 'be taken only with a grain of salt' [106]). Reading the past in terms of the present in this way does not mean proceeding 'in the manner of those economists who smudge over all historical differences and see bourgeois relations in all forms of society' (105). In order to avoid treating the economic forms of the past as if they are identical with those of the present, or as if the former are merely 'steps leading up to' the latter, we need to start from a *self-critical* understanding of the present (106). How are we to gain that self-critical understanding?

We already know that production predominates over distribution, exchange and consumption. Marx now tells us that '[i]n all forms of society there is one specific kind of production which predominates over the rest, whose relations thus assign rank and influence to the others' (106–107). In modern bourgeois society, it is capitalist production that is predominant. So, for example, it might seem to make sense to begin analysing society by looking at forms of landed property, because agricultural production is historically the first form of production and all production and ultimately all life must come from the earth. But in modern societies '[a]griculture more and more becomes merely a branch of industry, and is entirely dominated by capital'. As such, we will not be able to understand landed property without first understanding capital, so it is with capital that we must begin. 'Capital is the all-dominating economic power of bourgeois society. It must form the starting-point as well as the finishing-point' (107). Hence the 'order and sequence of the categories' with which we analyse capitalism is not determined by history: the categories do not 'follow one another in the same sequence as that in which they were historically decisive. Their sequence is determined, rather, by their relation to one another in modern bourgeois society' (106, 107). Thus, for example, we start with capital rather than ground rent, even though the latter may have developed historically before the former, because capital is dominant within modern society. This does not, however, commit Marx to an ahistorical analysis – a purely structural analysis of the capitalist mode of production that ignores history – because the whole point is to understand capitalism as a *historical* mode of production that can be distinguished from earlier modes of production.

Marx ends the third section of the 'Introduction' by outlining a plan for his critique of political economy, in the light of the foregoing discussion of economic categories (108). This plan is recapitulated later in the *Grundrisse* (227–8):

1. General, abstract determinations which obtain in more or less all forms of society
2. The categories which make up the inner structure of bourgeois society: capital, wage labour, landed property
3. State: taxes, state debt, public credit, population, colonies
4. International relations of production
5. World market and crises

This schema reflects the method of ascending from the abstract to the concrete. The chapter on 'general, abstract determinations' is likely to have been a version of the 'Introduction' itself, with some discussion of 'production in general'. Further on in the *Grundrisse*, Marx offers a refined and more detailed plan, which starts with capital (264, 275–6). This new plan is a little confusing, but if we combine it with those outlined in letters written by Marx in March and April 1858 then we have something like this (CW40: 287, 298–303):

1. Capital
    - a) Capital in general
        - i) Value
        - ii) Money
            - Money as measure
            - Money as means of exchange
            - Money as money
        - ii) Capital
            - Production process of capital
            - Circulation of capital
            - Profit and interest

- **b)** Competition: the interaction of many capitals
- **c)** Credit
- **d)** Share capital

2 Landed property
3 Wage labour
4 State
5 International trade
6 World market

The separate chapter on general, abstract determinations has disappeared, though at least one abstract determination – money – now has its own section. Of this new plan, the *Grundrisse* is essentially a draft of the topics under 1(a), with scattered comments on 1(b), 1(c) and 2. It is not wholly clear what was to be included in 3; there is very little in the *Grunrdrisse* on wages as such, but there are discussions of types of labour and wage labour necessarily enters the analysis of capital.[16] Sections 4, 5 and 6 are present in the *Grundrisse*, but not in any systematic way.

In November 1858, the plan was modified so that it begins with the commodity rather than value (CW40: 358, 368, 376–7). This is what happens in *A Contribution to the Critique of Political Economy* (written November 1858 to January 1859 and published in 1859), whose 'Preface' now claims that we must 'advance from the particular to the general' – hence starting with the particularity of commodities. The basic plan as laid out in the 1859 'Preface' nonetheless remains the same: '*capital, landed property, wage-labour; the State, foreign trade, world market*' (CW29: 261).

Forms of consciousness in relation to relations of production

The 'Introduction' finishes with a series of highly condensed and often enigmatic notes on a variety of loosely connected topics. Very broadly speaking, we could say that what interests Marx in this short section is the relation between production and other social forms and relations, or (to borrow Marx's terminology from elsewhere) the relation between base and superstructure. Marx lists a number of topics that he would like to discuss, but does little more than list them. These include the relation of production to: the state; law; war; the family; education; historiography; religion; and race. It would be a colossal understatement to say that it is a shame that Marx did not pursue these themes in more detail.

The most famous and longest of the notes comes at the very end, where Marx offers some thoughts on art. He notes that different forms of social development give rise to different forms of art. The art of classical Greece, for example, was bound to a form of mythology that cannot be reproduced under different conditions: classical sagas and songs were rendered obsolete by the printing press and the feats of Greek gods and heroes are dwarfed by the powers of industrial machinery. In short, a mythology which 'overcomes and dominates and shapes the forces of nature in the imagination and by the imagination' is made redundant now that science and other forces of production have in reality mastered nature (110). This leaves Marx with a conundrum, however: if Greek art is tied to Greek society, then why is it that we still value that art and even hold it up as an ideal standard by which all other art must be measured? '[T]he difficulty lies not in understanding that the Greek arts and epic are bound up with certain forms of social development. The difficulty is that they still afford us artistic pleasure' even though we have achieved a far more complex level of social development. Marx's solution is that classical Greece was like the childhood of humanity: 'Why should not the historic childhood of humanity, its most beautiful unfolding, as a stage never to return, exercise an eternal charm?' (111) This simplistic answer is not much help: it elides the central issue (the relation between forms of production and forms of culture), draws a rather crude analogy between the development of history and the development of a human individual, and resorts to a faith in the prelapsarian naivety and innocence of children which is itself rather naive. The obvious inadequacy of this answer is often used – even by Marx's admirers – as evidence of the limitations of the materialist conception of history. Alain Badiou, for example, suggests that Marx reaches this 'feeble' answer because he cannot acknowledge that art can produce universal and eternal truths.[17]

We can defend Marx, however, by making a number of points. First, his notes on art are clearly unfinished – even further from publication than anything else in the *Grundrisse* – and it would be unfair to use them to discredit his views on art or anything else.

Second, although this is rarely noted, he does actually return to this topic later in the *Grundrisse*: not in much more detail, admittedly, but in a way that at least sheds more light on his argument (see 'Forms which precede capitalist production' below). Third, far from denying the universality of some works of art, the very point that Marx is making is that Greek art has a universal appeal that goes beyond its context. Indeed, fourth, he makes it explicit that what he is discussing here is the '*uneven development of material production relative to e.g. artistic development*' (109). In other words, rather than assuming that cultural (or legal, political, or intellectual) forms are always strictly determined by an underlying economic foundation, he is overtly arguing that that their relative development can be highly complex and take different paths. Finally, the appearance of this concept of 'uneven development' should not come as a surprise because, *mutatis mutandis*, it is what Marx has just been discussing in the previous section: there we saw an uneven development of the categories of thought relative to the real social relations that they express; here we see an uneven development of artistic forms relative to social relations.

Study Questions

1. What does Marx say about 'production in general'?
2. What according to Marx is the relation between production, distribution, exchange and consumption?
3. What does it mean to ascend from the abstract to the concrete?
4. Why does Marx resolve to begin his critique of political economy with capital?
5. To what extent and how is the 'Introduction' influenced by Hegel?

Chapter on Money

Having discussed his method, Marx now begins his investigation of the capitalist mode of production, starting with money. On the face of it, this starting point seems to accord with the 'scientifically correct method' of ascent from the abstract to the concrete:

money is an abstract category, common to most societies but only reaching its full development as abstraction under capitalism. Yet as abstract categories go, money is in fact fairly complex: we cannot understand money (at least as Marx understands it) without first examining the even more abstract category of value. For this reason, in his correspondence of Spring 1858 Marx made it clear that he would start with value before reaching money (*CW40*: 287, 298). In fact, this is essentially what happens in the 'Chapter on Money': starting with money, Marx quickly moves to distinguish money from value before then working back to money. At the very end of the final notebook of the *Grundrisse*, Marx started a section called 'Value', which like *Capital I* introduces the category of value by examining the commodity. It begins: 'This section to be brought forward', clearly reflecting Marx's revised plan to place value before money (881). The section breaks off after only a couple of pages, however, and there is no clear and extended discussion of the theory of value in the *Grundrisse*.

In other words, it may be that Marx begins with money simply because he is still working out the correct order of categories. Or, drawing on a distinction made in the 1873 Afterword to *Capital I*, we might say that what we see in the *Grundrisse* is Marx undertaking his inquiry, which is necessarily going to look different from the presentation in later works of the results of that inquiry.[18]

However, there is perhaps a more compelling, conjunctural and political, reason for stating with money. Marx was writing during a monetary crisis: he wanted not only to understand this crisis, but also to combat socialist solutions to such crises. Socialists like Proudhon and his followers were advocating monetary reforms as a response both to crises and to the ills of capitalism more generally. In order to demonstrate that these proposed reforms were fundamentally misguided, Marx needed to develop his own theory of money.[19]

If this helps to explain why Marx begins his analysis with money, it also goes some way to explaining why the 'Chapter on Money' can be such a difficult read. Marx (writing only for himself) does not bother to explain the socialist proposals that he is criticizing and those proposals have no direct equivalent today. As we shall see, he spends a lot of time attacking proposals for a form of 'labour money', but almost no one today advocates anything like labour money. In addition, he develops his theory of money using a Hegelian framework and terminology. Whatever rewards this might bring, using Hegel is never a recipe for clarity.

Nonetheless, the 'Chapter on Money' is valuable for its insights into both Marx's work (as his first attempt to develop a comprehensive theory of money) and the workings of capitalism. Although the socialist ideas that he criticizes may have no direct equivalent today, parallels can be drawn with proposals for banking reforms that were put forward in the wake of the crisis that began in 2007. In contrast to those proposals, Marx's broad point is that if we are to understand capitalism and its frequent periods of crisis and instability, then we need to look beyond circulation to production.

Money and value

The opening of the 'Chapter on Money' makes immediately obvious the status of the *Grundrisse* as a set of notebooks for personal use. Marx begins abruptly with a critique of a book on banking reform written by the now largely forgotten Proudhonist Alfred Darimon. Assessing the causes of economic crises, Darimon argued that bullion drains meant that the supply of money did not meet the needs of circulation, which forced up interest rates, making it harder to borrow and thus precipitating crises. Following Proudhon, Darimon's solution was '*crédit gratuit*', that is an appropriate credit supply would prevent crises and so a central people's bank should be established to issue interest-free credit on demand. Marx presents various specific criticisms of this plan, showing that Darimon's statistics do not support his own theories, that he fails to distinguish between money and credit, that he misunderstands the causes of bullion drains and their role in crises, and that ultimately he does not get much further than recognizing the relation between supply and demand.

Marx soon reaches what he sees as the 'fundamental question'. The Proudhonists argued that their proposed banking and monetary reforms would 'create entirely new conditions of production and circulation', in the same way that the introduction of banks revolutionized the conditions of production by facilitating the development of large-scale industry (122). Marx asks: (a) will the proposed changes to the organization of circulation fundamentally alter the relations of production; (b) can these changes to circulation even be effected without first transforming the relations of production? Given his argument in the 'Introduction' concerning the predominance of production, it should not be too difficult to anticipate his answers: (a) tinkering with circulation will have little effect on the basic organization of society, because it will not alter the underlying relations of production; (b) far-reaching changes to circulation are not possible without prior changes to the relations of production.

Rather than simply asserting the priority of production over circulation, Marx continues to engage in detail with Darimon, whose basic position is summed up by the quotation from his work that opens the 'Chapter on Money': 'The root of the evil is the predominance which opinion obstinately assigns to the role of the precious metals in circulation and exchange' (115). Given this, in addition to *crédit gratuit* he proposed a more radical transformation of money itself. Because (Darimon argued) economic crises are ultimately caused by the privilege that belongs to gold and silver as the only authentic means of exchange, then this privilege should be abolished. The gold standard should be ended, so that any commodity can be exchanged directly for any other commodity. This would mean that gold and silver become commodities like any others. As Marx points out, this does not so much get rid of money as elevate all commodities to the status of money. As he sarcastically remarks: 'Let the pope remain, but make everybody pope. Abolish money by making every commodity money' (126).

In practice, the Proudhonists proposed to end the gold standard by introducing a form of labour money, a policy earlier supported by some of the Ricardian socialists. Given that labour time determines the value of products, they argued, why can't the price of those products be expressed in money that represents labour time? Thus, gold money would be replaced with 'time chits', a currency based on labour time: a worker would arrive at the bank with a commodity which took (for instance) eight hours of labour to produce and leave with a time chit representing exactly eight hours of labour, which she could then exchange for other commodities. Hence if the productivity of labour increased – the Proudhonists argued – then it would be the workers who benefited, because the chit would rise in value (because each chit would now represent more labour) and so increase in buying power. Marx rejects this plan first of all because the time chit is simply a form of money and so would bring with it all the problems of money. Like money, time chits could be accumulated and hoarded – meaning that when the value of the chits increased with rising productivity, non-working hoarders of chits would benefit just as much as workers. Like money, chits could also be loaned – an increase in the value of chits would disadvantage the indebted (because the value of their debt would increase with the value of the chits).

For the socialists, the advantage of labour money is that it matches value and price: 'by expressing value in units of labour time itself instead of in a given objectification of labour time, say gold and silver', 'every commodity would be directly transformed into money' and the privilege of gold and silver would be ended (138). For Marx, in contrast, the problem with labour money is precisely that it does not recognize the necessary distinction between value and price. The price of a commodity is its exchange value expressed in money and it varies according to supply and demand. Thus (drawing on a distinction already made by Smith) the price – also referred to by Marx here as 'nominal value', 'money value', or 'market value' – differs from 'real value': the price of a commodity fluctuates above and below the real value of a commodity. '[T]he two are constantly different and never balance out, or balance only coincidentally and exceptionally' (137). Not only does price differ from value, value itself will vary according to changes in productivity.

Distinct from price, the real value of a commodity is determined by labour time, but this labour time is an *ideal* measure. 'The value of commodities as determined by labour time is only their *average value*' (137). As Marx puts it in *Capital I*, the value of a commodity is measured by the 'socially necessary labour time' needed to produce it, averaged out over a period of time (*C1*: 129). Although the exact phrase 'socially necessary labour time' does not appear in the *Grundrisse*, the concept is present: 'What determines value is not the amount of labour time incorporated into products, but rather the amount of labour time necessary at a given moment' (135). Because the time chit represents *average labour time*, it 'would never correspond to or be convertible into [the] *actual labour time*' contained in an individual commodity (139). The commodity that took me as an individual 8 hours to make might therefore exchange for a time chit equal to 7 or 9 hours.

Marx summarizes his critique of labour money:

> *Because price is not equal to value [...] the value-determining element – labour time – cannot be the element in which prices are expressed, because labour time would then have to express itself simultaneously as the determining and non-determining element, as the equivalent and non-equivalent of itself.* Because labour time as the measure of value exists only as an ideal, it cannot serve as the matter of price-comparisons. (140)

For this reason, 'the value relation obtains a separate material existence in the form of money [...] The difference between price and value calls for values to be measured as prices on a different standard from their own' (140). Hence Marx has shown that 'the bourgeois system of exchange itself necessitate[s] a specific instrument of exchange': it 'necessarily create[s] a specific equivalent for all values', namely money as an independent commodity (127).

There might seem an irony in the fact that while he demolishes the labour money scheme by showing that it fails to recognize the distinction between price and value, throughout the *Grundrisse* Marx himself assumes that commodities are sold at their value. He does this not because he thinks that it always happens, but because – as we shall see – he wants to show that capital generates profits by forcing labourers to perform surplus labour and not by selling commodities above their value.[20] But what this means is that in effect Marx purposely identifies price and value. Partly for this reason, even sympathetic readers have suggested that his theory of value poses problems when we try to use it for the empirical study of actual societies, where we necessarily have to rely on information and statistics concerning actual prices: although it is clear that Marx wants to distinguish value and price, the exact relation between them is not always clear.[21] More broadly, it has been argued that because Marx derives the category of money dialectically, he fails to engage with the empirical reality of money. To an extent this is true: there is, for example, little discussion in the *Grundrisse* of the links between money and political authority (such as the institutional role of the state in issuing and regulating money). Marx himself was clearly aware of the potential limits of his work in the *Grundrisse*, writing with reference to his discussion of money: 'It will be necessary later [...] to correct the idealist manner of the presentation, which makes it seem as if it were merely a matter of conceptual determinations and of the dialectic of these concepts' (151). In other words, it can seem as if Marx falls prey to the mistakes of which he accuses Hegel and others, 'as if the task were the dialectic balancing of concepts, and not the grasping of real relations!' (90). (Indeed, it is precisely for this reason that so many Hegelian-inclined Marxists value the *Grundrisse*.) Elsewhere in his oeuvre, Marx does trace the historical derivation or development of money. While this also happens (though to a lesser extent) in the *Grundrisse*, it can seem there as if history is being used only in order to illustrate what has already been established logically via the dialectical unfolding of concepts.[22]

As we know from the 'Introduction', however, it is not Marx's intention simply to offer a historical narrative. His aim is to ascend from the abstract to the concrete, with the development of categories determined by their relation to one another in bourgeois society rather than the order in which they appear in history. That is exactly what Marx does next: leaving his critique of the labour money theorists to one side, he uses his dialectical method to make essentially the same point, namely that exchange value necessitates money. He starts this demonstration by looking at the nature of a commodity.

Remember that a commodity is a product that is produced in order to exchange it. Any commodity is thus a 'unity of two aspects' (881). On the one hand, every commodity has certain properties that distinguish it from other commodities and make it what it is. Though he does not use the term at this specific point, what Marx is referring to is the *use value* of each commodity: each commodity has distinctive properties that make it useful to someone. As use values, commodities are qualitatively different: a loaf of bread is used in a very different way from a pen. On the other hand, as *exchange values* 'all commodities are qualitatively equal and differ only quantitatively' (141).

In the *Grundrisse*, Marx tends to use the terms 'value' and 'exchange value' interchangeably, whereas in later works he distinguishes between these two categories.[23] To say that a commodity has an exchange value is to say that it can be exchanged for another commodity, or has value in exchange. If it is possible to exchange two commodities, this must be because they have something in common, so that they can be measured against each other. That common thing is value. Exchange value is the form of appearance that value takes when a product is exchanged: it is only in exchange with other commodities that the value of a commodity can appear. This is why '[t]he concept of value is entirely peculiar to the most modern economy': only under capitalism, when the commodity becomes the general form of the product, do the products of labour take the form of value, because only under capitalism are products in general produced for exchange rather than for use (776).

Considered as exchange values, the different properties or potential uses of commodities – their use values – are irrelevant and they differ only because one is (for example) worth twice as much as the other. This must mean that each commodity also differs from itself: a loaf of bread as use value is different from a loaf of bread as exchange value. As a use value, it is qualitatively different to other use values; if as an exchange value it is qualitatively the same as all other use values, then it must also differ qualitatively from itself. Thus each commodity 'achieves a double existence' – as use value and exchange value. As a use value, a commodity is a natural thing with material properties; value, in contrast, is a *social* relation, distinct from any natural properties and which appears only in the social relation of exchange (141). In exchange, the value of the commodity must appear or present itself somehow. While the use value of the commodity appears in the natural or material form of the commodity itself (e.g. the use value of bread appears in its natural form as an edible and tasty thing), the *value* of the commodity cannot be expressed in the natural form of the commodity itself: we have just seen that *as value* the commodity differs from itself as use value or natural thing, and to say that one loaf of bread is equal to one loaf of bread would not tell us anything about its value. Hence if the value of a commodity is to be expressed, or take objective form, it must do so in another commodity. Ultimately that other commodity is money. In other words, we have reached the conclusion that we reached via the critique of labour money: 'The definition of a product as exchange value thus necessarily implies that exchange value obtains a separate existence, in isolation from the product' (145). There must be a separate, independent commodity that objectifies the exchange value in any commodity and that independent commodity is money.

This objectification of exchange value in money is necessary to overcome the contradictions between the commodity as use value and the commodity as exchange value. As use value, a commodity is *particular* – it meets particular needs, it must be transported in a particular way, can only be divided and used in particular ways, etc. – while as exchange value it is *general*: it can in principle always be exchanged with any other commodity. There is a contradiction here between the general character of the commodity as exchange value and its particular character as use value and this contradiction can impede or undermine any intended exchange. For example, as exchange value, every commodity is equally divisible: a pen may be worth twice as much as a loaf of bread, or one millionth the value of a house. In practice, however, it is obvious that commodities cannot easily be divided up in this way (no one wants to buy one millionth of a house, or half a pen). Thus, two potential exchangers may possess commodities of equal value but cannot exchange them because they cannot be physically divided up appropriately. Money overcomes this contradiction between the particular and the general by allowing the general exchange value of a commodity to be separated or freed from its particular use value: e.g. I can first sell my pen for money and then buy one loaf of bread. Money thus acts as the general equivalent of all commodities, allowing each commodity to be exchanged with all others: I can sell any commodity for money and buy any commodity with money. 'Money is labour time in the form of a general object, or the objectification of general labour time, labour time as a *general commodity*' (168).

We can say, then, that money is the necessary material existence or objectification of the commodity as exchange value. This does not mean that money is simply a 'thing', however: it is a *form* of value, specifically the form in which the value of commodities appears as exchange value. As such, 'it is impossible to abolish money itself as long as exchange value remains the social form of products' (145).

While money overcomes the contradiction between the two aspects of the commodity, it nonetheless introduces contradictions of its own – or, more accurately, it gives a different form to the contradictions of the capitalist mode of production. Marx identifies four contradictions inherent to the money relation. First, in order to overcome the contradictory double existence of the commodity as both a use value with particular natural properties and an exchange value with general social qualities, money was needed as the objectification of the latter. But it is precisely because the exchange value of the commodity is now objectified as money – meaning that the exchangeability of the commodity now exists as something different from and external to the commodity itself – that it may not be possible to realize its exchangeability. To do this, I have to convert my commodity into money, i.e. I have to sell it. But, in practice, the commodity can only be exchanged under certain conditions: there must be a demand and a market for that object's particular properties, it must be transported to the market, must be stored and then used by a certain date and so on. These conditions have nothing to do with the commodity *as exchange value* (because as exchange value the qualitative properties of the commodity are irrelevant), yet they simultaneously dictate the circumstances under which the exchange value is exchangeable. Thus, realizing the exchangeability of the commodity, by exchanging it for money, 'becomes dependent on external conditions, hence a matter of chance' (148). The two aspects of the commodity are brought into contradiction, with one aspect (its status as an object with natural properties) potentially frustrating its other aspect (its capacity to be exchanged).

A second contradiction is located in the act of exchange itself. As the commodity itself is split in two – it is a particular, useful object and it is an exchange value, now objectified as money – so is the act of exchange split into two: commodities can be sold to gain money, or money can be used to buy commodities. In the forms of barter that might have taken place in earlier societies, there was an 'immediate equality' between the two sides of the exchange: the 'sale' and the 'purchase' take place immediately and simultaneously, balancing each other out. When exchange value is objectified as money, sale and purchase are separated: I can sell my commodity for money, but it might be several months later and in another place that I use the money to buy another commodity. The exchange is dislocated and unbalanced, 'split into two mutually independent acts' (148). Although he does not exactly make it explicit, Marx is here opposing the assumption of classical and neo-classical economics that the market produces an equilibrium of supply and demand, often formulated as 'Say's Law', after the French political economist Jean-Baptiste Say, who argued that supply creates its own demand. With the division of the act of exchange, Marx argues, there is the possibility of a disequilibrium of supply and demand, of overproduction or underproduction, instability and, ultimately, crises.

This contradiction leads to a third. With the division of exchange into independent acts of sale (to gain money) and purchase (to gain commodities) comes the possibility that I can enter into exchange not in order to buy commodities for my use, but merely in order to make money. This 'exchange for the sake of exchange' marks the appearance of *commerce*. Rather than the producers of commodities selling them in order to buy further commodities for consumption, we can have merchants who buy commodities only in order to sell them and make money: 'the overall movement of exchange itself become[s] separate from the exchangers, the producers of commodities' (148). Now there exist two types of exchange with 'different laws and motives' that may contradict each other, producing the possibility of commercial crises. Under capitalism, this exchange for the sake of exchange becomes generalized, such that the aim of production is no longer the production of use values for consumption: 'production works directly for commerce and only indirectly for consumption' (149).

In addition to the development of commerce, we also see the development of money markets. This is the fourth and final contradiction – the double status of money itself. Money is the general commodity, because it represents exchange value in general and can be exchanged for any and all commodities, but money is also a particular commodity: it has a value, determined by the labour time necessary to produce it, and this value can change. Like any other commodity it can be traded, becoming one commodity among others. Hence, it is not only the case that (as in the first contradiction described above) money as objectified exchange value comes into contradiction with particular commodities with their natural properties; because it is itself a particular commodity, money also 'comes into contradiction with itself [...] It becomes a commodity like other commodities, and at the same time it is not a commodity like other commodities' (150–1).

In summary, money has 'overcome' the contradictions of the commodity form only by reproducing and generalizing them. The contradictions of money are 'the development of the relation of products as *exchange values*' (152). Marx now returns to the socialist proposal of labour money: can time chits overcome the contradictions of money?

How might time chits work? A central bank would be needed to issue them. Unless the owners of commodities want to 'await the chance arrival or non-arrival of a buyer', then they will go to the bank to redeem their commodities in exchange for time chits (154). The bank would, therefore, be the general buyer of commodities and hence it would also be the bank that stores and sells all commodities. In order to establish the correct exchange value of every commodity, the bank would also have to authenticate the amount of labour that goes into commodities. To do this, it would not only have to know average production times in each industry, it would also need to 'place the producers in conditions which made their labour equally productive (i.e. it would have to balance and to arrange the distribution of the means of labour)' (155). Because it would have to organize production in this way, every worker would in effect be working for the bank. In other words:

> the bank would be not only the general buyer and seller, but also the general producer. In fact either it would be a despotic ruler of production and trustee of distribution, or it would indeed be nothing more than a board which keeps the books and accounts for a society producing in common. (155–6)

In short, the introduction of time chits would necessitate a revolutionary transformation of the relations of production. The proponents of labour money do not understand this because they fail to distinguish between the particular labour of an individual and general or social labour. They 'want to make the labour of the individual directly into *money*', i.e. to 'determine that labour directly as *general* labour', such that the products of the labour of those individuals can be directly exchanged for any other product. But 'the worker's particular labour time cannot be directly exchanged for every other particular labour time': in order to attain 'general exchangeability', and so be capable of being exchanged with any other commodity, the exchange value in a commodity 'has first to take on an objective form, a form different from itself', i.e. the form of money. This is what happens in capitalism: proceeding 'from the independent production of individuals', the *general* nature of that labour and hence the 'social character of production' is established only through exchange: 'mediation takes place through the exchange of commodities, through exchange value and through money'.[24] In contrast, in pre-capitalist or post-capitalist societies, based on communal production, in which production is socially rather than privately organized, '[t]he labour of the individual is posited from the outset as social labour': all labour here is social or general because it is 'determined by communal need and communal purposes'. The individual shares in the products of communal production, rather than (as under capitalism) producing an exchange value which then has to be expressed as money before it can be exchanged for other commodities (171–2).

Hence the two alternatives that Marx puts to the labour money theorists. Either their changes to the instruments of circulation will make little difference, because they will not have affected the underlying relations of production: labour money will prove incapable 'of overcoming the contradictions inherent in the money relation' and will simply 'reproduce these contradictions in one or another form' (123). Or, in order to achieve their aims, they would have to overturn existing relations of production and establish the 'common ownership of the means of production' – in which case the form of money becomes totally irrelevant (156). In short, Marx's critique of socialism is that it misguidedly thinks that the problems of capitalism can be remedied by reforming the means of circulation or exchange, without ever really addressing the relations of production. Thus Max has not only confirmed the predominance of production over circulation, as asserted in the 'Introduction', he has demonstrated the political significance of this predominance. Specifically, he has shown that it is futile to try to do away with money as long as production rests on exchange value:

> It is necessary to see this clearly in order to avoid setting impossible tasks, and in order to know the limits within which monetary reforms and transformations of circulation are able to give a new shape to the relations of production and to the social relations which rest on the latter. (145–6)[25]

Money as social bond

To show that exchange value must be objectified in money, Marx has moved dialectically from product to commodity to exchange value to money – though in the *Grundrisse* the sequence of these categories is still quite confused and it can seem as if, in idealist fashion, he is simply moving from concept to concept rather than tracing real relations. In much briefer and more scattered comments, he also offers a historical overview, showing that money emerges not by convention but 'out of exchange, and arises naturally out of exchange' (165). As exchange relations develop and as production is increasingly directed towards the production of exchange values rather than use values, 'to the same degree must *money relations* develop'. As this happens, 'so grows the power of *money*' (146). Marx here is not (or not simply) making the mundane point that money gives you power. Rather, he is talking about the development of money as the social bond or form of community.

We saw above that production under capitalism is privately organized, in contrast to communal societies in which production is under communal control and hence directly social. But while 'production is not *directly* social' under capitalism, nonetheless individuals 'produce only for and in society': it is just that their labour only becomes social through exchange (158). The products of labour are not consumed by the immediate producers but by another person who purchases that product in exchange: hence it is only through exchange that we can tell whether or not the labour was socially necessary. This is what characterizes bourgeois society: it is 'the society that rests on *exchange value*' (159). While forms of exchange exist in pre-capitalist societies, exchange relations 'only develop fully, and continue to develop ever more completely, in bourgeois society' (156). Given that money is the objectified form of exchange value, the dominance of exchange relations and production for exchange means that under capitalism all relations and activities become dominated by money. For example, where taxes and rent were paid in kind, they are now paid in money and all forms of labour develop into wage labour (146). This domination of social relations by money is of course readily recognizable in today's world and has if anything accelerated: we live in a world in which even friendship is monetized.[26] This 'dissolution of all products and activities into exchange value presupposes the dissolution of all fixed personal (historic) relations of dependence in production' (156). In earlier societies, it is the community which 'binds the individuals together' and power is exercised through '[r]elations of personal dependence': for example, the power of a tribal chief over his tribe, or of a lord of the manor over his serfs.

In contrast, in a society resting on exchange value in which money dominates, these relations of personal dependence are dissolved and it is 'the owner of *exchange values*, of *money*' who possesses the ability to exercise power 'over the activity of others or over social wealth'. To this extent, in a capitalist society the 'individual carries his social power, as well as his bond with society, in his pocket' (157, 158). This does not mean that community as such has been dissolved under capitalism: rather, money 'is itself the community, and can tolerate none other standing above it' (223).

As social power and bond, money is thus 'the god among commodities' (221). There is here an echo of the section on 'The Power of Money' in the *1844 Manuscripts*, where Marx writes of money as a 'visible divinity', and of his early works in general in which he draws a parallel between religious alienation and money as a form of alienation (*CW3*: 324). Yet the analysis in the *Grundrisse* also anticipates the theory of commodity fetishism in *Capital I*. Although production under capitalism is private and independent, the labour of the producers is still posited as social – it is just that 'the social character of production is *posited* only *post festum*', in exchange (172). While production is private, exchange 'presupposes the all-round dependence of the producers on one another' (158). But these exchange relations are between independent producers: they are not under any communal control and appear autonomous of any and all individuals. 'As the producers become more dependent on exchange, exchange appears to become more independent of them' (146). So while the 'social bond is expressed in *exchange value*', this is an alienated form of community, independent of any kind of collective control (156).

> The general exchange of activities and products, which has become a vital condition for each individual – their mutual interconnection – here appears as something alien to them, autonomous, as a thing. In exchange value, the social connection between persons is transformed into a social relation between things. (157)

Or as Marx puts it in the section on 'The Fetishism of the Commodity' in *Capital I*: 'To the producers [...] the social relations between their private labours appear [...] as material relations between persons and social relations between things' (*C1*:

165-166). The problem with capitalism is thus not that it dissolves all connections and leaves only isolated individuals, but rather that it generates an *alienated* form of mutual interdependence: it introduces 'the *connection of the individual* with all' but only on the basis of 'the *independence of this connection from the individual*' (161).

Marx recognizes that for some 'this is precisely the beauty and the greatness of it: this spontaneous interconnection, this material and mental metabolism which is independent of the knowing and willing of individuals, and which presupposes their reciprocal independence and indifference' (161). From Smith to Hayek to present-day neoliberals, this is indeed the beauty of the 'invisible hand' of capitalism according to its defenders: in pursuing their own private and competing interests, individuals simultaneously though unintentionally advance the public good, far more efficiently than any form of organized planning ever could. Thus a harmonious social bond is supposedly created through the pursuit of private interests. For Marx, this is to confuse things. There *is* a 'reciprocal dependence' in bourgeois society but it is not simply the sum of competing private interests, because 'that private interest is itself already a socially determined interest', 'given by social conditions independent of all' (156). This is an alienated form of social interconnection in which even and especially at the level of the individual we lack control, all of us submitted to an independent and estranged power materialized as money. In addition, the defenders of the free market erroneously universalize the social bond that exists under capitalism, as if it had always existed (and always will). For Marx, in contrast, 'it is an insipid notion to conceive of this merely *objective bond* as a spontaneous, natural attribute inherent in individuals and inseparable from their nature': while he agrees with the liberals that capitalism does create a kind of social bond, he insists that this is a historically specific bond (162).

In the face of frankly indisputable facts, some liberals do acknowledge that capitalism has not always existed, but they nonetheless argue that its arrival emancipated our natural dispositions and propensities by freeing us from the arbitrary restrictions of feudalism. Up to a point, Marx is sympathetic to this argument – not because he thinks capitalism accords with our human nature but because, as we have seen, he agrees that its development presupposed the dissolution of pre-existing social ties and bonds. Moreover, he also welcomes the destruction of those traditional ties: the 'objective connection' established by capitalism 'is preferable to the lack of any connection, or to a merely local connection resting on blood ties, or on primeval, natural or master-servant relations', as exist in pre-capitalist societies (161). Pre-capitalist societies – 'patriarchal, ancient or feudal' – are dominated by relations of personal dependence and the individual is subordinated to the community (159). Under capitalism, 'the ties of personal dependence, of distinctions of blood, education, etc. are in fact exploded, ripped up' and individuality can develop: 'a system of [...] universal relations, of all-round needs and universal capacities is formed for the first time' (163, 158). The problem, or contradiction, is that this personal independence is founded upon an objective, alienated dependence on exchange relations. At the same time, however, capitalism puts in place the conditions for a post-capitalist society in which we will find '[f]ree individuality, based on the universal development of individuals and on their subordination of their communal, social productivity as their social wealth' (158). While capitalism rests on privatization, competition and fragmentation, it simultaneously creates new forms of unity, cooperation and combination, in the production process – where many workers are gathered together – and in the creation of a world market. Therefore, 'within bourgeois society [...] there arise relations of circulation as well as of production which are so many mines to explode it'. Capitalism thus creates the conditions for the development of communism as the 'free exchange among individuals who are associated on the basis of common appropriation and control of the means of production' (159).

At this point in his work Marx expresses this argument not only in very condensed form but also in relatively crudely dialectical terms, in which (in effect if not entirely explicitly) feudalism is the thesis, capitalism is the antithesis (or capitalism is the antithesis to its own thesis) and communism the synthesis. Drawing on Roy Bhaskar, we could suggest that the influence on Marx here is not so much Hegel as Schiller, with a dialectic that moves from original undifferentiated unity (subordination of individual to community under feudalism) to fragmentation (competitive individualism within an alienated community under capitalism) to restored but differentiated unity (collective control of the means of production and the flourishing of the individual under communism).[27] Nonetheless, the argument has the value of both distinguishing capitalism from pre-capitalist societies and of making a political point about the growth of the conditions of post-capitalist society within capitalism: 'if we did not find concealed in society as it is the material conditions of production and the corresponding relations of exchange prerequisite for a classless society, then all attempts to explode it would be quixotic'. Though it is not made explicit here, this suggests that we need to wait for the right conditions to mature before we can successfully overthrow capitalism. At the very least, Marx's position here rules out the kind of anarchist voluntarism that thinks we can make a revolution at will. At the same time, however, socialist reformism is rejected: the 'antithetical forms' of capitalism 'can never be abolished through quiet metamorphosis' (159).

Despite his condemnation of bourgeois society, then, Marx's evaluation of capitalism is relatively positive: it is a progression from feudalism and a step towards communism. Yet he warns us not to get carried away. The destruction of the traditional ties of feudalism and the development of personal independence and freedom is what 'seduces the democrats' into championing capitalism: whereas under feudalism you were born into a position of personal dependence which defined you for the rest of your life, in a capitalist society as long as you have something to sell or buy then you are free to enter the market and in principle you are free to choose your place in society (163). This narrative – of ever-increasing freedom of choice – is seductive precisely because it is partly true: pre-capitalist societies rested on the 'natural or political super- and subordination of individuals to one another', whereas capitalism rests on free exchange (159). But while it is important to distinguish capitalism from feudalism, we should be careful of drawing *too* sharp a distinction or of seeing the transition from feudalism to capitalism too simplistically as purely an evolutionary progression.

In the first place, it is to an extent an 'illusion' that feudal social relations were 'purely personal relations' (165). They seem more 'personal' because they were more limited and 'primitive', but they are (like capitalist social relations) founded on a form of objective dependency: 'the individuals in such a society, although their relations appear to be more personal, enter into connection with one another only as individuals imprisoned within a certain definition' (163). More importantly, the individuals in capitalist society are equally imprisoned, such that their 'freedom' is only a 'semblance':

> [I]ndividuals [in capitalist society – SC] *seem* independent (this is an independence which is at bottom merely an illusion, and it is more correctly called indifference), free to collide with one another and to engage in exchange within this freedom; but they appear thus only for someone who abstracts from the *conditions*, the *conditions of existence* within which these individuals enter into contact (and these conditions, in turn, are independent of the individuals and, although created by society, appear as if they were *natural conditions*, not controllable by individuals). (163–4)

There seems to be less freedom under feudalism because 'the single individual cannot strip away his personal definition': if you are a serf, you'll stay a serf. But while the wage-labourer under capitalism, unlike the feudal serf, is free to choose their employer (though in practice even this freedom is often unavailable or is severely restricted), they are *not* free to choose whether or not to be a wage-labourer: if they want to live, they must sell their labour-power to a capitalist. It might be, of course, that a few workers manage to rise out of their class – '[a] particular individual may by chance get on top of these relations' – but they cannot all do so, because by definition capitalism needs a large mass of workers. Most workers must therefore remain workers: 'it is impossible for the individuals of a class etc. to overcome' the conditions of their existence '*en masse* without destroying them' (164).

In both feudalism and capitalism, therefore, there is a lack of freedom, but in different ways. Under capitalism, personal ties of dependence have given way to the impersonal rule of capital: 'individuals are now ruled by *abstractions*, whereas earlier they depended on one another. The abstraction, or idea, however, is nothing more than the theoretical expression of those material relations which are their lord and master' (164). If anything, the end of directly political subordination makes capitalism more brutal than feudalism. As Marx and Engels state in the *Manifesto*: 'for exploitation, veiled by religious and political illusions, [the bourgeoisie – SC] has substituted naked, shameless, direct, brutal exploitation' (*CW6*: 487).

By looking at his discussions of money as social bond, we can better understand what is dialectical about Marx's analysis of capitalism. Not only does he conceive of capitalism as a unity of opposites – simultaneously progressive and destructive – he insists that we view it as part of a broader historical movement: a social form that has emerged from previous social forms and on the basis of which will develop the new social form that will be communism. We can also see the originality of his political position, distinct not only from pro-market cheerleaders like Smith and his descendants (although to be fair Smith himself was far more subtle and critical than most of those who invoke his name today) but also from other critics of capitalism. Just as Marx rejects the perspective of bourgeois apologists, so he rejects that 'romantic viewpoint' – whether taken up by conservatives, socialists, or anarchists – which understands capitalism only in terms of loss (of tradition, community, individuality, etc.). 'It is as ridiculous to yearn for a return to that original fullness as it is to believe that with this complete emptiness history has come to a standstill' (162).[28] Capitalism may be highly destructive, but it is also progressive and necessary for the future development of communism and hence Marx has no time for nostalgic longing for what capitalism has destroyed.

Properties and functions of money

Marx now turns to the functions of money, in a section that can be seen as a rough draft for Chapter 3 of *Capital I*. Discussions of the different functions of money were common in political economy. Marx's difference is that he elicits the contradictions within and between these functions. In doing so, his aim is to move from money to capital. In his analysis of the functions of money Marx relies on a distinction between two different types of circulation (201). The discussion of these two types of circulation in the *Grundrisse* is neither very full nor very clear and there is a much more accessible analysis in Chapter 4 of *Capital I*.

On the one hand there is simple circulation, in which a commodity is sold for money and the money is used to buy a different commodity to consume. This is represented by the formula: C–M–C. On the other hand, we can have M–C–M, in which money is used to buy a commodity which is then sold for money. There would be little point in using money to buy a commodity which you then sold for the same amount of money, so the complete form of this process can be expressed as: M–C–M', where M' = M + ΔM, i.e. the original amount of money plus an additional amount. M–C–M' is the circulation of capital, or the 'general formula of capital' (*C1*: 257). The distinction between these two forms of circulation is a conceptual distinction that is used by Marx to identify the uniqueness of capitalism, rather than a historical distinction used to distinguish between pre-capitalist and capitalist societies. In C–M–C the aim of the exchange is consumption, or the satisfaction of some need and it does not matter how the commodities were produced: the 'C' that is sold for money may have been made by an artisan labourer working from his own home (rather than a wage labourer working for a capitalist). Yet, as we have just seen, exchange relations only develop fully in bourgeois society and, as we will see later, the circuit C–M–C plays a vital role in capitalism. In addition, while M–C–M' may be the general formula of capital, that does not mean that M–C–M' exchanges can not take place before the full development of capitalism: merchants, who buy goods only in order to sell them for money, can also exist in pre-capitalist societies.

Money as measure

The first function of money that Marx identifies is money as measure. In early societies, products could be exchanged through barter: we could decide between ourselves whether my apples are worth as much as your oranges. In those early societies, however, exchange was something that took place only rarely and at the borders of a society: one community may have exchanged its surplus with another, but exchange was haphazard and random rather than regular or continuous. As such, the products exchanged were only temporarily and accidentally exchange values: they were not produced as exchange values (204). As exchange develops, we are dealing not with products but with commodities – products produced for exchange – and each commodity must be brought into general relation to every other possible commodity rather than into a particular relation with only one other commodity: I am no longer looking to exchange my apples simply for some oranges, but for a potentially infinite range of possible commodities, all of which have to be measured against my apples. Given that all commodities are the product of human labour, we can measure their value according to the amount of labour time contained within them. However, rather than individually calculating what each commodity is worth in terms of every other commodity (what an apple is worth when converted into oranges, plums, pears, etc.), one commodity comes to stand as the common measure of all commodities. That one commodity is money.[29]

So it is not that money somehow creates the commensurability of commodities, i.e. gives commodities the capacity to be measured against one another. Commodities can be measured against each other because they all contain labour time (*C1*: 188). Gold can be used as money – as the standard of measurement – because it contains labour time (791). *Any* commodity could in principle be used as money, it's just that gold has certain advantages: durability, divisibility, uniformity, relative rarity, etc. (174–80).

Expressed in money, the exchange value of the commodity is its price (though we know from Marx's critique of the labour money theorists that price fluctuates around value). Money as measure thus expresses the price of commodities, but in this function it is not itself an exchange value, because it 'is not expressed as a relation [...] but as a natural quantity of a certain material, a natural weight-fraction of gold' (205).[30] Money is posited here as a definite and simple quantity of itself, as the material in which the value of all other commodities is measured and expressed as their price. As measure of exchange values, money does not actually need to be present: in order to know how many pieces of gold a commodity is equivalent to, we do not need to have those pieces of gold in our hand. Likewise, in order to know that the GDP of the UK is (say) £2 trillion, there does not actually need to be £2 trillion of money in the country. In this sense, money as measure is 'ideal': it does not need to be materially present to perform its function of measurement. Yet at the same time it must express some definite amount of a natural substance, such as gold: to give a price to something we have to know how much gold it is equivalent to, even though the gold does not have to be materially present.[31]

Money as medium

The second function of money is as medium of exchange: this is money as the 'M' in C–M–C, acting as the link between commodities by allowing one commodity to be exchanged for another. As we just saw, in its function as *measure*, the material substance of the money commodity is vital, whereas its actual presence is irrelevant. In contrast, as *medium* of exchange, the material substance of money is irrelevant, whereas its actual presence is vital (212). If, for example, gold is to act as the medium of exchange, then I need to have some pieces of gold in my hand in order to exchange them for a commodity. As measure, the amount of gold that exists is not important: as long as everyone knows what one gold coin is worth, it does not matter how many gold coins there are in existence. As medium, the reverse is true: in order that a certain number of commodities can circulate, there must actually be a certain number of gold coins in circulation, so that exchanges can take place. The exact quantity of money that must be in circulation is determined by the number of commodities circulating, their total price and the velocity of circulation (e.g. if circulation is rapid, then the same coin can be used for more exchanges in the same period of time). Marx's approach thus rejects the quantity theory of money (today supported by monetarists), which claims that it is the money supply that determines the price of commodities (because if the supply of money increases, the value of money falls and the prices of commodities increase). For Marx it is the reverse: 'the quantity of money required for circulation depends [...] on the sum total of prices to be realized', plus 'the rapidity with which money circulates' (194).

As medium of exchange, money also functions as the 'realizer of prices': if I sell a commodity for £1, I am realizing its price of £1 (208). In return for my commodity, I therefore expect to receive the exact equivalent value in money, otherwise I won't have realized its price. But this is important only if we consider 'this moment of circulation in isolation'. If instead we take the whole circular process of C–M–C (and its repetition in multiple acts of exchange: C–M–C–M–C) then it is of little significance whether or not I actually receive the exact equivalent value in money, because I am only going to use that money to purchase another commodity. In the process C–M–C, in other words, the price of my commodity is ultimately realized in another commodity and money 'serves only as a means to the end that all commodities are to be exchanged at equivalent prices' (211). The realization of the price of the commodity in money is only one fleeting and ephemeral moment (C–M) of a longer process (C–M–C) in which money is only a middleman, only a 'symbol' (209–10). Hence 'symbolic money can replace the real, because material money as mere medium of exchange is itself symbolic' (212). We can now see why, in its function as medium, the presence of money is essential but its material substance is irrelevant. This means that gold can be replaced with silver or copper coins of lesser value, or even with paper notes which in themselves have little value but which act as the symbol of money (810–11). It does not mean, however, that Marx is committed to a 'symbol' or 'nominalist' theory of money in which money itself has no value and acts purely as a symbol of value. As a *medium of exchange* money is a symbol, but that is only one of money's functions; as measure of value, Marx thinks money must ultimately exist as a commodity. In addition, whichever symbol is used as a means of exchange must ultimately be convertible into the money commodity gold (or whatever substance is used as money).

This second function of money is essential to bourgeois society, which is a society in which 'one produces only in order to exchange'. Without money, exchange would not be possible – and eradicating exchange would mean a fundamental transformation in the organization of society. It would mean either going backwards and reverting to a society of bartering, or overthrowing current society and establishing a society 'in which exchange value would no longer be the principal aspect of the commodity, because social labour, whose representative it is, would no longer appear merely as socially mediated private labour' (214).

Money as money

The third function of money is as an end in itself. This third function 'presuppose[s] the first two [functions – SC] and constitutes their unity'. Historically speaking, money as money appears with hoarding: I sell a commodity for money, but rather than then purchasing another commodity I hoard the money that I have made. But although gold (for example) can be accumulated before it has developed as money – i.e. before money has developed in its first two functions – if the first two functions have not yet developed then it is not really being accumulated *as money*: it is simply being collected as gold (216).

Money in this third function is both general and particular: it is the general form of wealth in a particular object (218). Money as money both *is* wealth (it is the realization of price) and it is the 'general material representative of wealth' (it represents the wealth found in all other commodities and it can purchase anything). All other commodities are a form of wealth, but they are only *particular* forms of wealth: they can be used only to satisfy a particular need, or their price can be realized (by being sold on the market) but only under particular circumstances (e.g. there must be a demand for that particular commodity). Money, on the other hand, *is* realized price and can be used to satisfy any and every need (because it can be exchanged for any and every commodity).

This is why money is 'the lord and god of the world of commodities. It represents the divine existence of commodities, while they represent its earthly form' (221). It gives power to the individual who possesses it because it can purchase anything. Money in this function is not merely the object of greed, it is also the very condition of possibility of greed as such: a person can crave particular possessions, but they can only have greed for wealth in general once wealth in general has been individualized in a particular object. (Thus greed is not somehow an essential feature of human nature, but a historical product of social development.) When Marx suggests that historically '[m]onetary greed, or mania for wealth, necessarily brings with it the decline and fall of the ancient communities', we should not take this as a moralistic claim that it was the greed of the ancients that was their downfall. Rather, we need to understand it in the light of Marx's argument concerning money as the social bond: the development of money as money undermines the traditional bonds of ancient societies, because money 'can tolerate none other standing above it' (223).

In bourgeois society, money has a productive rather than a dissolving effect: money, as the objectified form of exchange value, becomes the aim of production. In this sense, while money as money can exist in pre-capitalist societies, it can only fully develop where there is wage labour: 'money must be the *direct* object, aim and product of general labour, the labour of all individuals. Labour must directly produce exchange value, i.e. money'. Hence greed becomes universal in bourgeois society: it is 'the urge of all, in so far as everyone wants to make money', or rather everyone must have making money as their goal because all labour is directed towards the creation of money (224)

As well as dissolving pre-modern societies, money also plays a more active role in the development of bourgeois society. In the age of mercantilism, states and individuals went off in search of gold reserves and in this way 'colonization is improvised and made to flourish'. Preoccupied by the amount of gold each nation had – because they saw gold itself, rather than labour, as the source of all wealth – the mercantilists had a pre-capitalist understanding of money. But, without their understanding it ('behind their backs'), through their colonial adventures they helped the further development of wage labour and money as money by advancing its conditions: opening up new sources of and markets for commodities, 'draw[ing] distant continents into the metabolism of circulation, i.e. exchange' (225).

Although money as money develops *fully* in bourgeois society, it does not develop only there. Indeed, as we know from the 'Introduction', in its simple form money can play a dominant role in 'a less developed whole', i.e. in pre-capitalist societies (102). In the 'Chapter on Money', it can sometimes seem otherwise, because Marx develops the third function of money in terms of the circuit M–C–M, i.e. in terms of the 'general formula of capital', which might seem to suggest that money – at least in its third function – only develops under capitalism. But remember that M–C–M can take place in pre-capitalist societies. In addition, we can derive the category of money as money from simple commodity circulation (i.e. C–M–C), which is exactly what Marx does in *Capital I*. In *Capital I* Marx is also much clearer in identifying the three aspects of the function of money as money: (i) hoarding; (ii) means of paying debts; (iii) 'world money', i.e. the role of money as the means of payment in international trade (*C1*: 227–44). The first of these – hoarding, or the pursuit of money as money – can take place in both pre-capitalist and capitalist societies. It does so, however, in different ways: 'While hoarding, considered as an independent form of self-enrichment, vanishes with the advance of bourgeois society, it grows at the same time in the form of the accumulation of a reserve fund of the means of payment' (*C1*: 240). Although hoarding is a form of accumulation and can take place in capitalist societies, it is nonetheless quite different from capitalist accumulation. In the latter, as we will shortly see, value is created: the capitalist uses money to buy commodities to use in the production of value. In the former – the hoarding of money – no value is created: the hoarder sells without buying, but he has only withdrawn as much value from circulation (in the form of money) as he has put into circulation (in the form of commodities).

Money as an end in itself is in one sense the dialectical overcoming of the contradictions of money as measure and medium, as their negation and unity. Remember that as measure of value, money was the *ideal* measure of other exchange values, not because (as some economists argued) it is an imaginary value, but because it did not need to be materially present; as medium of circulation, money was a *symbol*, because its material substance was not important.[32] As end in itself, in contrast, money has both to be materially present and to be a definite material substance. 'As measure, its amount was irrelevant; as medium of circulation, its materiality, the matter of the unit, was irrelevant: as money in this third role, the amount of itself as of a definite quantity of material is essential' (229).

On the other hand, money as money introduces its own contradictions, which come to light especially when we consider its relation to circulation. In a sense, money in its third function is independent of circulation: when money is accumulated, it is withdrawn from circulation. And yet '[c]ut off from all relation to [circulation], it would not be money, but merely a simple natural object, gold or silver' (217). Removed from circulation, it is the general form of wealth, potentially able to buy anything, yet existing only as 'a mere phantom of real wealth': it can be realized as the material representative of general wealth only by re-entering circulation, leaving the hands of its owner and being exchanged for the particular forms of wealth (commodities). If I hold on to money, I am not necessarily increasing my own wealth: as a particular commodity itself, a product of a definite amount of labour, the value of the money commodity varies; in addition, its value will not increase if the general wealth of society does not also increase. In short, although independent of circulation – because withdrawn from it – money is also dependent on circulation: it comes out of circulation and it must return to it if it is to be realized. Yet in returning to circulation, it loses itself, in the sense that it loses its quality of being money as money (because money as money is precisely money withdrawn from circulation). 'Its independence is a mere semblance; its independence of circulation exists only in view of circulation, exists as dependence on it' (234).

As we should by now appreciate, when we encounter these kinds of contradictions in Marx's work we have reached not an impasse but rather the moment when one category develops into another. Having moved (albeit in a somewhat circuitous and digressive style) from the product to commodity to exchange value to money, we are now at the point when we must move from money to capital. Whereas money loses itself in circulation, capital, as we will see, preserves itself in circulation. With capital, 'exchange value deriving from circulation and presupposing circulation preserves itself within it and by means of it; does not lose itself by entering into it' (259–60).

Rather than overcoming the contradiction within the commodity between use value and exchange value, money replicated this contradiction. Money is the representative of general wealth, able to buy any and all commodities – yet this generality is contradicted by its quantity: money is always necessarily a definite amount of money, hence quantitatively limited and so only a representative of *limited* wealth. Money's 'quantitative limit is in contradiction with its quality. It is therefore inherent in its nature constantly to drive beyond its own barrier' (270).[33] This contradiction is overcome in capital, which is a form of value that increases itself. As Marx puts it:

> Money as a sum of money is measured by its quantity. This measuredness contradicts its character, which must be oriented towards the measureless. Everything which has been said here about money holds even more for capital, in which money actually develops in its completed character for the first time. (271)

As we might expect, however, and as we will see, the contradictions do not come to an end with capital.

Study Questions

1. Why does Marx begin Notebook I by looking at money?
2. What is the difference between use value and exchange value and in what ways do they contradict each other?
3. Why must exchange value objectify itself as money?
4. On what grounds does Marx reject the socialist proposal for labour money?
5. What are the three functions of money?

Chapter on Capital

At the start of his 'Chapter on Capital' – which fills most of the remaining 650 pages of the *Grundrisse* – Marx summarizes the difficulties of understanding money.[34] The central problem is that 'a social relation, a definite relation between individuals, here appears as a metal, a stone, as a purely physical, external thing which can be found, as such, in nature, and which is indistinguishable in form from its natural existence'. Appearing as a natural object that is mined from the ground, the attributes and powers of money appear to derive from its existence as this natural object. But '[n]ature does not produce money, any more than it produces a rate of exchange or a banker' (239). The Proudhonists and socialists think that the contradictions of money and of bourgeois society in general can be overcome simply by 'depriving money of its metallic form': removing its form as a natural object so that it becomes simply 'the expression of a social relation'. But this is to misunderstand the problem with money: it is to confuse money as a form of value with its appearance as a piece of gold, to think that the problems associated with money can be eradicated by eradicating the form of appearance:

> [P]olemics are directed against metallic money or money in general, as the most striking, most contradictory and hardest phenomenon which is presented by the system in a palpable form. One or another kind of artful tinkering with money is then supposed to overcome the contradictions of which money

> is merely the perceptible appearance [...] [O]ne strikes a blow at the sack, intending the donkey. (240)

The socialists have thus chosen the wrong target, attacking only the consequences and appearances of the social relations that are the real problem. Believing that exchange relations have been perverted by money, the socialists think that the solution must be to eliminate money in its current form: in effect, they want to get back to a time when exchange was uncorrupted by money (248).

To this extent, the socialists are not so different from bourgeois apologists for the status quo, for whom exchange is both a model for and justification of existing social relations. Both think that the exchange of exchange values is 'a system of universal freedom and equality': it is just that bourgeois economists think that exchange as it already exists is such a system, whilst the socialists look back to a money-free past or forward to a money-free future, wherein the essential or original freedom and equality of exchange is realized (248).

Superficially, at least, these views are plausible. In exchange – so it appears – each exchanger is indeed *equal*: they have the same social position (they are both exchangers) and they possess equivalent things (if they were not equivalent, why would they exchange them?). The exchangers are of course different, but this is the basis of their equality: it is because they own different commodities and have different needs that they enter into their equal exchange. In addition, each exchanger is *free*: they do not seize each other's property by force, but enter into exchange freely and voluntarily. Though each participant enters the exchange with only her own interests in mind, the exchange is mutually beneficial and serves their common interests. There is a sense in which I am compelled to enter into exchange, in that I am driven into exchange by the force of my own needs. But these are *my* natural needs rather than something imposed upon me from outside, and they affect everyone, forming the basis of the free and equal exchange (245).

Yet, contra Proudhon and the socialists, if we take this view then money is not a perversion of the exchange relation but its perfection (and, to this extent, the bourgeois apologists have a better understanding of the relation between exchange and money). As measure, money allows the equation of the two sides of the exchange. As medium of circulation, money presents one exchanger as equal to the other: 'A worker who buys commodities for 3s. appears to the seller in the same function, in the same equality – in the form of 3s. – as the king who does the same' (246). As end in itself, money can of course be accumulated. This seems to introduce inequality into the equality of the exchange relation, because the person who accumulates will become richer than the person who does not. But – the bourgeois apologist will argue – he who accumulates money only does so to the extent that he does not accumulate commodities of the same value, so no one is disadvantaged. Furthermore, the decision to accumulate is freely open to anyone: 'If one grows impoverished and the other grows wealthier, then this is of their own free will' (247). If, having accumulated money, a person then wants to pass that money on to his children, this does nothing to undermine the freedom and formal equality of the exchange relation: if a person has accumulated his money freely and justly, then there can be no objection to another person being chosen to step into their place as the owner of that money. Hence '[e]ven inheritance and similar legal relations, which perpetuate such inequalities, do not prejudice this natural freedom and equality' (247).

To see that these sorts of arguments have an enduring appeal and utility, one need only look at a late-twentieth-century thinker like Robert Nozick, whose basic arguments differ little from those that Marx here puts into the mouths of market apologists. Marx's response however, is not simply to reject the claim that the sphere of exchange is one of freedom and equality. To the contrary, he writes:

> Equality and freedom are [...] not only respected in exchange based on exchange values but, also, the exchange of exchange values is the productive, real basis of all *equality* and *freedom*. As pure ideas they are merely the idealized expressions of this basis; as developed in juridical, political, social relations, they are merely this basis to a higher power. (245)

This does not mean that it is only within bourgeois society that humans become free and equal, for different eras have their own versions of these ideals: the development of exchange based on exchange value is the foundation of the *bourgeois* versions of these ideals, but this same development is the destruction of ancient Roman ideas of freedom and equality. This suggests that, for Marx, we should not proceed by identifying some immutable and universal standard of freedom and equality and then seeing whether or not our exchange relations meet this standard.

On what basis, then, can Marx criticize bourgeois exchange relations? His basic answer is that focusing on exchange gives us only a partial and incomplete view. Defenders of the bourgeois system of exchange conceive of it in terms of the simple circulation of commodities: one commodity owner exchanging with another, their exchange mediated by money. But this tells us nothing about how those commodities were produced, how the exchangers became the owners of those commodities, or why they are entering into exchange. It is to examine only 'the surface process, beneath which, however, in the depths, entirely different processes go on, in which this apparent individual equality and liberty disappear' (247). These 'different processes' 'in the depths' are the relations of production upon which the exchange of commodities must rest. Commodity exchange can only be fully developed on the basis of *capitalist* relations of production. As such, it is those relations of production that we need to investigate. If we do so, we will find 'that the *presupposition* of exchange value, as the objective basis of the whole system of production, already in itself implies compulsion over the individual' rather than the freedom of the individual (247–8). The very fact that the individual is entering into exchange means that 'his immediate product is not a product for him, but only *becomes* such in the social process': he is alienated from the product of his labour and must enter the autonomous realm of exchange in order to meet his needs (248). These are the necessary conditions of exchange relations that all individuals are compelled to accept but which none of them has chosen or can control.

We can now see further why, from Marx's perspective, Proudhon and his disciples seem absurd. They 'want to depict socialism as the realization of the ideals of *bourgeois* society articulated by the French revolution' (a goal shared by many present-day socialists) (248). But Marx has shown that the 'real basis' of these ideals is the very exchange relations that socialists oppose. The Proudhonist will respond that these exchange relations are free and equal *in essence*, but have been undermined and perverted by later developments such as money and capital. Marx refutes this by showing that the 'perversions' that are supposed to undermine exchange are in fact an inherent part of it, because exchange can only become widespread on the basis of exploitative capitalist relations of production. The Proudhonists want to achieve justice on the basis of the law of value – i.e. the exchange of equivalents measured by labour time – but the operation of the law of value is necessarily exploitative.[35] 'It is just as pious and stupid to wish that exchange value would not develop into capital, nor labour which produces exchange value into wage labour' (249). We now need to understand what capital is and how it develops from money.

Section One: The Production Process of Capital

From money to capital

What is capital? For the classical political economists, capital is objectified labour which can be used as the means or instrument of further labour.[36] So, for example, an axe would be capital: it is objectified labour (it is an object produced by labour) and can be used as an instrument of further labour. The problem with this approach for Marx is that it looks only at the *material* side of a thing without considering its specific social *form* (257). If the approach of the classical economists was correct, it would mean that capital existed in every historical era, because any tool, from the simplest axe to the most complex computer, could be considered capital.[37] It would also mean that our bodies should be considered capital, as our bodies are used in labour and they are the products of labour (we feed ourselves, exercise, and practise and develop certain techniques and skills). This, in fact, is how most economists today still understand the term 'capital': think, for example, of the term 'human capital'. But such an understanding of capital is wholly dehistoricizing. It is thus typical of the approach of political economy: it takes something from the present, completely ignores the specific social form it has, and then projects it back into the past as if it had always existed. This dehistoricization works by seeing capital only as a thing (as the instrument of production), and a thing entirely abstracted from the social relations in which it is found: as if an axe produced and used within a hunter-gatherer society has the same social *form* as an axe produced and used within a capitalist society. '*Capital is conceived as a thing, not as a relation*' (258).

So the political economists are mistaken in thinking that they can move from labour and its products straight to capital. Instead, we have to follow the path that Marx has taken in the *Grundrisse*, moving from value to capital (via money):

> To develop the concept of capital it is necessary to begin not with labour but with value, and, precisely, with exchange value in an already developed movement of circulation. It is just as impossible to make the transition directly from labour to capital as it is to go from the different human races directly to the banker, or from nature to the steam engine. (259)

A slightly more sophisticated bourgeois understanding of capital characterizes it as 'a sum of values used for the production of values' (258). This is for Marx an improvement, because it does at least recognize that if we are going to get to capital we have to start with value. But the problem is that not every sum of values is capital: 'I cannot get from exchange value to capital by means of mere addition' (251). Attempts to define capital in terms of profit go a step further, but are ultimately confused:

> If it is said that capital is exchange value which produces profit, or at least has the intention of producing profit, then capital is already presupposed in its explanation, for profit is a specific relation of capital to itself. Capital is not a simple relation, but a *process*, in whose various moments it is always capital. (258)

Although we cannot define capital in terms of profit (because we need to know what capital is before we can know what profit is), in its crude way this definition does point to something important, namely that capital must increase or grow: capital is a process of the expansion of value. Marx has already told us that if we are to reach the concept of capital, we have to begin with 'with exchange value in an already developed movement of circulation'. In short, then, when we are looking for capital, we are looking for a form of value that preserves and increases itself through circulation. But which form of circulation?

In simple circulation, a commodity is sold for money and money is used to buy a commodity: C–M–C. Here, exchange value provides the form of the exchange (because in the exchange, commodity and money act as exchange values) but the real content and purpose of the exchange is the use value of the commodities: once the C–M–C exchange has happened, the commodity leaves circulation altogether and is consumed as a use value. 'If the commodity is exchanged via money for another commodity, then its value-character disappears in the moment in which it realizes itself' (260). So simple circulation is not a 'developed movement of circulation': once money has bought a commodity (M–C), exchange value disappears and this disappearance completes the circuit C–M–C. 'With that, circulation comes to an end' (262). That circuit can be repeated – another commodity can be sold for money and the money used to buy a commodity – but it would be a separate repetition rather than the continuous *process* that we are looking for. Simple circulation '*therefore does not carry within itself the principle of self-renewal* [...] Commodities constantly have to be thrown into it anew from the outside, like fuel into a fire' (254–5).

But what about money as money? Earlier, we developed this third function of money in relation to simple circulation: I can accumulate money as money by selling without buying (C–M). Yet we saw that here too exchange value disappears. Money persists as exchange value only by withdrawing from circulation and becoming independent of it, but it persists in this way only in an ideal form or 'a purely illusory realization', as a hoard which is basically useless until it returns to circulation (260). To realize itself, money has to return to circulation – yet as soon as it does so it returns to its two earlier functions (as measure and medium) and is dissolved in the purchase of commodities (254).

So we cannot reach capital through simple circulation alone (which is not to say that simple circulation is irrelevant: to the contrary, it is a necessary part of the process of capital). Capital develops from money and first appears as money, but it is more than money: we cannot reach capital just by accumulating money. We need to move from money as money to money as capital and to do so we must move from C–M–C to M–C–M. Whereas in C–M–C exchange value provided the form of the exchange but the consumption of use values was the content or purpose, in M–C–M exchange value is both form and content: exchange value is the purpose of the exchange. With C–M–C, each circuit ends with the consumption of a use value: in this sense, its end or purpose lies outside of circulation and although it can be repeated – another C–M–C exchange can take place – this repetition will be a new and separate circuit. In contrast, M–C–M is self-renewing or self-reproducing: it ends where it begins, with money, hence recreating its starting point and perpetuating itself. Whereas in C–M–C money loses itself as soon as it enters circulation – it loses its quality of being money as money – money as capital preserves itself in and through circulation. 'The immortality which money [in its third function as money – SC] strove to achieve by setting itself negatively against circulation, by withdrawing from it, is achieved by capital' (261).

We now have something like a preliminary definition of capital, or at least a definition of its first quality or aspect: '*exchange value which preserves and perpetuates itself in and through circulation*' (262). We do not yet know how capital does this, i.e. what its process involves or looks like. We have arrived at this point by deriving the concept of capital from that of money, moving from C–M–C and money as money to M–C–M and money as capital. Interweaved with this conceptual derivation in the *Grundrisse* is a (brief) historical discussion of the emergence of capital from money. 'Money is the first form in which capital as such appears': it appears first as merchant capital, with merchants buying in order to sell (253).[38] Initially, trade or commerce takes place only at the margins of society, or between societies. At this stage, exchange 'plays an accessory role to production itself': a community produces use values for consumption and will only trade whatever surplus it happens to produce (256). Gradually, however, exchange will begin to modify the ways in which they produce. At first this might just mean altering production to satisfy new needs: for example, a community may through trade with a neighbouring community discover coffee and having discovered it they may try to produce it for themselves. Eventually, however, circulation (as the sum of exchanges) will alter production more fundamentally, as a community moves from the production of use values for consumption to the production of exchange values for exchange. This is a move from 'a production in which only the overflow [or surplus – SC] was created as exchange value' to 'a production which took place only in connection with circulation, a production which posited exchange values as its exclusive content' (257).

Marx's point here is not just that the increasing circulation of exchange values will lead to the production of exchange values, but that the former can only exist on the basis of the latter. If exchange is to be anything other than an occasional series of isolated and sporadic acts, then it must take place on the basis of the production of exchange values, i.e. on the basis of *capitalist* production. In conceptual or formal terms, we can express this by saying that the simple circulation C–M–C can only exist in any continuous and generalized form on the basis of M–C–M. We can now see more clearly what Marx means when he says that simple circulation '*does not carry within itself the principle of self-renewal*': without capital circulation M–C–M, simple circulation cannot sustain itself, because it is unable to reproduce either commodities or money. Hence simple circulation '*is the phenomenon of a process taking place behind it*', i.e. the process of capitalist production (255). So having seen that simple circulation alone cannot explain capital, we can now see that in fact simple circulation itself presupposes a capitalist form of production. At the same time, however, capitalist production must itself presuppose circulation.[39] It is a form of '*production which presupposes circulation as a developed moment* and which appears as a constant process': as we will see, capital has to keep returning to circulation both to sell the exchange values that it produces and to buy the commodities it needs to produce those exchange values (255). 'As in the theory the concept of value precedes that of capital, but requires for its pure development a mode of production founded on capital, so the same thing takes place in practice' (251). In other words, both conceptually and historically we move from value to capital, but the former can only develop fully on the basis of the latter. (This is what confuses the political economists, who sometimes present capital as the source of all value and sometimes conceive of capital as nothing more than a sum of values.)

So far we have been thinking of capital in terms of money: money as capital. But capital circulation – M–C–M – also involves commodities: capital alternates between money and commodity (261). We can think about this by again contrasting capital circulation with simple circulation. In the latter, exchange value appears either as money or as commodity (266). If money is used to buy a commodity, then money is realized in that commodity, which is withdrawn from circulation and consumed as a use value. If a commodity is sold for money, then exchange value is realized, but only temporarily, before disappearing again in circulation. So in simple circulation, exchange value can emerge from circulation as commodity (in which case it disappears because it is consumed as a use value) or as money (in which case it disappears into circulation again). What we are looking for in capital circulation is money that preserves and increases itself as value through circulation. Hence the commodity that money as capital purchases – the 'C' in the centre of M–C–M – cannot be a commodity that is consumed in such a way that it drops out of circulation (as do the commodities in C–M–C): it must be consumed as a use value but maintain itself as an exchange value; it must be a commodity which can preserve and increase value:

> The only utility whatsoever which an object can have for capital can be to preserve or increase it [...] The only use value, i.e. usefulness, which can stand opposite capital as such is that which increases, multiplies and hence preserves it as capital. (270–1)

What is this commodity that 'stand[s] opposite capital'? At first this seems unanswerable, given that capital itself alternates between money and commodity: it is 'the unity of commodity and money', or 'money existing in all particular forms of objectified labour', i.e. in all commodities (266, 298). In other words it does not seem to stand opposite any commodities but to incorporate them into itself. If the commodity that stands opposite labour is not objectified labour, i.e. an object which is a product of labour, then there is only one option: 'The only thing distinct from *objectified* labour is *non-objectified* labour', or '*labour* as subjectivity', i.e. labour as it is present in 'the *living subject*, in which it exists as capacity, as possibility; hence as *worker*' (272). In other words, the commodity that capital must buy is the worker's capacity to labour, or what we call labour-power.

Marx has here gone round the Hegelian houses in order to arrive at what is a fairly simple point (and which is presented with greater simplicity in Chapter 6 of *Capital I*): the only way that capital can preserve and increase itself through circulation is by purchasing the one commodity that can create value, namely labour-power.

Therefore, we now need to look at this exchange that takes place between capital and labour.

(Having moved from money to capital, and before he examines the exchange between capital and labour, Marx opens a brief 'digression' on the type of labour with which capital must exchange [272–3]. We will return to this important digression later: see 'Productive and unproductive labour' below.)

Exchange between capital and labour

As we know, in simple circulation, a commodity is purchased and then consumed as a use value. This consumption takes place outside of circulation once the exchange has completed. In terms of the exchange, what counts is the *form* of the commodity as an *exchange value*: its *use value*, and its consumption as this use value, 'is irrelevant to the form of the relation' and is unimportant to economic analysis (274).[40] In the exchange between labour and capital, in contrast, '*the use value of that which is exchanged for money appears as a particular economic relation*' (274). Whereas in simple circulation the use value of the commodity and the use to which it is put has no bearing on the exchange itself, its use taking place outside of the exchange, in capital circulation the whole point of the exchange is the consumption of the very specific use value of the commodity that is labour-power. Hence in capital circulation '[t]he consumption of the use value itself falls within the economic process, because the use value here is determined by exchange value' (311).[41]

What this means is that the exchange between capital and labour is split into two separate processes. On the one hand, the worker sells his commodity – his capacity for labour – to a capitalist, just as he might sell any other commodity. With the money he receives, he buys commodities for consumption. This exchange takes place within simple circulation C–M–C: from the worker's perspective, the use that the capitalist makes of the commodity the worker has sold (his labour-power) is strictly speaking irrelevant to the exchange; and the exchange value that the worker receives is realized in the commodities that he buys, which are consumed outside of the exchange (282). On the other hand, the capitalist obtains labour-power: this goes beyond simple circulation, with the use value of labour-power appearing as an economic relation. Marx summarizes:

> *In the exchange between capital and labour, the first act* [the worker selling his labour-power – SC] *is an exchange, falls entirely within ordinary* [simple – SC] *circulation; the second* [the capitalist obtaining and using labour-power – SC] *is a process qualitatively different from* [simple – SC] *exchange, and only by misuse* could it have been called *any sort of exchange at all.* It stands directly opposite exchange. (275)

We will begin, as Marx does, with the simple exchange in which the worker sells his labour-power. As a simple exchange, the exchange between capitalist and worker meets the standards outlined above: each side of the exchange is free and equal. Thus the problem with the exchange is not that it is an unequal exchange according to the rules of simple circulation. The worker sells his labour-power and in return receives the value of that labour-power. How is that value calculated? In the same way that the value of any other commodity is calculated: by the amount of labour necessary to produce the commodity. In this case, 'the use value which [the worker – SC] offers exists only as an ability, a capacity of his bodily existence; has no existence apart from that' (282). As such, the value of labour-power is measured by the amount of labour required to reproduce the labourer: to keep the labourer going, meaning to feed him and clothe him etc., but also to develop his skills as labourer. This does not mean that the value of labour-power is an absolute bare minimum, or whatever is required simply to keep him alive. Marx says that the worker receives from the capitalist 'a means of subsistence, objects for the preservation of his life, the satisfaction of his needs in general, physical, social etc.' (284). Given that the worker's physical and social needs vary across time and from place to place, so the value of labour-power will also vary.

Although the worker receives 'means of subsistence' from the capitalist, he does not do so directly. This distinguishes him from the slave or serf: unlike them, the wage-labourer exchanges his labour-power for money, i.e. the general form wealth, which he is free to use as he wishes (283). Nonetheless, for the worker the exchange remains within simple circulation: the purpose of the exchange for the worker is ultimately the satisfaction of his own needs through consumption. As such, although the distinction between the worker and the slave or serf is real and significant, because the worker must use his wages to satisfy his needs he 'obtains not wealth but only subsistence, use values for immediate consumption' (288). The objection might be made that the worker does not have to spend his wages on subsistence: he could save the money he receives, by reducing the amount he spends on satisfying his needs, or by working longer hours. This, indeed, is one of the central platitudes of the liberal defence of capitalism, as common today as in Marx's day: by working hard and saving money can you pull yourself up. But while this option may be available to a few workers – as exceptions to the rule – if all workers acted in this way then ultimately they would only damage their own interests. First, if the worker consumed less and worked harder it would simply reduce the value of his labour-power and hence the level of his wages: if workers began to live on less, it would show the capitalist that wages are too high (286). Second, if consumption falls then production must also fall, which will increase unemployment: this will be bad for those workers thrown out of work as a consequence and bad for those workers who remain in work, because their bargaining power will be reduced. Falling production is, of course, unwelcome to capitalists as well; even the capitalists realize this, which seems to leave them in a double bind. On the one hand, capitalists want workers to save, not only because it pushes down wages, but also because it helps relieve them of certain burdens: if workers have saved, then in old age, illness, or times of crisis then they can fend for themselves rather than becoming a burden on capitalists or the capitalist state. On the other hand, capitalists want workers not to save but to consume, so that they buy their products. Each capitalist wants *his own* workers to save but all other workers to consume (287). (We will return to this point later: see 'Realization of surplus value' below.)

Above all, the claim that labourers can lift themselves out of the working class through hard work and thriftiness obscures the real nature of the relation between capital and labour. An individual worker may be able to leave the working class, but not all workers can do so: capital needs labour as its opposite. 'As capital it can posit itself only by positing labour as not-capital, as pure use value' (288). The worker remains within simple circulation, meaning that for the worker the product of the exchange between capital and labour is use value: although he does receive exchange value, in that he is paid wages in money, that money is spent immediately on use values which are withdrawn from circulation and consumed. The worker can withdraw money from circulation as savings, but ultimately those savings will be used in purchasing use values for consumption. If the product of the exchange for the worker was exchange value, then he would not be a worker but a capitalist. Capital purchases use value (the worker's labour-power) but obtains exchange value: it uses the use value of labour-power to create wealth. For the worker, in contrast, the exchange creates not wealth but poverty. Given that labour is the source of all value, this seems like a paradox: 'labour is *absolute poverty as object*, on one side, and is, on the other side, the *general possibility* of wealth as subject and as activity' (296). But this apparent paradox is presupposed as a condition of the exchange between capital and labour: when the worker sells his labour-power as a use value to the capitalist, he gives up all right to it and hence to whatever his labour produces. 'The separation between labour and property in the product of labour, between labour and wealth, is thus posited in this act of exchange [between capital and labour – SC] itself' (307). The impoverishment of the worker is therefore not an unfortunate but contingent fact that can be remedied by distributive reforms (e.g. progressive taxation or a minimum wage): it is rather a necessary condition of his being a worker.

The labour that confronts capital is '*labour pure and simple*, abstract labour' (296). When we looked at 'labour pure and simple' in the 'Introduction', we saw that it was unclear whether it referred to value-creating abstract labour or simply to concrete labour in general as the producer of use values in general (see 'Method of political economy' above). Now it is much clearer that Marx is referring to value-creating abstract labour: because the aim of capitalist production is the production of value rather than use values, capital is indifferent to the type of labour it employs. While any particular capital may require a particular kind of labour (e.g. a capitalist bakery still requires bakers), capital as such is interested in labour insofar as it is necessary for the production of products as values, i.e. abstract labour. The worker, on the other hand, is equally indifferent to what labour he does: what matters is that he can sell his labour-power to a capitalist, not what type of labour he performs. In contrast, in feudal times craftsmen would have developed a particular skill: a labourer would have been trained as a baker, or a blacksmith, or a clockmaker, etc. Marx argues that the economic relation between capital and labour 'develops more purely and adequately in proportion as labour loses all the characteristics of art': i.e. labour in reality becomes more abstract as it becomes increasingly deskilled and mechanized (297). This argument echoes that made in the 'Introduction', though as there we need to be careful: abstract labour may in reality become more adequate to its concept as it becomes deskilled and mechanized, but *any* labour – including highly skilled and specialized labour – is abstract insofar as it produces value, i.e. insofar as it is wage labour for capital (and, conversely, deskilled labour is not abstract labour unless it is labour producing value).[42]

The simple exchange between labour and capital is only one side of the process, or rather it is the start of a quite different and separate process: once capital has purchased labour-power as its use value, it can use it as it wishes. The labour-power it has purchased is *living labour* (labour as subjective activity, not yet objectified in any product) and capital puts it to work on *objectified labour* (the raw materials and instruments of production which are themselves the products of earlier labour). All three – living labour, raw material and instrument of production – are consumed in the production process, resulting in a product. This 'appropriation, absorption of labour by capital [...] brings capital into ferment, and makes it into a process, *process of production*' (301). Bourgeois economists see in this capitalist production process only the process of production in general, wherein 'capital' is the raw material and instrument of production, which labour consumes. Thus 'capital' – in this bourgeois sense of the means of production – is taken to be necessary to the production process as such. Accepting this bourgeois premise, the socialists demand that 'we need capital, but not the capitalist' – meaning that we need materials and instruments, but not the capitalist telling the workers what to do and taking the profits (303). From Marx's perspective this demand is fatuous, because the 'concept of capital contains the capitalist': we might be able to remove individual capitalists, but if there is capital then there must also be capitalists (512). Likewise, it is senseless to call for wage labour without capital, because 'wage labour as such presupposes capital' (308). The bourgeois apologists and their socialist critics understand 'capital' only as a thing – the materials worked on or with during the production process – and not as a *relation of production*: labour has been incorporated into capital not only in the sense that the materials worked on and with are the products of previous labour, but also in the sense that capital commands labour (514).

There is a limited sense in which the identification of the specifically capitalist production process with the production process in general is correct. Considered only in its material aspect, the capitalist production process may be indistinguishable from any other production process: a labourer works on some raw material using an instrument of production. 'But these material elements do not make capital into capital' (309). We need to consider not just the material aspect of the capitalist production process – its content – but its specific *form*. Thought of in this way, capital consists not of different objects of labour that are combined with labour, but of *values* (312). What distinguishes it is that it both preserves and creates value: capital is 'a *process of self-valorization*. Self-valorization includes preservation of the prior value, as well as its multiplication' (311, *tm*). The question that now arises is how capital does this: how does it create value?

At first, the question of how capital creates value seems unanswerable. Surely the value of the product that results from the capitalist production process must be equal to the value that went into it: the value of the raw materials, the instruments of production and the labour. But while this explains how capital might *preserve* value (albeit altering its form on the way, from raw materials, instruments and wages into a finished product), it does not explain the *creation* of value. And if we cannot explain the creation of value, how can we explain the capitalist: what does he live on? How is he paid? If all capital did was to preserve value, then the value that the capitalist got out at the end of the process would be exactly the same as the value he put in at the start. Maybe the capitalist pays himself a wage. But this doesn't address the problem: if he is not to make a loss then he'll have to replace the value of his wages with his labour. But if that happens then he is not a capitalist at all but a worker. 'If capital also had to work in order to live, then it would not maintain itself as capital but as labour' (324). So even if we think that the capitalist has a moral case to be remunerated for the money that he advances at the start of the process, then it is not clear from where his remuneration is going to come. Moreover, it is not clear why there should be any such moral case: given that the capitalist has not actually added any value, why should he receive anything in turn? He can work for it, but in that case he is not a capitalist. 'The existence of capital *vis-à-vis* labour requires that capital in its being-for-itself, the capitalist, should exist and be able to live as *not-worker*' (317).

Perhaps we can explain the creation of value through the circulation process. Let's say that the capitalist puts in £100 at the start of process and ends up with a product worth £100 at the end – but he cunningly sells this product on the market for £110, thus making a profit. But while this might explain how one individual capitalist could make a profit, it can't explain how all capitalists can make a profit: if they all sold their products at 10 per cent above their actual value, then they would cancel each other out; everyone selling at 110 per cent is the same as everyone selling at 100 per cent (315). It might be only a few capitalists who sold their products above their value, but they could only do so at the expense of those who bought those products: some would have gained, but only at the expense of others who would have lost. All that would have changed would be the *distribution* of value: value would not have been *created* (350).[43] Somehow, the capitalist production process creates more value than it begins with: a *surplus value* is created. It is in the *Grundrisse* that Marx first fully develops his theory of surplus value.

Surplus value

The secret of surplus value lies in the labour-power that the capitalist purchases from the worker. '[T]he labour objectified in the price of labour is smaller than the living labour time purchased with it' (321). To explain this, we need to remember the distinction between exchange value and use value. The worker sells her labour-power as an exchange value. Its value is determined in the same way as all commodities – by the amount of labour required to produce it. What the capitalist buys, however, is labour-power as a use value: he buys living labour, labour as an activity that creates value (673). The unique property of labour-power is that it can create more value than it is itself worth. This is why we cannot understand capitalism if we approach it only in terms of simple exchange. The exchange between worker and capitalist is fair and equal insofar as the capitalist pays the correct value of labour-power – but he receives more than he gives because labour-power can in one day create more value than the worker receives in wages.

'If one day's work were necessary in order to keep one worker alive for one day, then capital would not exist' (324). If, instead, £5 is required to meet a worker's needs for one day, then that is the value of her labour-power and what she will receive in wages; but if she can create £10's worth of commodities in one day, then she will have produced a *surplus value* of £5.

The creation of surplus value, then, cannot be explained purely by reference to exchange relations: in exchange there is an exchange of equivalents – but '[s]urplus value in general is value in excess of the equivalent'. Surplus value 'has to arise from the production process of capital itself' (324). Hence in *Capital II* Marx expands the formula for capital:

M–C ... P ... C'–M'

where M is the initial money advanced, C is the commodities bought (labour-power and means of production), P is the production process, C' is the commodity produced (including surplus value) and M' is the realization of that commodity as money once it has been sold on the market.[44]

The concept of surplus value is arguably the central category of Marxist economics, explaining both how capitalism works and what is wrong with it. Although it appears in a rudimentary form in earlier works and is developed further in subsequent works, it receives its first full development in the *Grundrisse*. Crucial to the concept of surplus value is the concept of labour-power. Because in 1857–8 the concept of labour-power is still a work-in-progress, in the *Grundrisse* Marx himself still sometimes confuses 'labour' and 'labour-power', using the former where his argument requires the latter. The distinction is vital, however, helping Marx both to overcome the limitations of political economy and to identify the workings of capitalism. The question of the value of labour became a stumbling block for classical political economy. If, as the labour theory of value states, value is determined by labour time, then what can the value of labour itself be? It looks like we have a vicious circle in which the value of one day's labour is one day's labour.[45] Perhaps we can say that the 'value of labour' means the value that labour produces. But (as the Ricardian socialists argued) if this is so, why is it that the value that the labourer receives (as her wages) is less than the value of the product that she produces?

Why is the value of the labour that the worker expends not equal to the value of the product in which that living labour is expended (560-1)?[46] The answer might be that the extra value contained in the product is created by something other than labour, but this answer cannot be given within the confines of the *labour* theory of value.

We already know Marx's solution to this puzzle: what the capitalist purchases is not a thing called 'labour' at all, but a *capacity* called 'labour-power'. Hence what needs to be determined is not the value of labour but the value of labour-power:

> The labour objectified in that use value [i.e. labour-power – SC] is the objectified labour necessary bodily to maintain not only the general substance in which his labour-power exists, i.e. the worker himself, but also that required to modify this general substance so as to develop its particular capacity. (282–3)

Without the distinction between labour and labour-power, it would be hard to see what wrong the wage-labourer is subjected to under capitalism. Under feudalism, there is a clear and obvious separation between the work that the serf does for himself and the work that he does for the master: for three days a week (for example) the serf performs *necessary labour*, i.e. the labour required to meet his own needs; then for another three days he performs *surplus labour*, i.e. labour performed in addition to necessary labour and for someone else (and on the seventh day he rests). In contrast, the wage-labourer under capitalism seems to have a good deal: he does a day's labour and he receives a day's wages in return, so he seems to be paid for all his labour. His exploitation is 'covered up by money' (772). Only if we recognize the distinction between labour and labour-*power* can we see that what the worker is paid for is the latter and that some of his labour is in fact unpaid. Once the capitalist has paid for labour-power, i.e. the capacity of the worker to labour, he can make use of this capacity by requiring the worker to perform labour. Some of this labour will be necessary labour: it will reproduce value equivalent to that needed to meet the worker's needs; the worker is returned this value in wages and so this necessary labour is paid labour. The rest of the day's labour will be surplus labour: it produces value beyond that which the worker needs and beyond that which he has been paid and so it is unpaid labour. In short, although he may be paid a day's wage, the wage-labourer still performs unpaid labour.

Absolute and relative surplus value

We now know how surplus value is created: the capitalist gains one day's labour by paying the worker the value of his labour-power; but the worker can reproduce this value in, say, half a day's labour; thus in the other half of the day the worker is creating *surplus value* which the capitalist appropriates. The labour that the worker expends on reproducing the value of his labour-power – in this case half a day – is called necessary labour. The additional labour that he performs for the capitalist – the other half of the day's labour – is called surplus labour: it is labour 'in excess of his requirements as worker, hence in excess of his immediate requirements for keeping himself alive' (324–5).

But what can the capitalist do to *increase* surplus value? There are two ways to do this: to increase the total amount of labour performed; or to reduce the necessary labour performed. The former produces absolute surplus value and the latter produces relative surplus value, based respectively on absolute and relative surplus labour. In the *Grundrisse* Marx begins with the latter before reaching the former. This makes sense, given that Marx's basic aim is to identify the distinguishing features of the capitalist mode of production: whereas absolute surplus labour takes place in all class societies, relative surplus labour, though not unique to capitalism, only develops consistently under capitalism and is capitalism's characteristic form of surplus labour. Nonetheless, the category of absolute surplus labour is simpler and easier to understand, so to clarify things I will here depart slightly from the sequence of Marx's analysis.

Absolute surplus value is produced by increasing the total amount of labour performed, i.e. by extending the working day, making the labourer work 10 hours instead of 8, for example. Clearly there is a limit to absolute surplus value. Not only are there only 24 hours in any one day, no labourer can work all 24 hours day after day: each worker needs time to replenish his labour-power by sleeping and eating. In addition, the working day is subject to legal restrictions (the subject of detailed analysis in *Capital I*). In our own time, similar legal limits exist, though employers can of course find ways around these laws, for example by requesting or demanding unpaid overtime. Technological developments can also help lengthen the working day: if you have a laptop or a smartphone, for instance, then you can work on the way to and from work or at the weekend, outside official working hours. Breaks can also be removed or shortened, in effect lengthening the working day by other means. Rather than passively accepting these exploitative practices, workers can resist and fight back (e.g. by joining trades unions, lobbying for legislative changes and protections, or through minor acts of subversive idleness). There is thus a struggle between capital and labour over the working day – a class struggle to which a major chapter of *Capital I* is devoted but which is not discussed in detail in the *Grundrisse*.[47]

Absolute surplus labour is not unique to capitalism: the ruling classes have always made the exploited classes perform surplus labour, whether the latter are wage-labourers, serfs or slaves. Given that the value form is unique to capitalism, however, absolute surplus value is produced only under capitalism. In contrast, although relative surplus labour can exist in pre-capitalist societies, it only develops fully under capitalism and it represents the 'distinguishing historic character of the mode of production founded on capital' (769).

Relative surplus value is produced by reducing necessary labour and hence increasing *relative* surplus labour, i.e. the amount of surplus labour relative to necessary labour. This requires developing the productive forces of labour in those industries which, directly or indirectly, produce commodities consumed by workers. If, for example, productivity doubles, it means that it will now take half as long for the worker to reproduce the value of his labour-power, because the use values consumed by the worker will have halved in value (because it takes half the time to produce them). As such, he now needs to spend only a quarter of a day rather than half a day reproducing the value of his labour-power. In theory, this could mean a reduction in work for the labourer: if he only needs to spend a quarter of a day working for his subsistence, then he could work three-quarters of a day and the capitalist would still have his half day of surplus labour. Of course, it does not work like this: the capitalist makes the labourer work a whole day and increases his return, because the worker now spends three-quarters of a day producing surplus value for the capitalist. The time working for his subsistence – necessary labour – is reduced, but surplus labour – the time spent producing surplus value for the capitalist – is increased.

This happens not because the capitalist is evil or greedy: it is simply the logic of capital. Capital must not only preserve but also create value: it must increase itself, which means increasing surplus value. Here and elsewhere in the *Grundrisse* Marx frames this point in more philosophical – and specifically Hegelian – language: capital constantly strives to move beyond its own barriers. 'Every boundary [*Grenze*] is and has to be a barrier [*Schranke*] for it', i.e. has to be a surmountable obstacle rather than an insurmountable limit: 'capital is the endless and limitless drive to go beyond its limiting barrier' (334).[48] This is not simply a bad thing for Marx; to the contrary, it is the genius and the value of capitalism:

> Capital's ceaseless striving towards the general form of wealth drives labour beyond the limits of its natural paltriness, and thus creates the material elements for the development of the rich individuality which is as all-sided in its production as in its consumption [...] This is why *capital is productive; i.e. an essential relation for the development of the social productive forces*. It ceases to exist as such only where the development of these productive forces themselves encounters its barrier in capital itself. (325)

It is perhaps tempting to see Marx here as being in thrall to a nineteenth-century (or proto-Stalinist) productivist ideology, blindly celebrating the production of things as an end in itself. But his point is to distinguish capitalism from other social forms and to highlight the value of capitalism in creating the conditions for post-capitalist society. In pre-capitalist societies, in which the production of use values dominates, the production of wealth will be limited, not least by the needs which those use values are to satisfy: here 'wealth itself has value only as gratification, not as wealth itself' and hence these societies will never produce '*general industriousness*' (326). In contrast, under capitalism the production of use values is only a means to another end, namely the production of exchange value: its aim is the general form of wealth. However, as the final line of the long quotation above suggests, there nonetheless comes a point when capital reaches a barrier that is a boundary, the overcoming of which would mean the dissolution of capitalism or rather its transformation into something else.

We have seen that capital can increase relative surplus value by increasing the productive force of labour – but in doing so, capital faces diminishing returns. In our example above, if necessary labour is originally half a day, then a doubling of the productive powers reduces necessary labour to a quarter of a day: hence surplus labour does not double, but rather increases by half, from half (or two-quarters) to three-quarters of a day. Now necessary labour is a quarter of a day, so another doubling of the productive powers of labour would increase surplus labour by only one-eighth of a day – because necessary labour would fall to one-eighth of a day and surplus labour increase from three-quarters (or six-eighths) of a day to seven-eighths of a day. Another doubling of productive powers will reduce necessary labour from one-eighth of a day to one-sixteenth of a day, thus increasing surplus labour from seven-eighths (or fourteen-sixteenths) of a day to fifteen-sixteenths of a day, i.e. by only one-sixteenth of a day. And so on. In short, surplus value does not increase in the same proportion as productive forces. The exact increase in surplus value depends not just on the amount by which productive forces increase, but also on the proportion of the working day that is already taken up by necessary labour. It becomes increasingly difficult to increase surplus labour: the more that necessary labour has already been reduced, the smaller are the gains from reducing it further. 'The self-valorization of capital becomes more difficult to the extent that it has already been valorized'. Yet this only pushes capital on further, to develop its productive forces more intensely: 'the more terribly must it develop the productive force in order to valorize itself in only smaller proportion' (340, *tm*).

There is, however, an absolute limit or boundary here. Necessary labour cannot be reduced to zero: 'a certain part of the working day must always be exchanged for the labour objectified in the worker' (337). We could argue that even this limit can be overcome, or at least suspended: in 'workfare' schemes, for instance, the state pays the worker's subsistence through benefits and the capitalist, therefore, receives an entire day of surplus labour. It is true that capital will indirectly contribute to those costs of the worker's subsistence, via the taxes it pays to the state (though the workers themselves also contribute through taxes on consumption), but then think about unpaid internships, in which capital receives labour for free. Equally, however, this is not simply a one-way process. The value of labour-power, and hence the proportion of the day given to necessary labour, is the result of a *struggle*: workers can fight back against the devaluation of their labour-power (by demanding higher wages, further benefits, shorter working hours, etc.).[49]

Productive and unproductive labour

We can now see more clearly the type of labour with which capital must exchange (and hence return to the 'digression' that we postponed earlier). The labour that stands opposite capital must be '*value-creating, productive labour*' (272). From the perspective of capitalism – which is what Marx is interested in – productive labour is wage labour which, as well as producing a use value, creates surplus value for capital.

> Labour itself is *productive only* if absorbed into capital, where capital forms the basis of production, and where the capitalist is therefore in command of production [...] Labour, such as it exists *for itself* in the worker in opposition to capital, that is, labour in its *immediate being*, separated from capital, is *not productive.* (308)

Marx adapts the distinction between productive and unproductive labour from Smith, who distinguished between 'the labour of a manufacturer' which 'adds to the value of the subject upon which it is bestowed' and '[t]he labour of a menial servant' which 'adds to the value of nothing': 'A man grows rich by employing a multitude of manufacturers: He grows poor, by maintaining a multitude of menial servants'. As an advocate of the emerging commercial society, Smith was keen to contrast the productivity of industry and manufacturing with the profligacy of the landed gentry and their army of servants. As well as the labour of menial servants, however, Smith's category of unproductive labour includes that of government officials, lawyers, doctors, entertainers, etc. What these workers have in common is that while their labour *has* 'value' in the sense that it is useful and even necessary, it is 'maintained by revenue' and so does not replace capital or *create* value.[50]

Marx accepts Smith's basic definition: 'A. Smith was *essentially* correct with his *productive* and *unproductive* labour, correct from the standpoint of bourgeois economy' (273). Marx uses the example of a capitalist who hires a woodcutter to cut some wood. Though the capitalist pays the woodcutter money for his labour, that labour does not in any way augment his capital: it is a service that the capitalist consumes and which is paid for out of the capitalist's revenue. As such, this exchange is merely a simple exchange of exchange value (the money the capitalist pays to the woodcutter) for a use value (the service of cutting wood) that is immediately consumed: the two parties confront each other as simple exchangers rather than as capital and labour.

Though 'essentially correct', according to Marx, Smith nonetheless 'misses the mark' (846). For having defined productive labour as that which produces value, Smith confused things by going on to claim:

> [T]he labour of the manufacturer fixes and realizes itself in some particular subject or vendible commodity, which lasts for some time at least after that labour is past [...] The labour of the menial servant, on the contrary, does not fix or realize itself in any particular subject or vendible commodity. His services generally perish in the very instant of their performance.[51]

Smith has conflated adding value with creating a material product, thus excluding the service industries from his definition of productive labour. But, as Marx later points out, if productive labour is that labour which adds value, then the type of use value produced – whether material or immaterial – is irrelevant: service labour can be just as productive as factory work. For example, although they do not produce a material commodity, '[a]ctors are productive workers, not in so far as they produce a play, but in so far as they increase their employer's wealth' (328–9). This point can get lost in the *Grundrisse*, because the examples that Marx uses of unproductive labour tend to be taken from the service industries ('From whore to pope, there is a mass of such rabble' [272]). Thus, for instance, he tells us that a piano maker is productive because he reproduces capital; the piano player, on the other hand, may produce music, but he is not productive because he does not reproduce capital but 'only exchanges his labour for revenue' (305). But the point is that the piano player *would* be productive if, like our actors, he worked for a capitalist to produce value instead of being hired by the capitalist out of the latter's revenue. (Likewise, sex workers – like Marx's 'whore' – are productive if they work for capitalist enterprises.)

What this means is that '[l]abour may be necessary without being productive' (533). Labour that reproduces labour-power – including housework and childcare, but also labour related to healthcare, education, housing, etc. – is not productive if it is provided within families or for free at the point of access by the government, even though such work is absolutely vital in any society. Increasingly, of course, such services are being provided as commodities sold on the market, transforming the labour involved in these services into productive labour. Often it can be hard to determine the status of a single worker (not least because the blurring of lines between public and private can make the identification of value-producing work difficult), but some workers can never be productive. Two categories in particular are important. First, those who help maintain the social order, including the army, police, judiciary, civil service, and those such as priests who undertake ideological functions, may be wage labourers and may even work for private companies, but they do not produce commodities and so are not productive. Second, surplus value is produced only within production: circulation (the M–C and C'–M' of the expanded formula of capital) adds no value (an argument we will come to in more detail when we look at Section Two of the 'Chapter on Capital'). This means that labourers involved in the activities of circulation cannot be productive: this of course includes a massive range and number of workers, in finance, legal services, retail, advertising and so on. These workers must be paid for through the redistribution of the surplus value created in production. Hence the majority of workers in the UK today, for instance, are 'unproductive' in Marx's sense. This does not mean, however, that they are not exploited, for like other wage labourers they will perform surplus labour (533).[52]

Preservation of value and constant and variable capital

We know that labour creates value. But the production process does not involve only living labour: the worker labours on raw materials, using instruments of labour. These materials and instruments, which together make up the means of production, are both use values (because they are used in the production process) and values (because they are themselves the products of previous labour). In the production process, the form of these use values will change – for example, from sheets of cotton into shirts – but their status as use values is preserved: at each stage, some product of labour (the raw materials and instruments) serves as a use value for further labour, until finally it is transformed into a use value who use is direct consumption. '[L]abour has the property of preserving the existing use value by raising it, and it raises it by making it into the object of new labour as defined by an ultimate aim' (362). Likewise, the *value* of the means of production is preserved: the commodity produced contains the new value added by the worker's labour and the old value found in the materials and instruments (356). 'The quantity of *objectified labour*' contained in the means of production, i.e. their value, 'is preserved in that its *quality* is preserved as *use value for further labour*, through the contact with living labour' (363).

The worker preserves the old value simply by doing his day's work, in the process of creating new value. (In the *Grundrisse* Marx states that this means that the preservation of value is not the result of a specific kind of labour [359]. In contrast, in *Capital I*, where he has refined his distinction between concrete labour, which produces use values, and abstract labour, which finds its expression in value, he is able to show that it must be concrete labour that preserves value, because the value of the means of production is transferred and preserved only in so far as they serve as use values that are put to use through a specific form of labour such as spinning or weaving.[53]) The creation of new value and the preservation of existing value are part of the same act (357). As such, the capitalist does not need to pay the worker extra for preserving value: the capitalist gains this preservation of value free of charge (356). Living labour-power is not paid for its capacity to preserve value, any more than it is paid for its capacity to create surplus value (363). Moreover, because capital owns both labour-power (because it has purchased this in the exchange with the worker) and the raw materials and instruments, from its point of view the powers of labour (to preserve and create value) appear as powers of capital. Vulgarized versions of this claim remain commonplace today: we often hear that it is capital that is creative – of wealth, of jobs, of ideas and inventions – and hence that the rest of us (as workers) should be humbly and eternally grateful to capital for its generosity in providing us with these things.

On the face of it, Marx seems to make a meal of this question of the preservation of value. His point appears fairly simple: in the production process the value of raw materials and instruments of production is preserved. To understand why he spends so long discussing it, we have to think about who Marx is (sometimes implicitly) responding to and what consequences the preservation of value has for his wider theory.

According to the labour theory of value, labour is the source of value. But then where does that leave the two other parts of the production process, namely raw materials and instruments? Imagine a capitalist who makes an initial investment of £100: £50 on raw materials, £10 on instruments and £40 on wages. Let's say that the worker can reproduce that £40 in 8 hours, but that his total working day is 10 hours: hence he produces a total value of £50, which includes £10 surplus value. So the capitalist expects to end up with £110: his original £100, plus a surplus of £10. Yet the labour theory of value tells us that only labour can create value, and in a 10-hour day the worker produces only £50 of value – so it looks as if the capitalist is going to lose £50 on his initial £100 investment, rather than making £10. As Marx notes, this apparent problem formed the basis of (unfair) objections to Ricardo: 'that he regarded profit and wages only as components of production costs, not the machine and the material' (354). Hence later political economists insisted that machine and material must be included as components of production costs along with wages and profits. According to this perspective, however, if the capitalist makes a 10 per cent profit – generating £110 from his initial £100 investment – then this reflects a 10 per cent profit on each of the components, as if each of the components has grown by 10 per cent: £55 raw material, £11 instruments, £44 wages (374, 567).

Marx does not accept this: for Marx, the means of production – which are themselves the products of earlier labour – have transferred rather than increased their value. To show why this point is important, we will need to begin to look at Marx's theory of profit, which he starts to bring in at this point but which he only develops more fully later in the *Grundrisse*, and even then only in a limited way compared to later writings (see 'Section Three: Capital as Fructiferous' below).

In our example, the capitalist has made a 10 per cent profit: he started with £100 and has ended with £110. But how has this profit been made? The raw materials and instruments have not added any value: their value has simply been preserved. 'The worker took nothing away from them and added nothing to them' (376). The extra £10 has come from surplus labour. In a 10-hour day, the worker has performed 8 hours necessary labour, in which he produces £40 of value, and 2 hours surplus labour, in which he produces another £10 of value. Whereas the rate of profit is 10 per cent, the *rate of surplus value* is something different. The relevant ratio for the rate of profit is the ratio of profit to total capital advanced (£10 to £100). To calculate the rate of surplus value, the relevant ratio is that of the value created by surplus labour to the value created by necessary labour: £10 to £40, or 25 per cent. We can see that the rate of surplus value is necessarily also that of surplus labour to necessary labour: 2 hours to 8 hours, or 25 per cent. Hence what the rate of surplus value measures is the rate of exploitation: the more the worker is exploited – the more surplus, unpaid labour he performs in relation to necessary, paid labour – the greater the rate of surplus value. (Hence, for Marx, exploitation has nothing to do with 'unjust' or 'unfair' distributions of income and everything to do with the performance of surplus labour.) What this means is that the rate of profit cannot tell us the extent of the worker's exploitation: the same rate of surplus value can give rise to different rates of profit.

To understand this, it will help to bring in some specific terminology that Marx begins to develop at this point. He calls raw materials and instruments of production 'constant capital' and he calls the part of capital that pays for necessary labour (i.e. wages) 'variable capital' – because the value of the former is merely preserved in the production process, hence remains constant, while the value added by living labour will vary according to the rate of exploitation of the worker, hence is variable (389).[54] These concepts are first worked out in the *Grundrisse*, where they remain in a relatively rudimentary form. In *Capital*, Marx expresses the ratio between constant and variable capital in terms of the *composition* of capital: the *technical composition of capital* is the ratio between constant and variable capital considered in material terms, i.e. the ratio between the mass of means of production and the mass of labour or number of workers; the *value composition of capital* is the same ratio considered in terms of value, i.e. the ratio between the value of the means of production and the value of labour-power or the total wages. Thus, two branches of industry may have the same technical composition but different value compositions, if the proportion between labour-power and means of production is the same for both but the means of production in one industry has greater value than in the other (because, for example, it uses raw materials of a higher value). The *organic composition of capital* is the value composition of capital in so far as it is determined by its technical composition.[55]

Different organic compositions of capital will therefore give rise to different rates of profit. In our example above, the composition of capital of £100 was £60 constant capital (£50 raw materials and £10 instruments) and £40 variable capital. With a rate of surplus value of 25 per cent, this produced a 10 per cent rate of profit. But suppose a different capital of £100 which employs fewer workers and a greater mass of machinery: let's say it's composed of £80 constant capital and £20 variable capital. With the same rate of surplus value of 25 per cent, this second capital will produce a surplus of only £5 and hence a rate of profit of only 5 per cent, or half as much as the first capital. Or consider a third capital which employs the same number of workers and the same mass of means of production but these means of production are of a higher value (because it has to use more expensive machinery or raw materials): it is composed of £40 variable capital and £160 constant capital, producing (at the same rate of surplus value of 25 per cent) a surplus value of £10 but a rate of profit of only 5 per cent (a profit on £10 on a total capital of £200). Contra Ricardo, therefore, smaller rates of profit do not necessarily mean a larger share of the wealth for the workers (385). To the contrary, exactly the same rate of exploitation can give rise to varying rates of profit.

Given that it seems to reduce his rate of profit, we might ask why the capitalist would increase constant capital relative to variable capital. But we already know why: the production of relative surplus value means increasing the productivity of labour, which means an increase in the mass of means of production relative to living labour, because more machinery is brought in to increase productivity or because a greater mass of raw materials is now being worked up:

> An increase in the productivity of labour means nothing more than that the same capital creates the same value with less labour, or that less labour creates the same product with more capital. That less necessary labour produces more surplus labour. The necessary labour is smaller in relation to capital. (388)

In other words, 'an increase in the productive force means that the constant part of capital [...] grows relative to the variable' (389).[56]

We also need to introduce another distinction here: between the rate of surplus value and the *mass* of surplus value, i.e. the total amount of surplus value produced. For example, our capital of £100, composed of £60 constant capital and £40 variable capital and with a rate of surplus value of 25 per cent, produces a mass of surplus value of £10; but a capital of £1000, composed of £600 constant capital and £400 variable capital and with the same rate of surplus value of 25 per cent, will produce a mass of surplus value of £100. In other words, the capitalist has an incentive not merely to increase the *rate* of surplus value but also the *mass* of surplus value.

How can the mass of surplus value be increased? As Marx puts it in *Capital I*, if 'the mass of surplus-value which a single worker produces [...] is determined by the rate of surplus-value', then the total mass of surplus value that a capital produces will be 'determined by the product of the number of labour-powers [i.e. workers – SC] simultaneously exploited by the same capitalist and the degree of exploitation of each individual labour-power' (*C1*: 418). Hence the mass of surplus value can be increased either by increasing the rate of exploitation or by increasing variable capital and thus the number of labourers working, such that 'more workers are employed *at the same time*, so that the real working day is simultaneously multiplied instead of only lengthened': 100 workers can produce a greater mass of surplus labour than ten workers (assuming an equal rate of exploitation) (386).

So it looks like capital has an incentive to employ as many workers as possible, i.e. to increase the number of simultaneous working days. But we also know that, on the other hand, capital has an incentive to increase relative surplus value by reducing necessary labour. Imagine six workers are employed by a capitalist:

each works a 12-hour day, of which 10 hours are necessary labour and 2 hours are surplus labour, meaning the rate of surplus value is 20 per cent. If there are 6 workers each working 12 hours, then in any one day there is a total of 72 working hours, of which 60 hours are necessary labour and 12 hours are surplus labour. Now imagine that productivity improves, such that necessary labour drops from 10 hours to 9 hours. This means that in each 12-hour day, 3 hours are now surplus labour: so to produce the same total of 12 hours of surplus labour in one day, the capitalist needs to employ only 4 workers instead of 6. These 4 work a total of 46 hours in a day, of which 12 hours is surplus labour and 36 hours is necessary labour, with a rate of surplus value of 33 per cent. In short, the capitalist can achieve the same amount of surplus labour, producing the same mass of surplus value, with a higher rate of surplus value, with less necessary labour and hence fewer workers: he can dismiss 2 workers. Of course, if possible the capitalist will continue to employ all 6 workers working at the higher rate of surplus value, but the point remains: there is 'a tendency of capital – just as in the case of the single working day – to reduce the many simultaneous working days [...] to the minimum, i.e. to posit as many as possible of them as *not necessary*' (400).

The more working days that capital can add – by employing more workers – the more it can increase the mass of surplus value. Yet capital also tries to reduce the number of these days which are necessary: if 4 labourers can produce the same mass of surplus value as 6, then so much the better. So the tendency that operates with respect to a single working day – increasing the absolute labour time as much as possible (extending the working day as far as it will go) whilst simultaneously reducing necessary labour as much as possible – also appears when we consider many workers together: capital seeks to increase the overall labouring population whilst simultaneously reducing its necessary part. 'It is therefore [...] a tendency of capital to increase the labouring population, as well as constantly to posit a part of it as surplus population – population which is useless until such time as capital can utilize it' (399). In other words, capitalism creates unemployment. We will return to this topic later (see 'Surplus population' below).

Study Questions

1. How does Marx define capital and how does his definition differ from that of the classical political economists?
2. How is surplus value created?
3. What is the difference between absolute and relative surplus value?
4. How does Marx distinguish productive labour from unproductive labour?
5. What are constant and variable capital and what relevance does this distinction have for the rate of profit?

Section Two: The Circulation Process of Capital

So far we have considered production in its narrow sense, or what Marx calls the 'immediate production process': the preservation and creation of value within the capitalist production process, in which living labour worked on and with objectified labour (619). But we cannot consider the immediate production process alone. We know from the 'Introduction' that circulation, as the totality of exchanges, is a moment of production in the broader sense. More specifically, we also know that capital is a process, and we have considered only one part of this process: we have only really considered 'P' of the general formula of capital M–C ... P ... C'–M'. Section Two of the 'Chapter on Capital' is devoted to circulation and to that extent it broadly corresponds to *Capital II*. It is a long and often poorly organized section, interrupted by an important and influential discussion of 'original accumulation' (which if anything corresponds to Part VIII of *Capital I*). We will follow Marx's order of presentation as closely as possible, while trying to keep the consequent repetition to a minimum.

Realization of surplus value

In the general formula of capital M–C ... P ... C'–M', M' must be greater than M. Capital must be *valorized*: its value must be increased. At the point that we have reached in this process, however, capital has not yet managed to do that. To the contrary: up to this point the valorization process has been a *devaluation* process (402). This is because we have not yet completed the circuit of capital. We have assumed that capital has purchased means of production and labour-power as commodities (though we have not examined that purchase in any detail) and has used them to produce another commodity. This commodity contains more value than the capitalist put into it – because it contains surplus labour, which the capitalist has not paid for. 'This value as such is *money*', but at the moment it 'exists only ideally as a certain sum of money', because it exists in the form of a commodity (402). If the capitalist left the process here then he would have lost money: he would have put some money into a process and ended up with a lot of commodities. In order to *realize* the value of the commodity, capital has to re-enter the circulation process: the commodity must be sold for money. This is why the production process up to this point can be described as a devaluation process: the capitalist began with value but now has a commodity which contains value but is stuck in the form of a use value. If he cannot sell this commodity, then the capitalist has lost his value. 'As a *commodity*, capital now shares the fate of commodities in general; it is a matter of accident whether or not it is exchanged for money, whether its *price* is realized or not' (404).

The realization of the value created now depends on a process of circulation that lies outside the production process. This process of circulation is thus a potential barrier to the realization of value, in at least two ways. First, the new commodity that has been produced 'is an exchange value only in so far as it is at the same time a *use value*, i.e. an object of consumption' (404). For its value to be realized, the commodity must be sold to someone who wants to consume its use value: there must be a need and a demand for it. This problem reflects the contradiction that we have already encountered between the use value and the exchange value of the commodity (see 'Money and value' above). The commodity must be realized as exchange value, but to achieve this there must be appropriate demand for its specific use value. The first barrier, then, is the capacity for consumption. The second barrier is the availability of money to buy the commodities. The production process has created *new* value and requires an equivalent value to realize it: where is this to come from? It can only come from production: 'The *surplus value* created at one point requires the creation of surplus value at *another* point, for which it may be exchanged; if only, initially, the production of more gold and silver, more money'. If the new value produced by one capital is to be realized – exchanged for value – then it must be matched by the production of new value by another capital. 'Hence, as value, [capital] encounters its barrier in alien production, just as, as use value, its barrier is alien consumption' (407).

We have already seen that capital is driven to increase surplus value by increasing absolute labour time. We can now see that capital is driven to expand the sphere of circulation, in order to realize the value that is created. If capital is to increase absolute surplus value then it needs other capitals also producing absolute surplus value, so that the value newly created can be realized in exchange with other values: it must create not only more absolute surplus labour but also more points of exchange. 'A precondition of production based on capital is therefore *the production of a constantly widening sphere of circulation*'. Hence circulation is 'expanded by production itself. Accordingly, it already appears as a moment of production itself' (407). This entails extending the capitalist mode of production itself, taking over pre-capitalist forms of production. These pre-capitalist forms, which produce directly for consumption rather than for exchange, are a barrier to the realization of surplus value, because they reduce 'the number of those engaged in exchange, as well as the sum of exchange values thrown into circulation, and above all the production of surplus values'. Hence '[t]he tendency to create the *world market* is directly given in the concept of capital itself. Every limit appears as a barrier to be overcome' (408).

We saw that relative surplus value, on the other hand, is produced by increasing productive forces and reducing necessary labour. This frees up both capital and labour: if productivity doubles, then capital need spend (for example) only £200 instead of £400 as variable capital. The newly released labour and capital can be used in new branches of production. But if the value produced in those new branches of production is to be realized then there will need to be a demand for the commodities created therein. Hence the sphere of consumption will need to expand, through the expansion of existing needs and the creation of new needs. This drive to find new use values and create new needs also pushes capital across the globe, producing the 'exploration of the earth in all directions, to discover new things of use as well as new useful qualities of the old' and the 'universal exchange of the products of all alien climates and lands'. This creation of new needs alters our very nature as human beings: 'the cultivation of all the qualities of the social human being, production of the same in a form as rich as possible in needs'. Our relationship to nature is also fundamentally transformed, because our understanding and control of nature is advanced through 'the development [...] of the natural sciences to their highest point' and because capital penetrates the natural world to an ever greater extent: the 'exploration of all of nature in order to discover new, useful qualities in things' (409). Thus nature itself is submitted to capital's power: '[f]or the first time, nature becomes merely an object for humankind, purely a matter of utility; ceases to be recognized as a power for itself' (410).

Some commentators have seen in these pages of the *Grundrisse* a critique by Marx of capital's subjugation of nature. In one sense this is certainly accurate: Marx argues that the capitalist mode of production creates

> a system of general exploitation of the natural and human qualities, a system of general utility, utilising science itself just as much as all the physical and mental qualities, while there appears nothing *higher in itself*, nothing legitimate for itself, outside this circle of social production and exchange. (409)

It is clear that Marx is condemning this domination of capital over nature and humanity (which are both even more advanced in our own time than in Marx's). But it would not be very dialectical *only* to condemn: the expansion of the capitalist mode of production *also* lays the foundations of a post-capitalist society, breaking the ties, bonds and beliefs of pre-capitalist societies. The domination of nature is a development, in other words, that is to be welcomed as well as condemned. It is part of the 'the great civilizing influence of capital': 'its production of a stage of society in comparison to which all earlier ones appear as mere *local developments* of humanity and as *nature-idolatry*' (409-410). Later in the *Grundrisse* Marx makes it clear that communism will be characterized in part by a collective 'mastery' over nature: the use of machinery will mean that the worker 'inserts the process of nature, transformed into an industrial process, as a means between himself and inorganic nature, mastering it' (705).

Thus, the problem for Marx is that capital sees nature as nothing more than a possible source of value, not that under capitalism nature has been objectified or controlled. Marx's understanding of the relation between humanity and nature is subtle and useful for informing present-day debates, but we should also be careful of retrospectively and anachronistically claiming Marx as an eco-socialist. Certainly Marx does not lament the loss of some more authentic relation to nature: he contrasts capital's domination of nature favourably with the 'nature worship' of earlier societies and celebrates the overcoming of traditional attitudes towards nature:

> In accord with this tendency, capital drives beyond national barriers and prejudices as much as beyond nature worship, as well as all traditional, confined, complacent, encrusted satisfactions of present needs, and reproductions of old ways of life. It is destructive towards all of this, and constantly revolutionizes it, tearing down all the barriers which hem in the development of the forces of production, the expansion of needs, the all-sided development of production, and the exploitation and exchange of natural and mental forces. (410)

These pages are among the most interesting, even exhilarating in the *Grundrisse*. They are reminiscent of the well-known passages from the *Manifesto* in which Marx and Engels write about the revolutionary and cosmopolitan character of the bourgeoisie, 'which draws all, even the most barbarian, nations into civilisation' (*CW6*: 488).

Although in this drive to expand production and circulation '[e]very limit appears [to capital] as a barrier to be overcome', this does not mean that these barriers really are overcome. Capitalist 'production moves in contradictions which are constantly overcome but just as constantly posited' (410). One barrier – which we have already implicitly been discussing – is that of *overproduction*: supply may outstrip demand, because the commodities which have been produced may not be able to be sold and hence realized as money. In contrast to Marx, his predecessors and contemporaries in political economy either denied the possibility of general overproduction or recognized it only as an occasional occurrence resulting from miscalculation, to be corrected through the self-regulating mechanism of the market. They did not recognize that the possibility and indeed inevitability of overproduction is inherent to capitalism and productive of regular crises 'in which this contradiction of capital discharges itself in great thunderstorms which increasingly threaten it as the foundation of society and of production itself' (411).

There is thus a contradiction in the capitalist production process, which is a valorization process and simultaneously a devaluation process: the value of the commodities produced may not be realized in circulation. Now Marx tells us:

> The contradiction between production and valorization – of which capital, by its concept, is the unity – has to be grasped more intrinsically than merely as the indifferent, seemingly reciprocal independent appearance of the individual moments of the process, or rather of the totality of processes. (415, *tm*)

In other words, we have to find the roots of this contradiction within the production process itself. Although capital is driven to create as much value as possible – 'to drive beyond every barrier to production' – there is nonetheless '*a limit, not inherent to production generally, but to production founded on capital*' (415). Capital 'restricts labour and the creation of value', 'it posits a *barrier* to labour and value-creation', in that it will only produce value at all insofar as it can create surplus value and will posit necessary labour only insofar as it forms the basis of surplus labour (421). Moreover, it seeks to reduce necessary labour, and the value it exchanges for necessary labour, as much as possible, hence reducing 'the worker's exchange capacity' and his capacity for consumption, thus increasing the difficulty of realizing the value that has been created (422).

One way to try to overcome these barriers is through the credit system. This can happen at the level of nations: 'e.g. the English forced to *lend* to foreign nations, in order to have them as customers' (416). It can also happen at the level of individual consumers, as we know from recent credit-fuelled booms (and subsequent crashes). Increasing the supply of credit is a way to stimulate consumption without having to increase wages. Ultimately, however, and as we have already seen (see 'Exchange between capital and labour' above), workers' consumption alone will always be inadequate to realize surplus value: 'the *demand of the labourer himself can never be an adequate demand*'. Each capitalist may want the workers of all other capitalists to consume as much as possible, but because he is driven to reduce necessary labour he also wants to *restrict* his *own* workers' consumption as much as possible. This relation of each capitalist to his own worker is 'the essential relation' – the relation between capital and labour that we are still considering here in our analysis of capital in general – and it is an 'illusion' that workers' consumption can be adequate to the demand to realize surplus value. An important illusion, nonetheless, because 'it *seems* to each individual capital that the demand of the working class posited by production itself is an "adequate demand"' (420).

It is equally an illusion on the part of certain critics of capitalism that overproduction occurs because – as Proudhon argues – capitalists overcharge the workers for the goods they consume, meaning that workers cannot afford to buy back the products they themselves have produced (424). This is an illusion because even if the capitalist sold his commodities at their value – which is the assumption that Marx has been making so far – then the value of the commodity will be more than the value that the worker has received in wages, because (in addition to the transfer of value from the means of production to the commodity) the commodity contains surplus value; there is a portion of the value of the commodity for which the capitalist has paid nothing (427). So the issue is not that the capitalist sets a price which is above the value of the product, thus denying the worker the opportunity to purchase. To the contrary, the price of a commodity can fall below its value and the capitalist can still make a profit (432). Moreover, if commodities were sold below their value, then a worker would benefit only if they happen to be a consumer of those products – and he will benefit only as a consumer, not as a worker, i.e. hardly at all (436–7). Equally, the capitalist does not increase surplus value by paying the workers below the value of their wage, by defrauding or tricking them somehow. More accurately, the capitalist *may* do this, but for the purposes of the analysis we assume that labour-power is paid at its value, in same way that we assume that commodities are sold at their value: 'We must always presuppose here that the wage paid is *economically* just, i.e. that it is determined by the general laws of economics'. If we assume that the capitalist pays the worker the value of the labour-power that he purchases, this is not because this always, or even usually, happens, but because Marx wants to show that surplus value – and hence profit – is created by exploitation within the production process, not by deception or dishonesty within exchange. 'The contradictions have to follow here from the general relations themselves, and not from fraud by individual capitalists' (426). The working class, in other words, are ultimately exploited not as consumers (by being overcharged) but as workers – and not because they are not paid the value of their labour-power, but because they have to perform surplus labour. This has important political consequences (though these are not explicitly drawn out by Marx here). Today it is often as consumers that people are urged to mobilize: the 'rights' and protections of consumers are affirmed against unscrupulous and predatory banks, electricity suppliers, train operators, etc. But if Marx's analysis is correct then it is, fundamentally, *as producers* that we must organize and resist.

In the following pages, Marx begins to look at the interaction of capitals, examining: (i) why commodities are not sold at their values and how profits are distributed among capitals (434–7); (ii) the circulation process of the total social capital (437–43). The first of these topics we will return to later (see 'General rate of profit' below). The second anticipates the famous reproduction schemas found in Part 3 of *Capital II*, where Marx examines the interlinking circuits of capitals producing means of consumption and capitals producing means of production. Because Marx only just begins to introduce this topic in the *Grundrisse*, and in a highly condensed fashion (what takes up almost 200 pages in *Capital II* is covered in about six pages in the *Grundrisse*), we will leave it to one side here.[57]

Surplus capital

Once surplus value has been realized by selling the commodities for money, at least some of this money must be reinvested as new capital: 'If the surplus value were simply consumed, then capital would *not* have valorized itself as capital, and not produced itself as *capital*, i.e. as value which produces value' (444, *tm*). The surplus value produced is posited as new capital, or what Marx calls 'surplus capital' (to distinguish it from the original capital) (451). Like the original capital, this surplus capital will be divided into constant and variable capital: some of it will be spent on raw materials and instruments, some of it will be spent of wages. This reinforces Marx's claim in the 'Introduction' for the priority of relations of production over relations of distribution: the capitalist cannot use all his profit as revenue for his own consumption, but must use it as surplus capital and reinvest it in means of production and wages; hence from the perspective of the capitalist, the forms of distribution that are profits and wages can be counted as relations of production, because they are used for further production (758).

When we originally analysed the capitalist production process, it seemed as if the capitalist just happened to have some raw materials and instruments and some money to spend on wages: we did not ask where the capitalist got these things. In Marx's terminology, they seemed to be 'external presuppositions' (450). Now we can see that capital itself posits these presuppositions: it has used surplus capital to reinvest in materials, instruments and wages. But where did that surplus capital come from? From surplus value. And where did surplus value come from? From surplus labour, i.e. from the unpaid labour of the worker. In other words, the presuppositions of capital are the products of labour. 'All moments which confronted living labour capacity, and employed it as *alien*, *external* powers, and which consumed it under *certain conditions independent of itself*, are now posited as *its own product and result*' (451).

The workers experience the production process as an alien process: not only do the materials and machinery that they use belong to someone else, they must work to the rhythms of that machinery, with no control over the whole process. In a bitter irony for the workers, it now transpires that those materials and machinery are the result of their own labour (i.e. of the labour of the workers considered collectively). What the worker has produced is not only the conditions of his alien labour (materials and instruments) but also his own submission to those conditions: labour has produced capital both in the sense of 'capital' as materials and machinery owned by the capitalist and 'capital' as a relation of domination to which the worker must submit. 'This social relation [between capitalist and worker – SC] [...] appears in fact as an even more important result of the process than its material results' (458). '[W]hile capital thus appears as the product of labour, so does the product of labour likewise appear as capital': the conditions of labour (materials and instruments) may have been produced by labour, but they are produced *as* capital (453). Some of the surplus capital that labour has created will be used for wages: but even this part will only be accessible to labour on the condition that it performs further surplus labour. 'The greater the extent to which labour objectifies itself, the greater becomes the objective world of values, which stands opposite it as alien – alien property' (455).

The objection from liberal critics will be that the worker and the capitalist engage in a free and voluntary exchange and so no exploitation has occurred: the capitalist pays the worker the value of his labour-power and in return the worker provides a day's labour. To an extent this claim is valid: we already know that, in terms of simple circulation, the two parties engage in 'an exchange entirely based on the laws of the exchange of equivalents as measured by the quantity of labour or labour time contained in them' (457). But we also know that this exchange, though it is formally free and equal, is an 'exchange without equivalent', because labour-power has the unique capacity to produce more value than it is itself worth: once the capitalist has paid for the labour-power, he makes the worker perform surplus labour for free. *In addition*, we can now see that the value that the worker has produced for free (the surplus value) is appropriated by the capitalist and realized as surplus capital, which is then used by the capitalist to pay the worker again. So even if we accepted that the original exchange between a worker and a capitalist is free and equal (which we could only do if we disregarded the unique character of labour-power as value-creating), in all following exchanges the capitalist pays the worker with value that the worker herself has created and for which she is never remunerated. The wrong done to the worker here is doubled and compounded: not only is she made to work part of the day for free, she is not even paid out of the capitalist's own pocket, but out of the very value that she created for free.

> Hence, by virtue of having acquired labour capacity in exchange as an equivalent, capital has acquired labour time – to the extent that it exceeds the labour time contained in labour capacity – in exchange *without equivalent*; it has appropriated alien labour time *without exchange* by means of the *form* of the exchange. (674)

Thus, the right of property – to which liberal apologists for capitalism attach so much importance – has undergone what Marx calls a 'dialectical inversion':

> The right of property is inverted, to become, on the one side, the right to appropriate alien labour, and, on the other, the duty of respecting the product of one's own labour, and one's own labour itself, as values belonging to others [...] The relation of exchange has thus dropped away entirely, or is a *mere semblance*. (458)

The liberal defence of the exchange between capitalist and worker fails, then. But what about the very first exchange between capitalist and worker? Even if we grant that the capitalist makes his money at the expense of the worker, doesn't the former at least make some initial investment? Clearly the capitalist needs some capital to begin with: where does he get it? Of the other side of the exchange we can ask a similar question: why is the worker a worker and not a capitalist? Why is she selling her labour-power rather than starting her own business? Granted that the central product of the capitalist production process is the relationship between capitalist and worker – '[t]he *production of capitalists and wage labourers is thus a chief product of capital's valorization process*' – how is that relationship established in the first place (512, *tm*)? These are the questions that Marx begins to address in his section on the original accumulation of capital.

Original accumulation of capital and pre-capitalist economic forms

If this section of the *Grundrisse* has a parallel in the three volumes of *Capital*, then it must be the final part of *Capital I* on 'So-Called Primitive Accumulation'. Having explained the process and law of capitalist accumulation – in which surplus value is created through capital and more capital is made from that surplus value, in a 'never-ending circle' of value creation – at the end of *Capital I* Marx asks how the whole process began. There must have been a 'primitive accumulation', or *original accumulation*: 'an accumulation which is not the result of the capitalist mode of production but its point of departure'. Political economy explains this primitive accumulation with the claim that once upon a time there was a 'diligent, intelligent and above all frugal élite' who carefully saved money and were thus able to purchase the means of production. This frugal élite became the capitalists, while the 'lazy rascals' who had saved nothing became the workers who had to work for the capitalists. Rejecting this 'insipid childishness', Marx instead details the highly violent measures that saw workers separated from the means of production and nascent capitalists accumulate wealth, showing how capital comes into the world 'dripping from head to toe, from every pore, with blood and dirt' (*C1*: 873, 926).

This part of *Capital I* thus examines the transition from feudalism to capitalism, above all 'the historical process of divorcing the producer from the means of production', which 'forms the pre-history of capital' (*C1*: 875). Some have argued that Marx's analysis of primitive accumulation also provides a model for analysing the *continued reproduction* of the separation of workers from the means of production and what David Harvey has called processes of 'accumulation by dispossession'.[58] The *Grundrisse* apparently lends credence to the latter interpretation, for Marx states: 'Once this separation [between workers and the means of production – SC] is given, the production process can only produce it anew, reproduce it, and reproduce it on an expanded scale'. However, he then immediately says: 'How it does this, we have seen': that is, it does it through the capitalist production process itself in which the conditions of labour are reproduced '*as independent values, i.e. values belonging to an alien subject, confronting this living labour capacity*' (462). In other words, it seems that for Marx the analysis of primitive or original accumulation is a historical analysis: its job is basically to tell us how capitalism emerged. As we will see, however, there is no clear break between capitalist and pre-capitalist societies, so that even a 'historical' analysis can have contemporary relevance.[59]

It might seem strange that Marx does not reach these historical questions until this point: would it not have made sense to begin his work by looking at the pre-history of capitalism? But remember that Marx is not offering a history of capitalism or a philosophy of history. According to the methodological principles laid out in the 'Introduction', the order of categories is determined by their importance and relation within bourgeois society. Because bourgeois society is the most complex and developed yet seen, from its perspective we can interpret and understand previous societies, without smudging over historical differences (see 'Method of political economy' above). This is the focus of this section of the *Grundrisse*: the examination of pre-capitalist forms in order to highlight the unique presuppositions and features of the capitalist mode of production. As such, and unlike in *Capital I*, in the *Grundrisse* Marx does not say much about the transition from feudalism to capitalism (indeed, as we will see, there is not much about feudalism at all).

Historic presuppositions of capital

Once the capitalist mode of production is up and running, capital posits its own presuppositions: the capitalist production process produces surplus value, which is then used as surplus capital to produce further surplus value and so on. But capital can only do this once capitalism is in place. While capitalism is in the process of developing or becoming, it must rely on external conditions for its development. So we have to distinguish between the *conditions of existence* of capital – the conditions it relies upon once it is in existence, conditions which it itself creates – and the *historic presuppositions* of capital: the conditions that need to develop in order that capital itself can come into being. Clearly these latter conditions cannot be produced by capital itself, because capital itself has not yet appeared.

This may seem an obvious point, but bourgeois economics sees things differently. The basic role of bourgeois economics – as far as Marx is concerned – is to legitimize capitalism, presenting it as 'an eternal and *natural* (not historical) form of production' (460). As such, it confuses conditions of existence with historical presuppositions. For example, it might have been that during the period of capitalism's development an individual was able to accumulate money through careful saving (although in reality careful saving was not the primary method by which nascent capitalists accumulated wealth). But this does not mean that this is how capitalists accumulate their money under capitalism. Under capitalism they accumulate wealth *as capitalists*, i.e. by exploiting labour to extract surplus value.

For capitalism to function, there are four historic presuppositions that must arise. First, there must of course be living labour capacity, in order to undertake the labour necessary to produce value. But the key is that this capacity must be 'separated from the *conditions* of living labour as well as from the *means of existence, the necessary goods*, the means of self-preservation of living *labour capacity*' (463). This means that labourers must be separated from the means of production. If a labourer owned these means – if, for example, they had a little piece of land, some seeds and a few tools or bits of machinery – then they would be able to work for themselves: they could reproduce the conditions of their labour-power, either by growing their own food and building their own shelter etc. or by making products and then exchanging them for food, shelter, clothing, etc., i.e. engaging in simple exchange as an immediate producer. Without these means of existence, however, the labourer is left with little choice: to survive, he must work for the capitalist.

To create value, the labourer needs something to work with and on: he needs objectified labour in the shape of materials and instruments. This is the second presupposition. There must be enough objectified labour for the labourer to reproduce value equivalent to the value of his labour-power and to absorb his surplus labour. Third, there must be a certain way of linking living labour capacity with objectified labour: the relationship must be 'mediated through exchange' (463). Hence money must be in circulation to buy labour-power. Fourth and finally, the side that owns the objectified labour must view it as value and must have as their aim the making of money (rather than the making of use values for consumption).

In summary, the four presuppositions are:

1. Living labour capacity separated from the means of production.
2. Objectified labour or means of production with which (1) can work.
3. Money to bring (1) and (2) together.
4. Owners of (2) aim to produce value, not merely use values.

Using these four presuppositions, we are able to distinguish capitalism very clearly from earlier modes of production. In the first place, the position of the wage-labourer under capitalism is quite different from that of workers in pre-capitalist societies. In the ancient world, a slave was the property of his owner: nothing more than the owner's 'labouring machine', little different from any other piece of machinery (464). In the Middle Ages, a serf was not so much a machine, but more like a farm animal: 'a moment of property in land itself' or 'an appendage of the soil' (465). In both cases, the slave and the serf are counted among the conditions of production, whereas '[f]or capital, the worker is not a condition of production, only work is [...] And [capital – SC] does not appropriate the worker, but his labour – not directly, but mediated through exchange' (498). Whereas the slave and serf are in effect pieces of property, the wage-labourer is not the property of someone else: the wage-labourer's labour-power is *his* property, which he then sells in an exchange with the capitalist. As we know, this exchange, in which formally both sides are free and equal, is 'a mere *semblance*, and a *deceptive semblance*': the capitalist has acquired alien labour without exchange (464).

For the worker, his 'labour capacity appears to him as his property [...] over which he, as subject, exercises domination' (465). On the one hand, this ownership of his labour-power *is* only an appearance, given that he is obliged to sell it to the capitalist: what kind of 'property' is it when the owner cannot dispose of it as he pleases? While the labourer may be free to pick and choose a particular employer – a particular capitalist to sell his labour-power to – he is not free to pick and choose whether or not he sells that labour-power to the capitalist class as a whole. On the other hand, the worker really does own his labour-power: he is forced to sell it to the capitalist not because he doesn't really own it, but because he owns nothing else; he owns no means of production and so cannot live unless he works for a wage, treating his labour-power as a commodity. This ownership of his labour-power distinguishes the wage-labourer from the slave and the serf. All three – slave, serf and wage-labourer – are exploited, because all three are made to perform surplus labour, but they are exploited in significantly different ways. Capitalist exploitation is indirect and economic, in that wage labourers are compelled to perform surplus labour not through direct political force but out of economic necessity.

Even if these historical differences between types of worker are acknowledged, some might still claim that capitalism has a much longer history than Marx claims. Marx argues that capitalism is based on an exchange between living and objectified labour

– but haven't some people always purchased the labour of others? Remember the fourth historic presupposition of capital, however: the aim of the exchange must be to create more value. It might have been that, for example, in ancient Rome or in feudal England someone paid another person to bake them a loaf of bread or weed their garden. But this is a simple exchange in which the person who pays for the service is not making any money: to the contrary, he has spent and lost money in order to gain a use value for his own direct consumption. He has purchased labour-power 'not as *value-positing* labour, but as an activity which creates utility, use value' (466). This is why, as we saw, even when such an exchange takes place in bourgeois society it is counted as 'unproductive labour': wealth is consumed and no value is created (see 'Productive and unproductive labour' above).

It might be that within pre-capitalist economic forms free day labourers are hired. For example, the lord of the manor might hire some labourers for a wage to work alongside his serfs. But the basic mode of production here would still be serfdom, i.e. a mode of production whose purpose is the production of use value rather than value. Even if the lord resells part of the workers' products – meaning that they have created values rather than merely use values – they would be sold only as surplus so that the lord could purchase luxury goods: the ultimate aim, in other words, would still be the consumption of use values rather than the production of value. So just because market exchanges are taking place, this does not mean that we have capitalism. Marx does claim that 'wherever these free workers increase in number [...] there the old mode of production – commune, patriarchal, feudal etc. – is in the process of dissolution, and elements of real wage labour are in preparation' (469). At this point, we might therefore want to ask: exactly when do we cross over from one mode of production to another? How many 'free workers' need to be hired before we can claim that a society is a capitalist one? When does the 'becoming' of capitalism end?

But Marx's goal is not to try to pinpoint the exact moment at which the capitalist mode of production came into being. Rather than arriving ready-made, capitalism develops within and out of previous modes of production and in different ways and at different rates in different parts of the world. As such, rather than existing in its 'pure' state, capitalism exists alongside pre-capitalist forms.[60]

What Marx wants to do is to identify capitalism's unique features in contrast with those pre-capitalist forms. With that aim in mind, he now looks at the latter.

Forms which precede capitalist production

We know that capitalism requires 'free labour and the exchange of this free labour for money, in order to reproduce and valorize money' (471, *tm*). 'Free labour' here has a double meaning. In the first place, it means labour that has been freed from the restrictions that operated in feudal times, when labour was constrained in various ways. Serfs would have been tied to a particular piece of land – required to work for one particular nobleman, without the possibility of moving to work somewhere else. Other types of labourer would have been constrained in different ways: craftsmen were required to undertake lengthy apprenticeships and to join guilds in order to practise their craft. In addition, crafts would often be passed down through generations, so employment was often not freely chosen. The masters within guilds would also have been permitted to employ only a limited number of workers. The first meaning of 'free labour', then, refers to the emancipation of workers from these feudal restrictions, an emancipation celebrated by the classical political economists.[61] But for Marx 'free labour' has a second, ironical meaning: under capitalism labourers are also 'freed' from the means of production, because they do not own them and have no access to them except through exchange with capital. The production of free workers in this second sense requires the dissolution of earlier societies in which labourers did own property, either as individual proprietors or as members of their community.

Marx's investigation of pre-capitalist forms of property is intended to highlight the distinctiveness of capitalist property ownership and in so doing to debunk the classical economic notion that capitalist property relations are somehow 'natural'. Bourgeois economics dehistoricizes capitalist property relations, projecting them into the past as if they had always existed. Marx counters this by demonstrating both that other forms of property existed in the past and that capitalism is based on the *dissolution* of property: its distinctive feature is that the vast majority are denied access to property. In order to do this, Marx looks at three forms of society, with three distinct forms of property ownership: the Asiatic, the ancient and the Germanic. At first glance these three forms seem to map onto those mentioned in Marx's '1859 Preface', which lists 'the Asiatic, ancient, feudal and modern bourgeois modes of production'. None of the three forms in the *Grundrisse*, however, can be fully identified with feudalism: the 'Germanic' form develops into feudalism, but in the *Grundrisse* Marx does not really explain how this development occurs or exactly how feudalism then develops into capitalism. Moreover, in the '1859 Preface' the modes of production listed are presented as 'epochs marking progress in the economic development of society' (*CW29*: 263). In contrast, the three forms found in the *Grundrisse* are best viewed as three alternative routes from what is later in the text referred to as 'naturally arisen [or primitive – SC] communism', i.e. early stateless and classless communal societies (882). In other words we should think of the three forms not as successive steps leading up to capitalism but as overlapping and coexisting pre-capitalist forms. Commentators have thus argued that in the *Grundrisse* we see the emergence of a 'multilinear' theory of history.[62]

The accuracy of Marx's historical overview of pre-capitalist forms is open to question. He was dependent on the knowledge and sources of his day, which have since been surpassed. But his primary aim is to shed light on capitalism, not to provide a detailed historical narrative: while this does not mean that the question of accuracy is irrelevant, it does mean that the inaccuracies that may exist in his account do not necessarily invalidate the entire analysis.[63]

The first form that Marx examines is the Asiatic (though it is not limited to Asia: in relation to this form Marx also mentions Mexico, Peru, Romania and the Celts).[64] It emerged on the basis of spontaneously arising groups: first families, then combinations of families within tribes or clans, would have formed communities. Initially these groups would have been nomadic, but eventually they would have settled in one place to appropriate and use a particular piece of land. Hence the community is here the presupposition of property: the community views the earth as its property and individuals possess property and so appropriate the conditions of life only insofar as they are members of the community. Within this form of property there are various possible developments. In most cases it develops into what Marx calls 'oriental despotism', in which many different communities are unified under a despot as 'the higher *proprietor*' or '*sole proprietor*' and who extracts surplus labour as tribute (472). While there can be 'a more despotic or a more democratic form of this community system', the typical form of this Asiatic mode of production is thus a despotic state based upon and collecting tribute from a network of self-sufficient villages (473).

The second form of property is the ancient, as found in the city states of ancient Greece and Rome. Although also beginning from communal clans, it developed in a different way to the Asiatic form. In the latter, the community itself owned property and individuals could consider themselves property owners only as members of the community: individuals were therefore merely 'possessors' of property owned by the commune (475). In the ancient form, in contrast, there are private individual proprietors: although some land may be set aside for common purposes or use (the *ager publicus*, or public land), one man or family may own and cultivate a particular plot of land. Nonetheless, membership of the community is in this case still a precondition of property ownership. This may be true in a legal sense – in that, for example, only Roman citizens can own land – but also in a wider material sense in that the community protects its property from other communities by engaging in war. 'War is therefore the great comprehensive task, the great communal labour' (474). There is thus a reciprocal dependence between individual property owners and the community: the ability of individuals to use particular pieces of land is sustained by the community's defence of that land from external threats; but equally the community can only be sustained by the labour of its members, who both cultivate the land that constitutes the community and dedicate their surplus time to the military service that defends the community. This ancient form was based on slavery: only citizens were property owners, and slaves were themselves property. In contrast to the Asiatic form, in which cities formed 'only at exceptionally good points for external trade', in the ancient form the town or city was the centre of the community, although the city is 'founded on landed property and on agriculture' and agricultural work was more highly esteemed than commerce and trade (474, 479).

The third form of property that Marx discusses is the one he calls 'Germanic'. In the ancient city states, individual property is still mediated by the commune. In the Germanic form of property, individual property owners are independent units and the commune exists only as the occasional 'coming together' of these units. 'The commune exists only in the interrelations among these individual landed proprietors' (484). Although the commune presupposes a common history, language, 'bloodline', and so on, as a real and material presence it exists only when its members gather together (in contrast to the ancient world, where the city is the material and economic unity of the commune). In the Germanic commune there is some land for common use, but whereas in the ancient world such land in effect belongs to the city state and individuals use it insofar as they are citizens, here the common land 'is really the common property of the individual proprietors, not of the union of these proprietors endowed with an existence separate from themselves' (485).

Having outlined the distinctions between these three pre-capitalist forms of property, Marx identifies their commonalities, in order then to distinguish all three from capitalist property relations. Each of them is ultimately based on agricultural labour whose aim is the production of use values rather than exchange values. In terms of their property relations, we find in each '[a]ppropriation not through labour, but presupposed to labour' (485). In other words, the labour that the worker performs presupposes an existing appropriation of the land: the objective conditions of his labour – principally land – do not appear as the product of previous labour but are already there before him as his own property or possession. In contrast, in capitalism the conditions of the worker's labour lie outside him: raw materials and instruments belong to capital and the food and shelter that he needs in order to live he has to purchase with the wage earned from labour. Whereas the wage-labourer under capitalism begins with no property and can only gain it through labour, a labourer in any of the three pre-capitalist economic forms finds the conditions of his labour before him – not because he exists in some sort of immediate unity with the earth, but because the land upon which he works is already his own property.

However, it is his own property only because he is a member of his commune: his relation to the conditions of his labour is mediated through the commune. These are the two fundamental characteristics of the pre-capitalist economic forms that Marx identifies: (1) the labourer owns the objective conditions of his labour; (2) but he does so only through membership of his commune (485). What varies is the 'specific form of the individual's property': it might be that there is communal property of which the individual is only a possessor (as in the Asiatic form); or that there is individual property ownership but only by citizens of a city state (the ancient form); or that there is 'communal property [...] only as a complement to individual property' (the Germanic form) (486). In each case, however, the members of these communities stand in contrast to the 'dot-like isolation' of the wage-labourer under capitalism (485).

As suggested above, Marx does not understand these three forms in terms of a linear chronological succession. In discussing why certain communities take one of the three forms in particular, he looks not at the level of historical development or civilization but at factors like climate, geography, soil type, 'the natural inclinations of the tribe' and its relations with neighbouring tribes (486). Given this, we should not expect some account of the transition between these forms, as if they were historical stages. We do, however, get some indication of why these forms decline and fail (though it is very far from a full historical analysis). The purpose of each of these communities is to reproduce itself and its members in the same form: to reproduce its conditions and individuals' relations to those conditions (541). As Marx presents them, therefore, these are societies that are static, or at most circular: the development of both the community and its individuals is restricted. Various changes can interrupt this stasis: population growth, poverty, war with or conquest by neighbouring communities. In particular, Marx highlights the corrosive power of wealth. In pre-capitalist societies, the aim of production is not wealth but use value and the perpetual reproduction of the society and its members. In ancient Rome, for example, commerce and trade were suspect and '[t]he question is always which mode of property creates the best citizens' (487).[65] As commerce develops, the traditional structure of society breaks down: production for exchange overtakes production for use and for the reproduction of the community and its members. The Asiatic form is most resistant to the development of capitalism because it subordinates the individual entirely to the community and so it 'hangs on most tenaciously and for the longest time. This is due to its presupposition that the individual does not become independent *vis-à-vis* the commune; that there is a self-sustaining circle of production' (486).

Some commentators have suggested that these passages of the *Grundrisse* are testament to Marx's nostalgia for pre-capitalist societies in which there was a harmonious unity between man and his natural conditions of existence.[66] There is some textual justification for these claims, not least in Marx's curiously worded claims about the earth as man's 'inorganic body', to which he relates as 'the inorganic nature of his subjectivity' (488, 485). The claim that '[n]ature is man's *inorganic body*' can also be found in the *1844 Manuscripts* and ultimately the concept of inorganic nature can be traced back to Hegel, which for some readers will only encourage their view that these pages of the *Grundrisse* are suspiciously humanist or reactionary (*CW3*: 276).[67]

Rather than covertly indulging in nostalgia, however, Marx explicitly recognizes its draw, without himself succumbing to it. Given that in ancient societies 'the human being appears as the aim of production', it is not surprising that such societies appear 'very lofty' from the perspective of capitalism, 'where production appears as the aim of mankind and wealth as the aim of production' – and, moreover, where that wealth is produced at the cost of the impoverishment of labour (487-8). In fact this gives us one answer to the conundrum that we encountered at the end of the 'Introduction': if the materialist conception of history is correct to propose that different socio-economic conditions give rise to different forms of culture, then why is it that we value ancient Greek art so highly when we long ago left behind ancient Greek social conditions? The answer is that Greek art arose from – and so reminds us of – a society for which humanity seemed to be an end-in-itself:

> This is why the childish world of antiquity appears on one side as loftier [than the modern, capitalist world – SC]. On the other side, it really is loftier in all matters where closed shapes, forms and given limits are sought for. It is satisfaction from a limited standpoint; while the modern gives no satisfaction; or, where it appears satisfied with itself, it is *vulgar*. (488)

Marx thus offers what we might call a materialist explanation for the persistence of nostalgia. But he is not himself nostalgic for the past: he does not long for some pre-capitalist harmony between man and nature, because no such harmony existed. There is a 'unity' between man and nature in pre-capitalist societies but, as we have seen, this unity is always *mediated* by his membership of the commune. Marx's point is not that man once existed in a more pure or direct relation with nature which capitalism has destroyed, but rather that prior to the advent of capitalism workers had not yet been separated from their conditions of production. It is this separation that in part defines capitalism and that needs to be explained.

If Marx is celebrating anything then it is not a lost past but rather capitalism itself. By making wealth the aim of production, capitalism may at first appear to be a retrogression from those pre-capitalist societies that made human beings the aim of production. But,

> what is wealth other than the universality of individual needs, capacities, pleasures, productive forces etc., created through universal exchange? The full development of human mastery over the forces of nature, those of so-called nature as well of humanity's own nature? The absolute working-out of his creative potentialities [...]? (488)

In other words, by pursuing wealth as an end in itself, capitalism frees us from the restrictions and limitations of the past and necessarily develops humanity's productive forces. The problem is that under capitalism wealth appears in its 'limited bourgeois form', i.e. as value, and the 'complete working-out of the human content appears as a complete emptying out, this universal objectification as total alienation' (hence the ancient world appearing loftier) (488). If anything, the *Grundrisse* is rather dismissive of, even contemptuous towards, pre-capitalist social forms. This position seems to be revised in later works, in which Marx suggests that certain 'archaic' communal forms of ownership could form the basis for the development of communism without first having to pass through capitalism.[68]

Although the aim of pre-capitalist societies is simply to reproduce themselves, in striving to achieve this aim those communities necessarily change and develop (493). As population grows, for example, villages grow into towns, more land is cultivated, other communities are conquered to absorb the extra people or obtain more resources, etc. As these objective conditions change, so too do the subjective capacities of the community members, as they develop new skills, ideas, needs, languages, etc. 'Thus the preservation of the old community includes the destruction of the conditions on which it rests' (494). In these passages, then, the emphasis is firmly on the 'development of the forces of production' as the motor of historical change (496). This does not mean, however, that Marx is indulging in a narrow form of technological determinism in which changes in tools, machinery, or use of land move history along: the community and its members are themselves a force of production and there are complex and multidirectional interactions between the community, its members, their forms of labour, and the technology they use. Altogether, the whole is what Marx calls a '*mode of production*' (495).

Dissolution of pre-capitalist relations

So far in the section on original accumulation we have seen Marx undertake a largely formal analysis of the four presuppositions of capital and a more historical analysis of three dominant types of pre-capitalist economic forms or modes of production. He will now begin to link the two by looking at how the presuppositions of capital were established through the *dissolution* of the pre-capitalist forms.

In order for capitalism to develop, certain forms of property must be dissolved 'before the worker can be found as a free worker, as objectless, purely subjective labour capacity confronting the objective conditions of production as his *not-property*, as *alien property*, as *value* for-itself, as capital' (498). There must, therefore, be dissolution of all property relations in which labourers: own land (this ownership mediated by the community, as in the Asiatic, ancient and Germanic forms); own their instruments of production (as in the case of artisan labourers); are themselves pieces of property, counted among the conditions of production and the owners only of the 'necessaries of life' (as in slavery and serfdom) (500). As we might by now expect, Marx does not straightforwardly condemn the dissolution of these forms. Although they mark a moment of loss for the labourer – loss of property – they also represent something else: 'release from the earth'; independence from the restrictions of the guild system; freedom from relations of bondage or slavery (502). This is the double sense of 'freedom' that we have already come across: workers who are 'free from the old relations of clientship, bondage and servitude, and secondly free of all belongings and possessions, and of every objective, material form of being, *free of all property*', 'liberated but also *homeless* and *empty-handed*' (507, 509).

What we are left with now is workers 'whose only property is their labour capacity' and who are thus 'forced solely by their lack of property to labour and to sell their labour' (502, 503). On the other side, we have the objective conditions of production (land, raw materials, instruments, necessaries of life, etc.). What we do not yet have is capitalism: the conditions are only *potentially* in place. At some point capital must gain ownership and control of the conditions of labour that have been separated from the workers. This is the 'original accumulation' to which Marx refers, and he is in agreement with the classical economists about the need for such an accumulation. The classical economists misrepresent things, however, in at least two ways. First, they confuse this original, pre-capitalist accumulation with the pattern of accumulation under capitalism. As we know, once capitalism is in place capitalists accumulate by exploiting labour: the raw materials and instruments used in the capitalist production process, and the commodities and profits produced by it, are all ultimately the products of labour. Classical political economists obscure this reality by taking the original accumulation, 'which is independent of labour', and shifting it 'from the prehistory of capital into the present' (504). Second, they present this accumulation as a peaceful process in which capitalists accumulate through the virtuous means of hard work and saving, thus disregarding the fact that in order for capitalists to gain ownership of the conditions of production, their original owners had to be dispossessed of them.

In Part VIII of *Capital I* Marx details the violent and coercive measures that, from the end of the fifteenth century onwards, first saw workers expropriated from their property (as a result of land clearances, usurpation of common lands, sale of state lands and other methods) and then disciplined into becoming wage labourers for capital.[69] In the *Grundrisse*, some of these measures are briefly mentioned, but there is more emphasis on the role of urbanization and the growth of markets and trade in ushering in capitalism, with usurers and merchants identified as nascent capitalists. Marx describes how merchant wealth was used to purchase the conditions of production once they had already been separated from workers as a result of the dissolution of earlier modes of production, though he notes that wealth is itself 'one of the agencies of that dissolution', acting as 'a highly energetic solvent' (506, 507). The growth of exchange encourages production for exchange rather than for use and 'money transforms itself into capital' when, for example, a merchant induces some previously independent weavers and spinners to work for him, transforming them into wage labourers for capital (510). Once capitalist production has developed in some branches of industry, then capital itself can act as a solvent, spreading through all branches of industry, dispossessing workers of their means of production and subordinating them to the command of capital: it is 'the effect of capital [...] to conquer all of production and to develop and complete the divorce between labour and property' (512).

The emphasis here on the growth of commerce and the role of merchant capital echoes the analyses in *The German Ideology* (as well as other texts of the 1840s, such as the *Manifesto*), which locates the origins of capitalism in 'the extension of trade through the merchants beyond the immediate surroundings of the town' (*CW5*: 67). At the same time, however, the emphasis on the *separation* of the labourers from the means of production anticipates *Capital I*, where the focus is not on the development of trade and markets out of the towns but on the expropriation of the rural peasantry, who after being expropriated are forced into towns to look for employment. In this way, as in many others, the *Grundrisse* marks a kind of point of transition in Marx's thinking between *The German Ideology* and *Capital*.[70]

In general, however, the *Grundrisse* does not tell us much about how exactly capitalism developed (or why feudalism collapsed). What it offers is an analysis of the distinction between pre-capitalist and capitalist societies. The essential presupposition of the latter is that labour has been separated from the conditions of production. Hence we can now better understand that 'dialectical inversion' that the right to property undergoes in bourgeois society (see 'Surplus capital' above). The right of property becomes the right (of capital) to appropriate alien labour on the basis that the worker has lost all property, hence has no choice but to exchange his living labour for objectified labour (i.e. a wage with which he can buy products to consume). '*The exchange of labour for labour – seemingly the condition of the worker's property – rests on the foundation of the worker's propertylessness*' (515). The exchange between labour and capital that forms the basis of the capitalist production process '*presupposes* alien labour capacity itself as an exchange value – i.e. the separation of living labour capacity from its objective conditions' (510). In other words, only when labour has been separated from the means of production and labour-power becomes a commodity that can be bought and sold on the market can capitalist production take place. So, while the development of exchange and exchange value (in its form as money) helps to dissolve previous forms of production and usher in capitalism, the domination of exchange value and commodity exchange can only develop on the basis of capitalism, i.e. on the basis of that mode of production whose aim is the production of exchange values. This is why we cannot understand capitalism simply by looking at the exchange processes of circulation: 'This exchange of equivalents [...] is only the surface layer of a production which rests on the appropriation of alien labour *without exchange*, but with the *semblance of exchange*' (509). On the basis of this analysis, Marx offers us as good a description as we find in the *Grundrisse* of capital as a relation of production:

> Production based on exchange value, on whose surface this free and equal exchange of equivalents proceeds, is at its base the exchange of *objectified labour* as exchange value for living labour as use value, or, to express this in another way, the relating of labour to its objective conditions – and hence to the objectivity created by itself – as alien property: *alienation of labour*. (514–15)

Circulation of capital and its costs

We have in place the historic presuppositions of capitalism: on the one side living labour separated from the means of production and on the other side owners of the means of production. These two must meet in exchange when the owners of the means of production purchase living labour in order to produce value. Hence we now need to return to the *circulation* of capital: capital has to enter into circulation in order to purchase the means of production and living labour. More than this, capital has to keep on entering into circulation. Its purpose as capital is self-valorization: having purchased labour-power and the means of production, it uses them to create value, which is realized as surplus capital, used to purchase more labour-power and further means of production, to create more value and so on. 'The circulation of capital is at the same time its becoming, its growth, its vital process' (517). Simple circulation began with one commodity, which was exchanged for money, which was then exchanged for a qualitatively different commodity, which was consumed and so dropped out of circulation, thus ending the process. The circulation of capital, in contrast, is circular and never-ending: it enters into circulation only so it can return with what it needs to enlarge itself. Beginning with capital, the process ends with (a larger amount of) capital, only to begin again. 'The circulation of capital constantly ignites itself anew, divides into its different moments, and is a *perpetuum mobile*' (516).

To establish the relationship between production and circulation, Marx considers different moments of the 'turnover' of capital, i.e. of one turn of the circle of capital. There are four such moments (520–1):

1. **The real production process**

   This is the period spent producing the product, in which living labour is put to work on the means of production.

2. **Transformation of the product into money**

   This stage involves selling the product as a commodity, having transported it to a market.

3. **Transformation of money into the means of production**

   Once capital has money from selling its commodity in a market, before it can produce more commodities it must spend some of that money on raw materials and instruments of production.

4. **Transformation of money into labour-power**

   Some of the money must also be spent on paying workers to perform new labour.

Together (3) and (4) make up the conditions of production, but Marx considers them separately because the labour market (to which the capitalist must go to buy labour-power) behaves very differently from the market in materials and instruments.

These four moments account for the turnover time, because each of them must be completed before the entire process can begin again. It is in capital's interest to increase the speed of turnover time as much as possible. Marx provides some calculations to show why, but the basic reason is fairly obvious: given that capital creates surplus value in each turnover cycle, the more cycles that can take place in any one year, the greater the mass of surplus value that can be created that year.

We have so far examined (1): the production of the product. In order to reach (2) – transformation of the product into money – it is usually necessary to transport the product to its market. This is not always the case, 'since a product may be bought and even consumed at the point of its production' (534). In *Capital II*, Marx gives the example of property: 'A house that is sold by A to B circulates as a commodity, but it does not get up and walk' (*C2*: 226). But in most cases, before a product can be sold it needs to be transported. This particular moment of the process (bringing the product to market so that it can be sold) is distinct from 'the real production process' (the making of the product in the first place). But it can nonetheless be considered part of the production process because '[t]he product is really finished only when it is on the market': transporting the product to the market achieves 'the transformation of the product *into a commodity*'. Although Marx terms this transportation of the product '*real* circulation (in space)', this is only to distinguish it from 'the economic process of circulation' as such: transportation is a *condition* of circulation rather than the moment of circulation as such, which begins when the product has been taken to market and is ready to be sold (534). Transportation is thus a branch of production: as *Capital II* puts it, 'what the transport industry sells is the actual change of place itself' (*C2*: 135). This is not always very clear in the *Grundrisse*, because Marx often discusses transportation as if it is a moment of circulation rather than of production.

Like any other branch of production, the transportation industry can generate surplus value for capital. This is achieved not by employing the transport workers 'during transport for a longer time than is required for the transporting', but by ensuring that 'the workers are *not paid* for a part of the transportation time, because it is surplus time, time *over and above* the labour necessary for them to live' (522–3). The capitalist who benefits from this, however, will be the one who employs the transportation workers, not the capitalist who owns the factory making the products that are being transported. For the latter, transportation is a *cost*, the same as if he had to spend more money on means of production: transportation adds value to his products (because value is transferred from the means of transport and added by the labour of the transport workers) but it does not produce surplus value for him (but only for the capitalist who owns the transportation business).

There are two obvious ways in which capital can lower transportation costs. The first way is to sell goods closer to their point of production. Ultimately, however, this is not a viable solution, because capital is from the start globalizing: it creates new markets not merely by commodifying new goods and services, but by extending its reach into new regions, nations and continents. If my factory is in Manchester, I cannot be content only to sell my commodities in Manchester. Given this, capital needs to rely on a second way of lowering transportation costs, which is to make the means of transportation more effective: to build faster railways, roads, ships, aeroplanes, etc. With more effective transport come more efficient communication systems and networks: better transport routes improve communication, and new communications technologies, from the telegraph to the satellite, are developed to facilitate transportation.

Marx puts this argument in striking terms: 'Capital by its nature drives beyond every spatial barrier. Thus the creation of the physical conditions of exchange – of the means of communication and transport – the annihilation of space by time – becomes an extraordinary necessity for it' (524). The 'annihilation of space by time' is as good a summary as any for what gets called 'globalization': the world becomes a smaller space as the speed of travel and communication increases. The advantage of Marx's analysis is that it identifies the mechanism that drives the whole process: advancing technology facilitates rather than causes a process which is ultimately driven by capital.

Although it is capital that benefits from and drives transport and communications developments, it may not be capital itself which directly funds or undertakes such developments. The state may instead construct them on behalf of capital, paid for out of what Marx calls '*deductions from the social revenue*, [i.e.] the state's taxes', 'out of the government's treasury' (532, 533). Given that capital contributes towards taxation, if transportation is funded in this way then it must count as a cost for capital. Although capital is here acting in its own interests (because in the long run it needs that infrastructure in place) it is not strictly speaking acting *as* capital: capital always augments itself, whereas these are *costs* taken from the capitalist's *revenue*. Because they are not employed directly by capital, the labourers who undertake this work will be performing necessary but unproductive labour.

The alternative is for capital to fund and build the transportation and communications infrastructure itself. For this to happen, a couple of conditions need to be in place (529–30). First, capital has to have the power and capacity to carry out the task: it has to have the resources to employ the large number of workers needed and the large-scale machinery that will be required. Second, there must be enough trade and traffic to make such undertakings profitable for capital, either directly (e.g. by charging tolls on roads) or indirectly (by sharing in the surplus value created and realized as a result of the improved transport). When the *general conditions of production* – i.e. those things which all capitalists require, as opposed to the conditions of a particular capital – are constructed by capital acting as capital, then this indicates that we have reached

> the highest development of production founded on capital. The separation of *public works* from the state, and their migration into the domain of the works undertaken by capital itself, indicates the degree to which the real community has constituted itself in the form of capital. (531)

So far we have still only considered the 'real circulation' of transportation. Once the product has been transported to market and thus transformed into a commodity, that commodity must be sold for money (and that money used to purchase further means of production and living labour). This is the moment of circulation as such. 'The production process cannot be begun anew before the transformation of the commodity into money' (535). To this extent, '[a]ll capital is originally circulating capital': both a product of circulation and producing circulation, emerging from circulation and returning to it (536). The 'real circulation' of products through space can be speeded up through improvements to transportation.

The time of circulation as such can be reduced through *credit* (535, 549). By borrowing money, a capitalist can in effect realize the value in his products before he even sells them (or even before he produces them). The aim of credit is thus to reduce the time of circulation to zero. Given that this is the aim of capital, Marx presents credit as a uniquely capitalist institution.

Why exactly does capital want to reduce circulation time, however? It is not because circulation itself produces value: we know that for Marx value is created by living labour in the production process. 'The circulation of capital *realizes value*, while living labour *creates value*' (543). Circulation time must be reduced because it is a 'time of devaluation': if my commodities are simply sat waiting to be sold then their value is not being realized and I will have to wait longer before I can produce more value (538). So circulation does not create value, but it is a potential barrier to the realization of value (539, 543). As we have repeatedly seen, capital will always work to destroy the barriers that stand in the way of its valorization. In addition to the use of credit, capital can make it easier to sell commodities and thus reduce circulation time through 'the *creation* of a continuous and hence an ever more extensive market', while at the same time striving to reduce transportation times (542):

> Thus, while capital must on one side strive to tear down every spatial barrier to intercourse, i.e. to exchange, and conquer the whole earth for its market, it strives on the other side to annihilate this space with time, i.e. to reduce to a minimum the time spent in motion from one place to another. (539)

Formal and real subsumption

Marx does not condemn this tearing down of barriers. To the contrary, it represents 'the universalizing tendency of capital, which distinguishes it from all previous stages of production' (540). As we saw, pre-capitalist societies have as their purpose the reproduction of their specific conditions of production and the individuals 'as living carriers of these conditions'. As such, in those societies there is a limit to the development of the productive forces: any development of the productive forces (an increase in population, say, or revolutionary new technology) would potentially threaten the continued reproduction of the conditions of production. In contrast, '[c]apital posits the *production of wealth* itself and hence the universal development of the productive forces [...] as the presupposition of its reproduction': by having the production of wealth in the form of value as its aim, capital is driven towards 'the universal development of the productive forces' (541, 540). We have now seen how this can operate in practice, with the creation of a 'world market' and the annihilation of space by time through improvements to transportation and communications (542).

The problem is that this tendency towards the *universal* development of productive forces – which puts in place the conditions for a new, post-capitalist mode of production – is in contradiction with capitalism's own *limited* form and purpose. In its own way, bourgeois society is as limited as pre-capitalist societies, subordinating the development of productive forces to the reproduction of its own conditions. Thus while capitalism offers the potential of 'the universal development of the individual' (in contrast to the limited development of individuals in pre-capitalist communities), this potential cannot be achieved under capitalism because the capitalist mode of production rests upon the alienation of individuals (542). The aim of capitalism is wealth, and wealth is ultimately 'the *development of human productive forces*'– but it is wealth in the form of value, to which labourers relate as '*alien wealth*' and as productive only of their own poverty (540, 541). Productive forces are ultimately 'the productive powers of labour', but they appear as 'the *productive power of capital.* The collective power of labour, its character as social labour, is therefore the *collective power* of capital'. All the powers of labour are subordinated to and enrich only capital (585).

In their combination and cooperation, workers are able to undertake unprecedented tasks and projects. But for 'the individual worker, the combination appears accidental. He relates to his own combination and cooperation with other workers as *alien*, as modes of capital's effectiveness' (585). This is a form of alienation not because each worker is alienated from some essential human capacity to engage in creative labour, but because the workers are alienated from their own collective powers: working in combination with each other, they possess enormous powers of production, but capital appears as the source of these powers. What is social (the collective powers of labour) appears as what is private (as a product of privately owned capital).

Cooperative labour on a large scale is of course not unique to capitalism (the pyramids could not have been built without it), but it is accelerated and widened under capitalism. At first, capital 'takes over the accumulation and concentration of workers'. This is what Marx elsewhere terms *formal subsumption*, where '*the mode of production is not yet determined by capital, but rather found on hand by it*': capital imposes its command on an existing labour process without changing the character of that process (586). This happens in the early stages of capitalism, as when, for example, a capitalist will employ a number of weavers who previously worked for themselves: they now perform surplus labour for the capitalist, but the nature of their work, and maybe even its location, does not change. *Real subsumption* occurs when capital imposes its own distinctive processes of production.[71] Rather than simply employing existing workers, who may be scattered over a wide area, capital collects its workers together 'in one spot under its command, into one manufactory, and no longer leaves them in the *mode of production found already in existence*, establishing its power on that basis, but rather creates a mode of production corresponding to itself'. The powers of labour are concentrated in one place and a complex division of labour allots different operations to different workers. With concentration comes '*regimentation, greater discipline, regularity*' as labour is submitted to the command of capital – not only because it performs surplus labour, but because capital takes control of the labour process itself, supervising and regulating its workforce now collected into one place (587).

Why does capital combine labour in this way? The short answer is: to produce surplus value. In the early days of capitalism's development, nascent capitalists needed to gather together a large enough mass of workers in order to produce enough surplus value such that the capitalist could live from the revenue and use some as surplus capital. With the development of manufacture, where many workers are gathered together in one place and there is a division of labour between tasks, absolute surplus value predominates: hence the capitalist brings together many workers in order to increase the number of simultaneous working days (588). The workers have little choice but to allow themselves to be concentrated in this way. They are not directly, physically forced into association, as were slaves under previous modes of production. But the conditions of production are 'present as *objective association*' in that they are in the hands of capital, so if the workers want to live then they have to come together under the capitalist (590).

As the capitalist mode of production develops, manufacture is replaced by large-scale industry, in which relative surplus value predominates: we see the introduction of machinery in order to increase the productivity of labour.[72] Thus there is a deskilling of labour, as labour is transferred to machinery (587). We shall return to the development of machinery below, in the 'Fragment on Machines'.

These remarks on the subsumption of labour to capital remind us that for Marx capital is not a thing but a particular economic form with a specific set of relations. If capital meant merely 'instruments of production', then 'every savage is a capitalist'. (As Marx sardonically notes, some economists do in fact assert this, such that 'the savage who throws a *stone* at a bird' is an owner of capital.) This is not merely a technical or analytical error on behalf of classical political economy but is rather reflective of bourgeois society and the interests of its ruling class. If capital is defined as the instrument of production, then it means that capital is a necessary feature of production throughout history (because *all* production requires instruments of production) (591). In other words, this definition dehistoricizes and universalizes capital. It also depoliticizes capital, obscuring its power dynamics. If 'capital' means only the instruments of production, then the exchange between capital and labour looks free and fair: the owners of capital (the instruments of production) exchange with the owners of labour; the former gain labour and the latter gain access to 'capital'. But for Marx 'capital' refers not merely to one side of the exchange, nor even to the exchange *between* capital and labour, but to the relations of production of which the exchange is only one moment. If we investigate those relations, as we have repeatedly seen, then we find that there is only a 'semblance of exchange': 'the bourgeois system of equivalents turns into appropriation without equivalent' (593, 596).

Surplus population

The worker under capitalism is what Marx calls 'a virtual pauper': he is totally reliant on capital for his livelihood. If he wants to live, he must work for the capitalist (and if he lives without working for the capitalist, 'it is only because alms are thrown to him from revenue', e.g. only because he can pick up unemployment benefit from the capitalist state) (604). Though he may not live constantly in poverty, he lives always at the risk of poverty: he can be thrown out of work at any time and even *in* work he impoverishes himself. In the case of the wage labourer, therefore, the usual relation between 'surplus' and 'necessity' is overturned: under capital, if the worker wants to perform necessary labour – and hence earn a wage with which he can buy the goods necessary to live – then he must perform surplus labour for the capitalist. 'In production resting on capital, the existence of *necessary* labour time is conditional on the creation of *superfluous* labour time' (398). This reverses the situation that existed in pre-capitalist societies, in which production was dominated by necessary labour – the labour necessary to produce use values to meet a community's needs – and any surplus that happened to be produced was exchanged with neighbouring communities.

For many of Marx's contemporaries, pauperism was best understood as 'overpopulation': paupers are an excess that the population of a nation cannot sustain. Marx does not exactly reject this category of 'overpopulation', but he wants to rethink it in terms of *surplus population*, thereby relating it to surplus labour and historicizing the analysis of population. For Marx there can be no constant law of population because in 'different modes of social production there are different laws of the increase of population and of overpopulation [...] Thus, what may be overpopulation in one stage of social production may not be so in another, and their effects may be different' (604). Previous modes of production acted as a check on population. As we saw above, the aim of pre-capitalist societies was to reproduce themselves and their members in the same form. They were static communities, which developments in the forces of production could threaten to undermine and so such developments were kept in check. This means that there was a check on population, because population is itself a force of production: if you have more people, you not only have a larger potential labour force, you also have a potentially more productive labour force, with greater capacity for advanced divisions of labour, cooperation, the development and manufacture of machinery, etc. (608). Under capitalism a quite different logic is at work: because its purpose is the production of exchange value, capitalism is motivated to develop all of its productive forces, and this includes population.

In insisting on the historical relativity of the limits of population, Marx has a specific target in mind, namely the theories of Thomas Malthus – theories which today retain their original notoriety and influence. Malthus's argument is relatively simple: 'Population, when unchecked, increases in a geometrical ratio. Subsistence increases only in an arithmetical ratio.'[73] If a couple have two children and each of those children, in turn, has two children and so on, then there is a geometric progression in the population: 2, 4, 8, 16, 32, etc. Malthus does not deny that food production can also increase over time, but he claims it cannot keep pace with population increase because it increases only arithmetically: from 2 tonnes of grain, to 4, 6, 8, 10, etc. When the population inevitably outpaces the means of subsistence, some people will go hungry – but their eventual deaths from starvation will act as a useful check on a population that would otherwise be unsustainable. So Malthus's theory does not completely ignore history: indeed, its central argument is that over time the pressures of population will increase. But for Marx the theory ignores the historical specificity of different modes of production. Specifically, there are two reasons why Marx thinks the theory 'false and childish' (605).

First, Malthus 'transforms the historically distinct relations into an abstract numerical relation' between 'the natural reproduction of humanity [...] on the one side, and the natural reproduction of edible plants (or means of subsistence) on the other'. But there is no purely 'natural' reproduction, whether of humans or of plants: the rate at which the population grows and the rate at which we can grow food is going to depend not on some constant, natural law, but on the specific conditions pertaining to a particular historical period. There is likewise a historical variation in the definition of 'overpopulation': the size of population that is called 'overpopulated' changes ('How small do the numbers which meant overpopulation for the Athenians appear to us!') and the consequences of overpopulation vary (in one period it might lead to emigration to other lands, while in another it might lead to an internal displacement of people into workhouses). Marx is not denying that there are limits to human population growth. To the contrary, it is Malthus who thinks that the population would grow unchecked if it were left alone in its pure state, increasing geometrically were it not for the supposedly external barrier that is the inferior, arithmetic rate of growth of our food supply. For Marx, this is ludicrous. There is no 'natural' rate of population growth: what Malthus sees as the external, 'natural' barriers to the supposedly natural or normal rate of population growth are in fact the 'inherent conditions of population'; population is always dependent on the historically variable conditions of production that humans themselves maintain and reproduce (605–6). In addition, there is no reason to suppose that the edible plants that form our basic food supply are naturally limited by an arithmetic growth rate: the only barriers to the growth of plants are those that we impose on them; without human interference they would likely grow at an increased rate. (As Marx puts it, in a weirdly science-fiction tone: 'The ferns would cover the entire earth'.) Hence Marx can say of Malthus:

> He transforms the immanent, historically changing limits of the human reproduction process into *outer barriers* [because he views the necessary but historically variable conditions of population as external checks on a purportedly natural geometric rate of population growth – SC]; and the *outer barriers* to natural reproduction into *immanent limits* or *natural laws* of reproduction [because he views the human limitations that are placed on the growth of food as natural limits – SC]. (607)

Second, Malthus argues that population growth is checked when the means of subsistence can no longer support a population – simply put, when there are more people than food available. But things are not this simple. Malthus ignores the fact that our access to means of subsistence is always socially mediated: if there is a 'surplus population', this is not necessarily because there is too little food or too many people, but because there are people who have no *access* to the food available (because they have no property, no job, or no money). What determines whether or not there is a surplus population, therefore, is not the quantity of food available but the broader mode of production and people's place within it: not the means of subsistence, but 'the mode of producing them' (608). A surplus of food may coexist with a surplus population. For example, in ancient Greece there was a surplus population because there was a large group of people who had access neither to food nor to the means to produce it. In other words, it was their specific place within the mode of production that made them surplus, not a shortage of food. In general there was more than enough food for the population, as demonstrated by the demands to increase certain sections of the population, namely slaves. As Marx notes, 'we never hear there were *surplus slaves* in antiquity'. Similarly, there may be surplus population even where the population level is extremely low. For example, 'among hunting peoples' there was overpopulation not because there was a large number of people but because their manner of production – i.e. roaming around hunting animals – needed a vast amount of territory to support only a very small number of people (607). This point of course remains relevant today: in a world in which so much food is simply wasted, if people die of famine it is not because we lack food or have too many people but because certain people lack *access* to food and the means to produce it.

In general, Marx's compelling criticisms of Malthus remain pertinent to the twenty-first century, when Malthusian-style concerns about population growth are raised not simply by those on the right (who have responded to changing patterns of migration by provoking anxieties about the population levels of individual nations) but also by some on the left, who are concerned about the consequences of a growing global population for environmental sustainability. Positions within these debates obviously vary, but often there is an assumption that the global population is reaching some kind of natural limit. What Marx shows is that there is no 'natural' limit that is not historically mediated: a sustainable population is that which can be sustained by present conditions of production.

Earlier, we saw Marx argue that the pursuit of surplus value causes capital both to increase the labouring population and to reduce its necessary part, to posit it as surplus population (see 'Preservation of value and constant and variable capital' above). He now links this argument more explicitly to capital's need to increase productive forces. Capital wants to increase the population as much as possible, because population is a productive force. But it will employ that population only if it can generate a profit out of their labour. If it cannot, then part of the population will be superfluous to requirements: a surplus population. As productive forces develop, then a smaller number of workers can perform the same amount of work, so more workers are made superfluous: they are pauperized. As capital develops, however, it may employ or reemploy more workers. Hence 'capital has the tendency both to posit and equally suspend this pauperism' (610). The surplus population of the unemployed are required by capital not just to go home and die, but to wait in abeyance or reserve until needed by capital. Without a wage from the capitalist, the reserve worker is supported 'out of the revenue of all classes' – in our day, supported by unemployment benefits:

> [S]ociety in its fractional parts undertakes for Mr Capitalist the business of keeping his virtual instrument of labour – its wear and tear – intact as reserve for later use. He shifts a part of the reproduction costs of the working class off his own shoulders and thus pauperizes a part of the remaining population for his own profit. (609-10)[74]

Before we return to circulation, it is worth looking at some brief remarks that Marx makes about the nature of work itself. He notes that for Smith labour is the measure of the value of all other things because the value of labour never changes. Regardless of what I produce in one hour of work, an hour's work always has the same value for me: assuming that I work at roughly the same rate and with the same intensity, I always give up the same amount of freedom and tranquillity when I settle down to work for one hour. So labour can give things a price because we always pay the same price for labour: when I work I always make the same sacrifice. It might be that at different times one hour's labour can buy me a larger or smaller number of goods, but that is because the value of those goods has changed, not because the value of labour has changed.[75]

From Marx's perspective, there are a number of confusions contained in Smith's argument, not least a failure to distinguish labour from labour-power and concrete from abstract labour. But Smith is also mistaken about the nature of work: for Marx, work is not merely sacrifice. To define it as such is to define it only *negatively* – as a negation of our freedom and tranquillity. But this alone could not explain how labour creates value: 'Something that is merely negative creates nothing' (612). Standing alone in a cold field whipping oneself with branches might count as sacrifice, but it would create no value. Products can be measured by labour time because they are objectified labour. Hence labour cannot be merely sacrifice, but is 'a *positive, creative activity*'. Smith certainly captures something with his negative view of work, but what he captures is the experience of the labour performed under conditions of exploitation by workers in class societies. As with political economy in general, Smith universalizes from bourgeois society: he 'correctly expresses the *subjective relation of the wage worker to his own activity*' (614). Many of us no doubt experience our work as tedious, tiring, or oppressive – as a form of sacrifice – but that has more to do with the conditions under which we perform that work than the inherent nature of work itself.

While wage-labour 'always appears as repulsive', in a classless society labour can become 'attractive work, the individual's self-realization'. Yet this does not mean that we can ever conceive of work in naively romantic or utopian terms as play or 'mere fun, mere amusement' (611). Even when work is rewarding and satisfying, this is not because it is fun; rather, it is because even serious and intense work can leave us with a sense of achievement and self-realization. When Smith claims that in working the labourer gives up '*his tranquillity, his freedom*, and his *happiness*', he identifies freedom and happiness with tranquillity (Smith, cited 610–11).[76] But this is a strange idea, implying that we are most free and happy when at rest. Even under conditions of exploitation, however, for most of us work is often preferable to the 'tranquillity' of doing nothing: *absence* of work can just as well mean boredom, lethargy and self-disgust as it can freedom or happiness.

Some may object that Marx's view of work remains too optimistic. The question that is often put to communists is: even in a post-capitalist society, won't some work (e.g. cleaning the sewers) simply be unpleasant? Who will undertake that work and will it really be a form of self-realization? This question can only be asked from a position of privilege, because it disregards or underplays the fact that under capitalism work for the vast majority is already unpleasant. But it need not be so: in order to reduce necessary labour time, capitalism develops the productive forces, introducing machinery that can perform work in place of humans. By reducing necessary labour time in this way, machinery creates '*a large quantity of disposable time*' which could potentially be used for the 'free development of individualities'. The problem is that under capitalism necessary labour time is reduced only so that surplus labour time can be increased, such that the free time created through the introduction of machinery is 'not-labour time, free time, for a few', while the many are simply forced to perform more surplus labour. Under communism this contradiction will be overcome and disposable time can become free time for all individuals to pursue their 'artistic, scientific etc. development' (706, 708). Machines cannot do everything and some 'necessary' labour will remain, but it will be transformed: under communism, 'direct labour time itself cannot remain in the abstract antithesis to free time in which it appears from the perspective of bourgeois economy'. The labouring subject will be transformed – because her needs will have developed (hence transforming what counts as 'necessary' labour) – and labour will have transformed, because it will now be directly social (712, 612).

This understanding of the future of labour is rather different from that found in *Capital III*. Whereas in the *Grundrisse* the antithesis between labour and freedom is overcome, *Capital III* claims that under all modes of production the 'realm of freedom really begins only where labour determined by necessity and external expediency ends' (*C3*: 958–59). The *Grundrisse*'s notion of labour thus sits somewhere between *Capital III* and the *1844 Manuscripts*, in which we are told that in work 'man proves himself a conscious species-being' (though of course this capacity is alienated from us under capitalism) (*CW3*: 276).[77]

Turnover time

'Now back to our subject' – namely circulation (618). We know that '[t]he total production process of capital includes both the circulation process proper and the actual production process [...] Capital appears as this unity-in-process of production and circulation'. Up until now, we have looked mainly at the individual phases of this process, or at the unity of these phases insofar as they make up one turnover. Marx begins now to consider the process in its 'totality', i.e. not merely as the completion of one turnover but many turnovers: a continuous process that is constantly renewed and repeated (620). Thought of in this way, it is clear that capital does not simply go through successive phases, first as money capital, then as productive capital, then commodity capital, then back to money capital, etc. The capitalist does not suspend the production process while he waits to sell the commodities produced: he continues producing commodities while those already produced are waiting to be sold. In other words, capital exists in its different phases and forms simultaneously. With this in mind, Marx clarifies the main phases of the process (619):

1 Immediate production process: creation of products that contain surplus value.

2 Transforming these products into commodities by taking them to a market to be sold. Earlier we referred to this phase as 'real circulation (in space)' and saw that it is part of the production process rather than the circulation process.

3a Capital circulates as commodity: capital as commodity enters into circulation and is transformed into money.

3b Capital circulates as money: capital as money enters into circulation in order to purchase conditions of production.

4 Renewal of the production process.

Marx proceeds by reflecting on the relation between these phases and the process as a whole. To do so, he draws upon the traditional distinction made within political economy between 'fixed' and 'circulating' capital. His analysis and use of these terms develops and alters over several pages and we will return in more depth to them later (see 'Circulating and fixed capital' below). At this point he adopts the terminology of circulating and '*fixated*' capital. The latter refers to capital in one of the different phases though which it must move, while the former refers to the movement of capital through the process as a whole: 'the process of going from one phase into the other' (620). In each of its phases capital is 'fixed' or tied down in some particular form: as productive capital in the immediate production process, as commodity capital looking to be sold, or as money capital looking for conditions of production.

> As long as it cannot be brought to market, it is fixated as product. As long as it has to remain on the market, it is fixated as commodity. As long as it cannot be exchanged for the conditions of production, it is fixated as money. (621)

The total turnover time will obviously be determined by the time it takes to move through each phase, so it is in capital's interests 'to abbreviate the phase of fixity' (623). If it gets stuck in one of these phases, then the process as a whole cannot flow or circulate: capital that remains fixated is devalued, unproductive, and crises will develop.

Therefore, we can see that circulation is an 'inescapable condition for capital' (658). If it cannot circulate then it cannot valorize itself and in this sense '[c]apital is therefore essentially *circulating capital*' (639). Given this, it would be easy to assume that the circulation process proper – points 3(a) and 3(b) in the schema above, distinct from the immediate production process – somehow creates or adds value. Superficially, it might appear as if the logic of Marx's argument would support this conclusion: if, as Marx claims, value is determined by labour time, then won't the labour time incurred in circulation – e.g. the labour involved in selling a commodity in a shop – increase the value of that commodity?

But we already know that for Marx circulation creates no value. Value is only created by living labour in the production process: circulation is needed to realize the value of the commodity as money and to use that money to purchase the conditions of further production. He now asks us to think more about why circulation cannot create value. Ultimately, circulation is nothing but a series of acts of exchange. As a capitalist, I enter circulation to exchange my commodities for money or my money for the conditions of production. And what happens in exchange? Remember that Marx assumes that exchange is an exchange of equivalents: if my commodity is sold for £10, that is because it has a value of £10, this value determined by the labour time put into producing it. The commodity's value has been *realized* through its sale, but its value has not somehow increased through its sale. Hence, if exchange cannot create value and if circulation is ultimately a series of exchanges, then we can say that circulation cannot create value (631–2). The one exception here, of course – and it is an 'exception' on which the entire capitalist system rests – is the exchange between capital and labour which leads to the production of surplus value, but we know that is only a semblance of exchange.

Circulation, therefore, is always a *cost* for the capitalist. To think about why this is so, think about a simple exchange between independent producers. If I catch a fish and I want to exchange it for a pheasant that you have caught, then we have to enter into exchange with each other. Clearly our exchange is not going to add anything to my fish or your pheasant or their respective values (624). To the contrary, for both of us there is a *cost* to the exchange: our exchange takes *time* and that is time that I could have spent fishing and you could have spent hunting pheasants (632). Similarly, the capitalist loses time in circulation. In the case of the capitalist, it is not his own time that he loses, because the capitalist himself does not spend any time creating value. Rather, it is the alien labour time that he appropriates: 'circulation time [...] interrupts the time during which capital can appropriate alien labour time' (634). This does not mean that while the capitalist's commodities are waiting to be sold production back in the factory grinds to a halt (although this might happen 'in crises and depressions of trade' [660]). What it means is that the value embodied in the commodities cannot be realized as long as those commodities are waiting to be sold. Circulation time is time in which those values are not being used as capital in the production process, i.e. in the process in which capital appropriates alien labour and creates further value. Circulation time is thus '*not*-production time': it is 'not time during which capital creates value, but rather during which it realizes the value created in the production process' (658–9).

The capitalist who produces commodities is not normally the capitalist that sells the commodities: the latter function is performed by commercial capital (e.g. retailers like Tesco or Walmart). Because circulation itself creates no value, the profits and wages of commercial capital must come from the redistribution of the surplus value produced in the production process (see 'General rate of profit' below).[78] These, therefore, are further costs of circulation for industrial capital. Hence circulation costs differ from productions costs, because the latter contribute to the production of value (659). In contrast, '[t]he *costs of circulation* as such *do not posit value*, they are *costs of the realization of values* – deductions from them' (625). Circulation time is needed to realize value, but it also acts as a 'barrier' to or 'negation' of 'the production time of capital' (634). It is therefore obviously in my interests as a capitalist to keep circulation costs as low as possible by reducing circulation time.

We can think of the capitalist's desire to reduce circulation time in terms of turnover time. The turnover of capital is the time that it takes for capital to go through one whole cycle. This first of all includes the production time. Note that 'production time' is not the same as 'labour time': in some industries the former can be much longer than the latter (668). For example, in the wine-making industry the labour time required to pick and press some grapes may be relatively short, but the production time will also need to include leaving the wine in a cellar for a few years to mature (which won't be counted as labour time, because no or minimal labour will be used). Similarly, in agriculture the labour time is that time spent sowing and harvesting crops, while the production time must include waiting for the crops to grow. If no labour is being used during a certain period of production time, then no value will be added to the product (669). However, the value of any means of production being used (e.g. the barrels and buildings in which a wine is maturing) will be transferred (*C2*: 319–20). Even where production time is determined by natural factors (such as the fermentation of grapes or the growth of crops), it can be brought closer to labour time – hence reducing turnover time – through various artificial methods (for example by introducing chemicals that allow wine to mature at a quicker rate or crops to grows more speedily) (*C2*: 317).[79]

Turnover time also includes, second, circulation time: to start making products again, the capitalist must have sold his completed commodities and used that money to purchase new conditions of production. The more turnovers that the capitalist can achieve within one year, the greater the mass of surplus value he is going to be able to create and realize. Achieving a quicker turnover time gives me the same advantages as beginning with greater capital: for example, if I as a capitalist can produce £1,000 worth of toy dolls five times a year, it is the same as if I were to produce £5,000 worth of dolls once a year. It is easy to see, therefore, why it does indeed *appear* as if circulation time is creating or adding value – because it looks as if somehow the more times my products enter into circulation the greater their value. But what is really happening is that a quicker circulation time is reducing the turnover time, which in turn increases the value that can be produced within a given period. For this reason, the capitalist tries to reduce turnover time as much as possible. He wants circulation '*without circulation time* – i.e. the transition of capital from one phase to the next at the speed of thought' (631). This would be the ideal situation for the capitalist:

a circulation time of zero, so that the production process could be begin again as soon as it had finished.

Circulating and fixed capital

'We divided capital above into *constant* and *variable value*; this is always correct as regards capital within the production phase, i.e. in its immediate valorization process' (649, *tm*). Now that we are considering the production *and* circulation processes, we need a different division, namely between circulating and fixed capital. In the previous section we saw Marx define 'fixated' capital as capital in each of its phases (money capital, productive capital, commodity capital) and circulating capital as the movement of capital as a whole through these phases. That distinction was useful for thinking about the whole process of capital as essentially circulating capital. But we also need to think about the immediate production process and its relation to the circulation process proper. To this end, Marx identifies three different aspects of circulation, or its 'threefold character' (678):

1 Total process
2 Small-scale circulation
3 Large-scale circulation

These three aspects of circulation give us three possible definitions of fixed and circulating capital. First, considered as a total 'unity-in-process', capital must be circulating in that it must constantly be going through its different stages or moments and starting all over again. This gives us the definitions of fixed and circulating capital that we have already established: circulating capital as the whole process and fixed capital as capital 'fixated' in its different phases. This distinction is useful, but it is not how Marx defines fixed and circulating capital in his later work: strictly speaking, therefore, this distinction does not actually refer to fixed and circulating capital. Remember that in the *Grundrisse* Marx is still developing these concepts and trying out different definitions: this can make things confusing, but it is also one of our best opportunities to see his mind at work.

Small-scale circulation refers to the exchange between the capitalist and the worker and gives rise to an alternative distinction between fixed and circulating capital, with the latter defined as the part of capital which is used to purchase the worker's labour-power. Whereas the part of capital that is used to buy the means of production will re-enter the production process (as raw materials or instruments of production), the part of capital used to purchase labour-power never directly enters the production process: the worker takes his wages and uses them to buy commodities which he consumes. Yet although it never enters the production process, it 'is simultaneous and interwoven with it', it 'constantly accompanies it', because production cannot take place at all if wages are not paid and living labour purchased and because the value of the wages is reproduced by the workers themselves within the production process (674–5). In this sense, circulating capital as wages is a precondition of capital: when the worker spends his wages on food and so on to keep himself alive and healthy, he reproduces not only himself but also the living labour capacity that is a condition of capital's functioning (676).

There is a confusion here, however, which means that we cannot use this particular definition of fixed and circulating capital. In the sense of small-scale circulation, Marx identifies circulating capital as that which 'enters directly into the worker's consumption, and is directly exchanged for it [...] Here is the only moment in the circulation of capital where consumption enters directly' (675). But we know that capital cannot leave circulation to be consumed in this way: capital is that which perpetually returns to circulation in order to valorize itself. Marx is confusing two different and separate things: on the one hand, the value that capital advances to the worker in return for labour-power; on the other hand, the use that the worker makes of that value in purchasing commodities to consume as his means of subsistence. As he puts it in *Capital II*: 'What the capitalist consumes productively in the labour process is labour-power and not the worker's means of subsistence. It is the worker himself who converts the money he receives for his labour-power into means of subsistence' (C2: 245). The distinction between capital advanced as wages and capital advanced as means of production *is* important, but this is the distinction between variable and constant capital (see 'Preservation of value and constant and variable capital' above). Whether or not this is also relevant to the distinction between circulating and fixed capital is yet to be established.

The third aspect of circulation is large-scale circulation, which is what we have been referring to as circulation proper, or circulation as such: 'the movement of capital outside the production phase' in which commodities leave the production process to be realized as money and that money is used to purchase further means of production. This gives us a definition of fixed capital as 'that which is fixated in the production process and is consumed within it' and circulating capital as that which leaves the production process (678). This is still not very clear, however. Does it mean that all of the means of production should be counted as fixed capital, or only things like machinery (which stay in the production process) but not raw materials (which enter the product and so leave the production process in the product)? Is the product itself circulating capital? Are wages?

To try and clarify things, Marx surveys the works of political economists. In doing so, he finds that within political economy the concepts of circulating and fixed capital have no agreed or consistent definitions (640–8). To achieve greater precision, he recalls the distinction between value and use value. He notes that for Smith and Malthus fixed capital is that which stays with the capitalist, while circulating capital cannot be profitable unless and until it leaves the capitalist's hands (679). This is for Marx partially true. It is true if we are considering *use values*: there are use values which never leave the capitalist – such as machinery – and use values that have to leave his hands if he is going to profit from them, such as the raw materials that go into the finished products. As Marx points out, however, the former do circulate *but as value*: although a machine will not physically leave the factory, a portion of its value is preserved by being transferred to the product and hence circulates with that product. In this way, a machine comes from circulation (because the capitalist has to purchase it) but it does not return to circulation, except as value (because it is used up in the production process, passing on its value as it is consumed in that process).

This is the definition of fixed capital on which Marx eventually settles in the *Grundrisse*: it is capital that is 'realized as value only through being used up in production' and so circulates as value but not as use value (738, 680). It takes Marx a while to reach this definition and there remains quite a lot of confusion and slippage. Furthermore – adding to the confusion – the definition is modified by the time we reach *Capital II*. In the *Grundrisse* the suggestion is sometimes that the commodities that emerge from the production process count as circulating capital. But although we are considering the production process insofar as it relates to circulation, the distinction between fixed and circulating applies only to productive capital and not to commodity capital or money capital (*C2*: 246–7). By *Capital II*, fixed capital is not defined primarily as that which enters circulation only as value, but as that which is used up only gradually in the production process and so transfers its value over the course of a number of production processes; in contrast, circulating capital is consumed entirely within one production process, transferring its entire value to the product. 'The value of the fluid [or circulating – SC] capital – both in labour-power and means of production – is advanced only for the time that it takes to produce the product' (*C2*: 245–6).[80] Fixed capital thus includes instruments of production or 'means of labour' such as buildings, machinery, canals, railways and improvements to the soil, while circulating capital includes variable capital, raw materials and 'ancillaries', i.e. things like coal and gas that are used to power fixed capital. In the *Grundrisse*, ancillaries are defined as fixed capital, because they are used up in the production process and so leave that process only as value, not as use values (680). With the refinement of the definition in *Capital II*, they are counted as circulating capital, because 'they are completely consumed in every labour process they enter into': unlike fixed capital they 'do not preserve their independent use-shape as they function' (*C2*: 238–9).

Our new definition of fixed and circulating capital, which is first developed in the *Grundrisse* but is not fully refined and finalized until later, supersedes our previous definition in terms of circulating and 'fixated' capital. The latter distinction – between capital as the total process and its different phases – is not invalidated and remains important, but it can no longer accurately be referred to as a distinction between fixed and circulating capital. Whereas circulating and fixed capital 'appeared earlier as changing forms of the same capital in the different phases of its turnover', now they appear '*as two particular kinds of capital*': 'they have now hardened into two particular modes of its existence, and fixed capital appears separately alongside circulating capital' (737, 702). When we first looked at the capitalist production process, we divided it into three elements: instruments of production or means of labour; raw materials; and living labour. While these three elements are physically or materially different, we did not establish any *formal* or *qualitative* difference between them: they appeared merely as 'quantitative subdivisions of capital'. As use values they are different, but formally speaking they are all *values*, differing only quantitatively (691). With the introduction of the concepts of fixed and circulating capital, however, a *formal* distinction can be made between capital as raw material and wages paid for living labour (circulating capital) and capital as the instruments of production (fixed capital): a distinction between different 'mode[s] of the presence of capital' (692). 'The split within capital as regards its merely physical aspect has now entered its form itself' (703).

This does not mean that it is some element of the material existence of a thing – how 'fixed' it is in the sense of how long it lasts, for example, or how easily it can be moved around – that makes it fixed capital: what makes something fixed capital is the function that it plays in the production process. Things in themselves are neither fixed nor circulating capital and to think that it is the natural properties of a thing that makes it one or the other is a form of what Marx calls 'crude materialism': it naturalizes qualities that a thing only has because of its place or role within social relations, confusing the material content of a thing with its social form (687).[81] The same material thing may be fixed or circulating capital, or neither, depending on its function. Take the example of a house (680–1, 723). Houses tend to last a long time and are not usually moved about, but this does not *necessarily* make them fixed capital. If I own a house-building firm, then for me houses are commodity capital, because they are the finished product that I put onto the market to be sold.[82] Likewise, machines are commodity capital for machine makers. If I use the house to set up a sweatshop, or even if I simply rent it out to tenants, then for me the house is fixed capital, because it is acting as an instrument of production. If I buy the house and simply live in it, then it is not capital at all, because I relate to it as a consumer. (Although in this last case things become more complex. First, because if I use a mortgage to buy a house then I do not really own it at all: the bank owns it and in effect acts as my landlord. Second, because – even if I do have a mortgage – the house can make me money if its value increases and hence can act as capital for me. '[T]his aspect,' Marx claims, 'will enter when we study interest', which is a topic that Marx never deals with consistently or in detail in the *Grundrisse* [687].)

Marx does nonetheless call things like buildings and railways 'the most tangible form of fixed capital': given that they are 'welded fast to the surface of the earth', their immovability as use value corresponds to their formal fixity within the production process (740).[83] Buildings and railways, and other forms of transport and means of communication, prove an interesting case, for a number of reasons. First, they can simultaneously serve as fixed capital and be directly consumed as a use value outside the production process. For example, a railway can at the same time be used to transport products or raw materials and be used for taking holidays; a house that is both lived in and used as the base for a business is simultaneously directly consumed and used as fixed capital. Second, whereas a machine is first put onto the market as commodity capital *and then* when it has been bought by a different capitalist it is put to use in the production process as fixed capital, with a railway or a rented building that is used as a business these two moments are simultaneous: the seller or provider realizes its value as commodity capital at the same time as the buyer uses it as fixed capital. Third, means of transport and communication and the general physical infrastructure are used as fixed capital by many capitals at once: rather than being 'locked within a particular process', they are 'the connecting artery of a mass of such production processes of particular capitals', acting as 'a general condition for production processes' (725, 739).

As a formal or qualitative distinction between two modes of capital, the distinction between fixed and circulating capital acts as 'a determinant of its total movement (turnover)' (692). It has, in other words, important consequences for turnover time and hence for the mass of value that capital can create and realize. Every time fixed capital – let's say a machine – is used in the production process, it transfers a little of its value to the product, which is then sold as a commodity and returned as money to the capitalist. But it is only once the machine is fully exhausted, and hence all of its value has been transferred, that the capitalist needs to use that money to replace or reproduce the machine. If my machine lasts five years, then only one-fifth of its value enters circulation every year, 'and only with the passing of the five years has it completely gone into circulation and returned from it' (682). So we can say that its circulation is determined by its reproduction time: the time it takes for its entire value to enter into and return from circulation is determined by the time needed before it must be reproduced or replaced. (And it is in my interests as a capitalist to have a machine that is as long-lasting as possible, because '[t]he more often it must be replaced, the costlier it is' [711]). In the case of circulating capital, in contrast, reproduction is determined by its circulation time. Labour-power, raw materials and ancillaries give up their entire value to the product, which then enters circulation and returns as money once it has been sold as a commodity. The time it takes before the product can be reproduced is determined by the time it takes for the commodity to be sold and the money used to purchase further circulating capital.

In short, fixed and circulating capitals have different turnover times: the average turnover time will depend on the amount of fixed capital relative to circulating capital. My fixed capital may have a turnover time of five years, because I only have to replace it every five years. But my circulating capital may have a turnover of four months, because it takes four months for them to be formed into products, those products sold as commodities and the money used as further circulating capital. Let's imagine that I begin the year with capital of £1,000. If all of my capital were circulating capital, then it could all be turned over three times in one year, so by the end of the year the total capital turned over would be £3,000. If all of my capital were fixed capital, however, only one-fifth of it could turn over in one year, so by the end of the year the total capital turned over would be £200. Clearly, I need *both* circulating and fixed capital, so the average turnover time is going to depend on the specific balance between fixed and circulating capital: the more fixed capital I have relative to circulating capital, the slower the turnover time is likely to be. The quicker my turnover, the more surplus value I can generate and realize and so the greater my profits will be. Hence a greater proportion of fixed capital has a detrimental affect on my profits: 'profit declines because the turnover time of capital increases in proportion as the component part of it which is called fixed capital increases' (684–5).

The fact that different ratios of fixed and circulating capital produce different rates of profit 'has strengthened the common prejudice that circulating capital or fixed capital through some mysterious innate power brings a gain' (684). What Marx wants to show is that a different ratio of fixed to circulating capital affects rates of profit only insofar as it coincides with a greater ratio of constant to variable capital (see 'Preservation of value and constant and variable capital' above) or insofar as it produces a slower average turnover time.[84]

Fragment on machines

Earlier we made a distinction between formal and real subsumption: the former refers to the imposition of capital's command on an existing labour process, while with the latter capital develops and imposes its own distinct processes (see 'Formal and real subsumption' above). We can now apply this distinction to our new concept of fixed capital. Initially, capital merely takes over existing means of labour and they become fixed capital by virtue of being used within a specifically capitalist production process. As it progresses, capital develops its own distinctively capitalist means of labour, namely the '*automatic system of machinery*' (692). The machine – which, as we know, is introduced in order to increase the productive force of labour and to reduce necessary labour – represents 'the historical reshaping of the traditional, inherited means of labour into a form adequate to capital' (693, 694).

With this, we reach the famous 'Fragment on machines', one of the most influential and celebrated parts of the *Grundrisse*. In a highly condensed set of arguments, Marx here discusses a wide range of issues, including the role of science and technology, work and free time, the nature of value, and post-capitalist society, as well as engaging with contemporary investigations of machinery such as those of Charles Babbage. The density and novelty of Marx's arguments in the 'Fragment', many of which are not found elsewhere in his work, leave it open to a variety of conflicting interpretations, which will be discussed in more detail in Chapter 4.

What really distinguishes the machine, at least in its 'most complete, most adequate form', from earlier means of labour is automation: the capacity to set itself in motion and to maintain that motion on its own (692). Whereas earlier means of labour – a hammer, say, or a scythe – facilitated or enhanced the powers of the worker, with the automatic machine the roles are reversed: the function of the machine is not to 'transmit the worker's activity to the object', but rather the worker 'merely transmits the machine's work, the machine's action, on to the raw material' (692). The worker becomes a 'watchman and regulator' who merely supervises the work of the machine and it is the latter 'which possesses skill and strength in place of the worker' (705, 693). The introduction of the machine signals the most complete form of capitalist production because it materializes that which is inherent in the concept of capital: capital is the appropriation of living labour by objectified labour and with the submission of the worker to the machine this appropriation becomes literally and materially manifest, it 'achieves a direct reality' (704). The labour process is now dominated not by (living) labour but by the (dead objectified labour of the) machines. The formal relation between living and objectified labour – the subsumption of the former as value-creating activity by the latter as value – is with machines made into a material relation directly experienced by workers in the labour process. Thus the machine is the form of the means of production 'adequate to fixed capital and to capital as such', 'a form posited by capital itself and corresponding to it' (692).[85]

The machine replaces not only the body of worker but also her brain: for the machine is not only a physical force but also an application and incarnation of scientific knowledge. Like living labour, this scientific knowledge is appropriated rather than created by capital: it is created by the collective labour of society, a product of 'the general productive forces of the social brain' or of the 'general intellect' (694, 706).[86] Intellectual labour thus becomes more important within the production process – but because knowledge is objectified in machines, it appears as a power of capital and comes to dominate the workers, appearing to the worker as 'an alien power, as the power of the machine itself' (693). We have already seen Marx argue that the productive powers of labour are appropriated by capital, which then appears as the source of those powers. With the machine, the submission of labour to capital is all the more complete, because those productive forces now appear in a material object which physically confronts the labourer during the production process. '[T]he entire production process appears as not subsumed under the direct skilfulness of the worker, but rather as the technological application of science' (699).

Marx's point here is not to bemoan the increasingly scientific and technical nature of production or the growing role of science within society. To the contrary, the progress of science is to be celebrated as an increase in society's productive forces. The problem is the appropriation of these forces by capital: science 'pressed into the service of capital' (704). Nor of course is Marx taking issue with machinery itself: to think this would be to lapse into that crude materialism or fetishism that confuses the material qualities of a thing with its social form. The problem lies not with machinery but with machinery *as fixed capital*:

> While machinery is the most appropriate form of the use value of fixed capital, it does not at all follow that therefore subsumption under the social relation of capital is the most appropriate and ultimate social relation of production for the application of machinery. (699–700)

As we saw above, as *use value* machinery can save labour, potentially creating more free time in which all individuals can develop themselves (see 'Surplus population' above). Not only is necessary labour reduced, the labour that remains becomes easier, as it 'is transformed more into a supervisory and regulatory activity' (709). In this sense, the use of machines will be a vital aspect of any future communist society (833). But, as we also saw, under capitalism the labourer does not benefit from the time-saving advantages the machine brings, because 'the *saving* of necessary labour' is identical to 'the creating of *surplus labour*' (389). '*The most developed machinery thus forces the worker to work longer than the savage does*' (708–9). Hence we need to be liberated from machinery *as fixed capital*, but at the same time machinery – by transforming and (at least potentially) reducing labour – is itself a precondition of that liberation and the establishment of a post-capitalist society.

The introduction of machinery thus indicates the highest development of capital, in a number of senses. First, as we have seen, it more completely subsumes living labour under capital, materializing the submission of the worker to capital. Second, fixed capital more and more becomes not simply the instrument of production but the *aim* of production: capital is increasingly directed towards the construction of machinery. This indicates that productivity must have reached a stage whereby enough capital can be withdrawn from production for consumption and redirected to the production of fixed capital. It also conforms more fully to the concept of capital: we have seen that for capital the production of use values is unimportant except insofar as they are also exchange values; with the production of machinery we can say that the aim of production is no longer 'direct objects of individual gratification' even as values, but rather the production of 'the means of value creation' itself (707, 710). Hence 'it is in the production of *fixed capital that capital posits itself as end-in-itself*' (710). Third, machinery both enables continuity of production – because a machine, unlike a human labourer, can operate 24 hours a day – and encourages it. The turnover time of circulating capital is increased if commodities cannot be sold and their value realized, or if the production process is delayed for some reason (see 'Circulating and fixed capital' above). But although this deferment reduces the mass of surplus value that can be created and realized within a given period, it cannot reduce the initial value invested: by postponing the creation or realization of value, it interrupts the growth of value rather than destroying value as such. In terms of circulating capital, then, value will only be destroyed if the commodities can never be sold or if their use value is ruined before they can be sold (as with, for example, bananas that begin to rot before they can be sold and consumed). In contrast, with fixed capital 'every interruption of the production process acts as a direct reduction of capital itself' (703). Machines that sit idle will lose their use value – because they will gradually deteriorate and fall into disrepair – and they will lose this use value without passing on any of their value. Hence any interruption in production time in effect destroys the value contained in fixed capital, meaning that capital is not merely enabled but compelled to maintain continuous production, so that machines never sit idle.

Finally, machinery can be considered an indication of the highest development of capital in the sense that it develops its contradictions to their highest level and creates the conditions for the supersession of capitalism. We have seen that there is a contradiction between, on the one hand, the transformation and reduction of labour that machinery allows and, on the other hand, the fact that for the worker this reduction of necessary labour entails only an increase of surplus labour. Another way of expressing this same contradiction is to say that there is a contradiction between the reduction of labour time and capital's need for surplus value – or between the reduction of labour time and the fact that capital posits labour time as the source of value. Capital 'presses to reduce labour time to a minimum, while it posits labour time, on the other side, as sole measure and source of wealth' (706). With the development of machinery, 'direct labour and its quantity disappear as the determinant principle of production', because the direct labour of individual workers is subordinated to and replaced by the work of machines that are the product of the general intellect and which harness the powers of nature (700). The application of science within the production process means that 'general social knowledge has become a *direct force of production*', replacing the direct labour of workers (706). Hence 'the creation of real wealth comes to depend less on labour time' the more that machinery comes to dominate the production process (704). Yet capital continues 'to use labour time as the measuring rod for the giant social forces' that its own mode of production has created, 'and to confine them within the limits required to maintain the already created value as value' (706). This contradiction is, according to Marx, fatal for capital: 'Capital thus works towards its own dissolution as the form dominating production' (700).

With the dissolution of capitalism, its contradictions are overcome: under communism, the free time created through machinery will allow for the physical, intellectual, scientific and artistic development of all individuals. By allowing and encouraging the development of the general intellect, the increase in free time will thus accelerate the development of the productive forces. 'The measure of wealth is then not any longer, in any way, labour time, but rather disposable time' (708).

What exactly is Marx arguing here? He seems to be claiming that capital itself is undermining the law of value: by introducing machinery, capital makes 'the creation of wealth independent (relatively) of the labour time employed on it', so that labour time can no longer be the measure of value (706). 'Real wealth manifests itself, rather – and large industry reveals this – in the monstrous disproportion between the labour time applied, and its product' (705). Direct labour becomes less important in the creation of wealth and machines become more important, eroding the whole basis on which capital rests, namely the production of surplus value through the unpaid surplus labour of the workers.

Attempts to establish Marx's meaning are not helped by some confusions – or least ambiguous phrasing – in Marx's presentation.[87] Marx tells us that the presupposition of capitalist production 'is

– and remains – the mass of direct labour time, the quantity of labour employed, as the determinant factor in the production of wealth' (704). As the role of machinery increases, however, we reach a situation in which 'labour in the direct form has ceased to be the great well-spring of wealth' (705). It is not entirely clear to what extent this situation is reached *within* capitalism and, hence, to what extent the law of value remains valid within capitalism. In addition, it is not really clear what Marx means at all, because the concepts that he uses here are, from the perspective of his later work, vague and rudimentary. Throughout the *Grundrisse*, when Marx speaks of 'wealth' it is often uncertain whether he means *use values* or *value*. If he means the former, then labour has never been the only source or 'well-spring' of wealth. Considered as *use values*, 'wealth' is anything that is useful to us, so includes things like water and air. Hence, as Marx puts it in a text written in 1875: 'Labour is *not the source* of all wealth. *Nature* is just as much the source of use values' (*CW24*: 81). If by 'wealth' Marx means *value* – the specific form in which wealth appears in capitalism – then it is true that labour is the source of wealth, but *abstract* labour, which includes both the 'direct' or concrete labour of the worker in the production process – including the labour of supervising machines – *and* the labour objectified in the machines. In other words, the introduction of machines – which by being used transfer their value to the final product – does not obviously undermine or contradict the law of value. Finally, even if there is a contradiction between capital's reduction of labour time and its use of the same as the measure of value, it is not obvious why this contradiction should automatically lead to the 'dissolution' of the capitalist mode of production.

These ambiguities in Marx's presentation are not necessarily simply weaknesses: it is in part the obscurity of the 'Fragment on machines' that makes it open to so many varying interpretations and thus such a fecund source of discussion and debate. That the 'Fragment' remains of interest today may also be because we are presently experiencing what some have called 'the third industrial revolution' or 'the second machine age', otherwise known as the digital revolution: if in Marx's day factory workers were being replaced by 'automatic systems of machinery', in our day 'white-collar' workers such as journalists, librarians and those in financial and legal services risk being replaced by computers, while robots perform all kinds of labour, from the supermarket checkout to warzone battlefields.[88] There are two typical responses to these kinds of developments: either we are urged to welcome them for liberating us from various kinds of drudgery; or we are warned that machines will render humans redundant and even (especially with the arrival of artificial intelligence) come to dominate or enslave us. From Marx's perspective, neither of these responses is adequate. The first correctly recognizes that machines have the potential to save labour, but (in addition to relying on a Smithian understanding of work as sacrifice) it does not acknowledge that in practice machines tend merely to extend and degrade labour (for example, for all the claims that computer technology makes our jobs and our lives easier, anyone who actually has to use computers in the course of their work knows that their principal effect is to create more work and lengthen the working day).[89] The second fails to acknowledge that to a large extent machines *already* dominate us, with the human labourer becoming an appendage of the machine. Both responses are crudely materialist, unable to recognize that the qualities that they attribute to machines in themselves – whether their capacity to emancipate or enslave – are not the natural properties of machines but result from the social relations within which machines are put to use. They thus reflect a kind of technological determinism (the belief that social developments are driven by technological change). In some of his earlier works, where he suggests that transformations in the relations of production are caused by developments to the forces of production, Marx himself comes close to these kinds of arguments, such that even some Marxists have claimed him as a technological determinist.[90] The 'Fragment on machines', however, makes it clear to what extent Marx rejects this position. He does argue that technological change, in the shape of machinery, transforms relations of production, both by facilitating the domination of labour by capital and by pushing capitalism to the brink of its dissolution. But he argues further that the introduction of machinery is itself driven by the appropriation of surplus value that is demanded by capitalist social relations. In other words, there is a reciprocal determination between technology and social relations. Marx never analyses technology 'in itself', but only in relation to the forms that it takes in different modes of production, distinguishing sharply between machinery as fixed capital and the potential uses to which machinery might be put in a communist society.

Study Questions

1. Why, having examined the production process, does Marx move on to the circulation process?
2. What are the historic presuppositions of capital and how do they differ from its conditions of existence?
3. What three pre-capitalist economic forms does Marx examine and what do they have in common?
4. Why does capital seek to reduce circulation time?
5. How does Marx distinguish fixed capital from circulating capital and what does he think will be the effects of the production process's increasing reliance on fixed capital?

Section Three: Capital as Fructiferous

'Capital is now posited as the unity of production and circulation' (745). Initially, we saw that the circulation of commodities and money alone could not explain the creation of value. So we entered the sphere of production to examine the creation of value and surplus value, considering circulation only in terms of the exchange between capital and labour. But capital then had to re-enter circulation, in order to realize the value created and to purchase the conditions of further production. Hence although the exchange operations of circulation 'produce no surplus-value', they 'are conditions for its realization. They are conditions of the *production of capital itself*, in so far as its *form as capital* is posited only to the extent that it passes through them' (742). Moreover, circulation is a determination of value insofar as it affects turnover time, which determines the amount of surplus value that can be produced in any one period.

Circulation and production can be seen as part of the same movement, therefore, and this is the movement *of capital*. As such, from the perspective of capital its relation to living labour appears as only one moment of its total movement. It appears to capital as if capital itself is the creator of value: 'capital relates to itself as self-increasing value; i.e. it relates to surplus value as something posited and founded by it'. From the perspective of capital, both labour and the means of production are simply parts of capital and (as we saw earlier: see 'Preservation of value and constant and variable capital' above) all parts of capital are equally productive of value: labour, as an activity incorporated into capital, is productive '*only in so far as the other parts of capital are posited together with it*' (822). Given this, capital 'no longer measures the newly produced value by its real measure, the relation of surplus labour to necessary labour, but rather by itself as its presupposition' (746). Viewing itself as the source of value, capital measures the value created against 'the total value of the capital presupposed to production' (762). Surplus value that is measured in this way – in relation to the total capital advanced rather than in relation to the portion of capital that pays for necessary labour – is known as *profit* (746).

Profit is therefore the mystified but necessary form of appearance of surplus value. It is how surplus value is understood by capitalists and political economists, for whom 'all parts of the capital bear profit simultaneously' (823). '*Profits* is only a secondary, derivative and transformed form of the surplus value, the bourgeois form, in which the traces of its origin are extinguished' (595). Earlier in the *Grundrisse* Marx had already started to work out the theory of profit. He now develops it more fully, though compared to *Capital III* – to which the third section of the Chapter on Capital corresponds (at least to the first three parts of *Capital III*) – the theory as found in the *Grundrisse* is underdeveloped.

General rate of profit

Profit in its '*immediate form* [...] *is nothing but the sum of the surplus value expressed as a proportion of the total value of the capital*' (767). The sum of profit – or the gross profit – will therefore be the same as the sum of surplus value: a surplus value of £10 is a profit of £10. It might be that an individual capitalist can sell his products at a price above their value – and this does indeed happen, as we will see below – in which case his profit will obviously exceed the surplus value created. But this relates only to the *distribution* of profits between different capitals, not the total aggregate value of profit created by all capitals. Remember that as a rule and up until this point in the *Grundrisse* Marx is looking at capital in general: not individual capitals in competition with other capitals but 'the capital of the whole society' (346). From this perspective, 'the *profit of the capitalist class*' considered as a whole '*can never be greater than the sum of surplus value*' (767).

Given this, why is the distinction between surplus value and profit significant? The answer is clear if we look not at the sum of profit but at the *rate* of profit. We have already seen that the rate of profit differs from the rate of surplus value (see 'Preservation of value and constant and variable capital' above). The rate of surplus value is that of surplus to necessary labour time. Expressed in a formula, the rate of surplus value = s/v, where s is the surplus value produced by labour and v is variable capital. In contrast, the rate of profit = s/C, where C is the total value of capital at the start of the process – not just v (variable capital) but also c (constant capital). So the rate of profit = s/C = $s/(c+v)$. What this means is that the rate of profit is always going to be lower than the rate of surplus value, because the former is measured in relation to the total value of capital presupposed to production, which is always going to be larger than the capital that is exchanged for labour: 'the surplus value s must appear smaller when measured against $c + v$ than when measured against its real measure, v'. As such, 'the rate of profit never expresses the real rate at which capital exploits labour [...] The rate of profit could express the real rate of surplus value only if the entire capital were exchanged for living labour', which is impossible (even in service industries there must be some objectified labour that acts as a means of production) (762). The same rate of surplus value can therefore give rise to different rates of profit and the same rate of profit can be based on different rates of surplus value, depending on the organic composition of capital.

Given that different branches of industry will have different organic compositions of capital – some will be more labour-intensive, some will rely on more machinery, or machinery of a greater value – they will indeed produce different rates of profit. However, there is a tendency for rates of profit to be equalized: if profits in one branch of industry were much higher than in another, then capital would simply move to the more profitable branches. 'The inequality of profit in different branches of industry with capitals of equal magnitudes is the condition and presupposition for their equalization through competition' (761). There is thus an average or *general rate of profit*. Marx does not discuss this general rate of profit in much detail in the *Grundrisse*, partly because his notes on profit are comparatively short and sketchy, but also because at this stage he believes that the discussion 'does not yet belong here', given that it involves competition between capitals rather than capital in general (760). As such, strictly speaking it 'belongs only in the chapter on competition' (762). Nonetheless, the basic theory is already present in the *Grundrisse* (although, confusingly, it is mostly worked out much earlier in the text, in Section Two [434–7]).

'A *general rate of profit* as such is possible only if the rate of profit in one branch of business is too high and in another too low' (435). Imagine three capitals of £100 – A, B, and C – in three different branches of production. Each has a rate of surplus value of 100 per cent but each has a different rate of profit: A has a rate of profit of 5 per cent, B 10 per cent, and C 15 per cent. This is explained by differences in the organic composition of the capitals: A is composed of £95 constant capital and £5 variable capital, B £90*c* and £10*v*, and C £85*c* and £15*v*. Given the rate of surplus value is 100 per cent, A is going to produce a surplus value of £5, B £10, and C £15: the total values produced by each capital will therefore be, respectively, £105, £110, and £115. If the commodities produced were sold at their values (which is the assumption that Marx has been making until now), then the prices of the commodities produced would also be £105, £110, and £115 respectively. But given the tendency for the rate of profit to be equalized, there is a general or average rate of profit of 10 per cent, which is determined by the ratio of aggregate surplus value (the total surplus value produced by all three capitals together, i.e. £30) to aggregate capital (£300). How can this general rate of profit 'exist in reality' such that the three capitals share equally in the profit produced (435)? 'Since the profit of capital is realized only in the price which is paid for it, for the use value created by it, profit is determined by the *excess of the price obtained over the price which covers outlays*', in other words the excess over the '*production costs*' (760). Given that each of the capitals has the same production costs, i.e. £100, then they can share equally in the profits produced only if they all sell their commodity at the price of £110, generating a rate of profit of 10 per cent for each capital. Elsewhere Marx calls this price the *price of production*: it is the production costs ($c + v$) plus profit.[91]

What has happened, therefore, is that C has transferred some of its surplus value to A. '[T]he individual capital's *profit is not necessarily restricted by its surplus value* [...] It can exchange more than its *equivalent, and then its profit is greater than its surplus value*', as in the case of A. Equally, '[p]rofit – the excess over the advances made by capital – may be smaller than surplus value', as with C (760). This example of the general rate of profit is illustrated in Table 1:

Table 1: General rate of profit and prices of production

Capital	A	B	C
Total capital, or production costs (*M* = *c* + *v*)	100 (95*c* + 5*v*)	100 (90*c* + 10*v*)	100 (85*c* + 15*v*)
Rate of surplus value (*s*/*v*)	100%	100%	100%
Surplus value (*s*)	5	10	15
Total value produced (*M*′ = *c* + *v* + *s*)	105	110	115
Rate of profit (*s*/(*c* + *v*))	5%	10%	15%
General rate of profit (*S*/(*C* + *V*))	10%	10%	10%
Price of production	110	110	110

Marx summarizes:

> The capitalist class thus to a certain extent distributes the total surplus-value so that, to a certain degree, it [shares in it] evenly in accordance with the *size* of its capital, instead of in accordance with the surplus values actually created by the capitals in the various branches of business [...] This is realized by means of the relation of prices in the different branches of business, which fall *below* the *value* in some, rise *above* it in others. This makes it seem as if an equal sum of capital in unequal branches of business created *equal surplus labour or surplus value*. (435–6)

There is a second way in which surplus value is redistributed among capitals. We know that only living labour within the production process can create surplus value and that '[p]rofit is nothing but another form of surplus value' (762). But there are forms of capital other than industrial capital – which produces the surplus value – and those other forms of capital need their profits. Hence some of the surplus value produced by industrial capital will have to be redistributed to landlords (as rent), merchant capital (commercial capital and money-dealing capital), and interest-bearing capital. The unproductive workers who work for these capitals (and that we examined earlier) also need to be paid: their wages also come from redistributed surplus value. In addition, a portion of surplus value will be paid to the state as taxation and the capitalist will consume some as revenue. He cannot of course use all of his profit as revenue, for at least some of it must be retransformed into surplus capital to produce more value (758). The distribution of the total surplus value among these different agents does not affect the amount of surplus value that is to be distributed (788). Because it brings in particular types of capital, Marx only touches on this topic in the *Grundrisse*.[92]

Marx's theory of the general rate of profit has led to what is known as the 'transformation problem', so called because the transformation of values into prices of production supposedly generates problems for his wider theory. In a nutshell, the problem is this: Marx has shown that the general rate of profit means that commodities are sold at prices of production which differ from their actual values; yet when he calculates production costs ($c + v$) he assumes that c and v are purchased at their values rather than at their prices of production. We will not dwell on the transformation problem, mainly because it would take us too far from the *Grundrisse*. Suffice it to say that price and value are two different, but not incompatible or contradictory, levels of analysis.[93]

It is difficult for political economists to understand the sources and nature of profit because they have not adequately distinguished it from surplus value or really understood the latter: 'surplus-value denies its own origin in this, its transformed form, which is profit; it loses its character and becomes unrecognizable' (*C3*: 267). The average rate of profit and the selling of commodities at prices above or below their value disguise the origins of profit in surplus labour, concealing the link between the production of value and the exploitation of labour. Because capitals of equal size yield equal profits, it looks as if the size of a capital is the determining factor in the production of profit and that the amount of labour employed in proportion to constant capital is irrelevant – hence it looks as if capital itself, and not labour, is the ultimate origin of profits. The average rate of profit is thus a good example of how competition, as the form of appearance of the laws of capital, can conceal the real nature of those laws: competition leads to the equalization of the rate of profit, such that it appears that capital is the source of profit. Things are further obscured by the redistribution of surplus value from industrial capital to other forms of capital, which makes it look as if these other forms of capital are themselves productive of value. Political economists are therefore forced to abandon the labour theory of value and have to resort to other explanations for the origins of profit, for example by claiming that selling goods above their value creates profit (rather than redistributing surplus value already created), or simply by ascribing 'to capital some magic power which makes something out of nothing' (761).[94]

Falling rate of profit

In our example above using the three capitals A, B, and C, we saw that a higher organic composition of capital – i.e. a higher proportion of constant capital relative to variable capital – will mean a lower rate of profit. This much is clear from the formula for the rate of profit: if we assume that the rate of surplus value (s/v) remains constant (an assumption to which we will return shortly), then the rate of profit – s/C or $s/(c+v)$ – is going to depend on the value of c, i.e. on the proportion of the total capital (C) that is made up of constant capital. As c increases relative to v, the rate of profit is going to decline. We know that c does indeed increase – because we know that the pursuit of relative surplus value leads the capitalist to introduce more machinery to increase productivity. Hence the pursuit of surplus value itself causes the rate of profit to fall. This is known as the law of the tendency of the rate of profit to fall.[95] Of this law, Marx states:

> This is in every respect the most important law of modern political economy, and the most essential for understanding the most difficult relations. It is the most important law from the historical standpoint. It is a law which, despite its simplicity,

has never before been grasped and, even less, consciously articulated. (748)

If this law has 'never before been grasped' it is because it has not been understood, not because Marx is the first to note a tendency for the rate of profit to fall. Both Smith and Ricardo recognized the tendency, but from Marx's perspective their explanations are inadequate. Smith thought it could be explained by competition among capitals.[96] In response, Marx notes approvingly, Ricardo argued that while competition can explain why the profits of individual capitals are lowered to the average level, it cannot explain the lowering of this average level itself (751).[97] For Marx, '[c]ompetition executes the inner laws of capital [...] but it does not invent them. It realizes them'. The falling rate of profit applies to capital in general, not merely to individual capitals. Competition may play a role in lowering profit rates, but only if 'a general and permanent fall of the rate of profit, having the force of law, is conceivable *prior to* competition and regardless of competition' (752). Nonetheless, Marx finds Ricardo's own explanation of the falling rate of profit no more convincing than that of Smith. Beginning 'from the presupposition that a given value is to be divided between wages and profit, between labour and capital', Ricardo must argue that if profits fall it is because wages rise. Wages have a tendency to rise, Ricardo claims, because agriculture becomes less productive relative to other industries, hence making the production of the means of subsistence increasingly difficult, pushing up food prices and thence wages (596).[98]

But given that productivity is growing in industry, falling productivity in agriculture must be explained in terms unique to agriculture: Ricardo's explanation is that the steadily deteriorating fertility of the soil produces increasingly poor crop yields, hence Marx's quip that Ricardo 'flees from economics to seek refuge in organic chemistry' (754). In other words, by focusing on the increasing difficulty of producing means of subsistence, Ricardo resorts to a Malthusian explanatory framework (see 'Surplus population' above). In addition, as many of Ricardo's critics before Marx had pointed out, Ricardo assumes a general or average rate of profit, which contradicts his assumption that the value of commodities is determined by labour time. If profits are inversely related to wages, then rising wages will have a differential effect on the profit rates in capital-intensive industries (in which wages are a lower proportion of total capital) and labour-intensive industries (which will have a relatively higher wage bill). As wages rise (as Ricardo claims they will), profits will fall at a lower rate in capital-intensive industries, so the prices of the products produced in those industries will have to fall in order to offset their higher rates of profit and bring them down to the average. But if this happens then it means that the price of commodities is being determined by something other than the labour time contained within them, contradicting Ricardo's labour theory of value.

With his analysis of the transformation of values into prices of production, Marx himself has shown that commodities do not sell at their values, but he has done so on the basis of his theory of surplus value. For Marx, if there is a relationship between wages and profits, it is only insofar as profit is a form of surplus value and surplus value varies in inverse proportion to necessary labour. But this does not mean that profits fall as wages rise: 'profits and wages, although determined by the relation of necessary and surplus labour, do not coincide with it, are only secondary forms of the same' (557). Ultimately, it is because Ricardo does not distinguish surplus value from profit that he has to link the latter directly to wages: 'since he confuses profit with surplus value, he was forced to make wages rise in order to let profits fall' (756).

Once we have distinguished profit from surplus value, as Marx does, then things look very different. As the productive power of labour rises, so necessary labour falls in relation to surplus labour and the rate of surplus value and of exploitation increases. But this growth in the productive power of labour is identical with 'the decline of the part of capital which exchanges… for living labour relative to the parts of it which participate in the production process as objectified labour and as presupposed value', i.e. it is identical with the decline of variable capital relative to constant capital (763). Given that the rate of profit declines as the proportion of constant capital to variable capital increases, this means that the falling rate of profit goes hand in hand with increasing productivity and increasing exploitation of the workers.[99]

Marx summarizes his findings as two 'laws of the transformation of surplus value into profit' (762–3):

1 'Surplus value expressed as profit always appears as a smaller proportion than surplus value in its immediate reality

actually amounts to.' This is because while surplus value is measured only against variable capital, profit is measured against the total capital advanced. Given that the rate of surplus value is the rate of exploitation, 'the rate of profit never expresses the real rate at which capital exploits labour'.

2 The 'tendency of the rate of profit to decline with the development of capital'. The rate of profit falls with the development of the powers of production, which is identical with both the growth of surplus labour in relation to necessary labour and the relative growth of that part of capital employed as constant rather than variable capital.

The falling rate of profit is a *tendency* rather than an empirical law or prediction, so we should not expect profits in reality to fall at a constant and uniform rate. In addition, we should not confuse the *rate* of profit with *gross profit* or the sum of profit. A capital of 100 with a rate of profit of 10 per cent will produce a gross profit of 10, whereas a capital of 1000 with a rate of profit of only 2 per cent will produce a gross profit of 20. Given that gross profit 'will grow on the average *not as does the rate of profit, but as does the size of the capital*', the tendency of the rate of profit to fall can to some extent be offset by increasing gross profits (748). Marx also identifies what in *Capital III* he calls counteracting influences or tendencies which work by 'checking and cancelling the effect of the general law [of the tendency of the rate of profit to fall – SC] and giving it simply the character of a tendency' (*C3*: 339). In the *Grundrisse* these include: 'the constant devaluation of a part of the existing capital: the transformation of a great part of capital into fixed capital which does not serve as agency of direct production; unproductive waste of a great portion of capital etc.'; the 'creation of new branches of production in which more direct labour in relation to capital is needed, or where the productive power of labour is not yet developed'; 'the omission of existing deductions from profit, e.g. by a lowering of taxes, reduction of ground rent etc.' (750–1).

As Marx explains in *Capital III*, an increased level of exploitation can also act as a counteracting tendency: an increasing rate of surplus value – s/v – will counteract the tendency of the rate of profit – $s/(c + v)$ – to fall.[100] Given this, it might seem strange, or even theoretically or mathematically inadmissible, that in calculating the rate of profit Marx assumed a constant rate of surplus value. This assumption seems especially inappropriate because machinery is introduced precisely in order to increase the rate of relative surplus value, so we would expect the rising organic composition of capital to be accompanied by an increasing rate of surplus value.

In response to this possible criticism of Marx's theory, we can say that, first, the rate of surplus value and the organic composition of capital are to some extent independent variables, in that there are cases in which one increases when the other does not: for example, the increase of (absolute) surplus value that results from the lengthening of the working day does not raise the organic composition of capital. Second, Marx's initial assumption that the rate of surplus value remains constant is not meant to reflect the real development of capital but is an abstraction used so that we can better understand the influence of the organic composition of capital upon the rate of profit. Finally, if we now assume that the rate of surplus value does increase with a rising organic composition of capital – as generally happens in reality – then we will see that this new assumption does not undermine the law of the tendency of the rate of profit to fall. This can be illustrated by altering our example from above. Instead of assuming that capitals A, B, and C all have a rate of surplus value of 100 per cent, let's assume that they have rates of 160 per cent, 130 per cent and 100 per cent respectively. Hence A has the highest organic composition of capital and the highest rate of surplus value and C the lowest, as seen in Table 2.

Table 2: Increasing exploitation and the rate of profit

Capital	**A**	**B**	**C**
Total capital, or production costs ($M = c + v$)	100 ($95c + 5v$)	100 ($90c + 10v$)	100 ($85c + 15v$)
Rate of surplus value (s/v)	160%	130%	100%
Surplus value (s)	8	13	15
Total value produced ($M' = c + v + s$)	108	113	115
Rate of profit ($s/(c + v)$)	8%	13%	15%

We can see that the higher rates of surplus value for A and B have increased their rates of profit, but these rates of profit are still lower than that of C: their higher rates of surplus value have not compensated for their higher organic compositions of capital. Of course, we could adjust the figures so that the rate of surplus value was so high that it *would* compensate: for example, if A had a rate of surplus value of 300 per cent then it would have a rate of profit – 15 per cent – to match that of C. But it is clear that an increasing rate of surplus value cannot fully or continually compensate for the falling rate of profit: in our example, the rate of surplus value of capital A has to treble just to match the rate of profit of capital C! We also know that there are limits to the increase of the rate of surplus value: in the case of absolute surplus value, there is a necessary limit to the length of the working day; in the case of relative surplus value, an increase in productive forces produces steadily smaller gains in surplus value the more that necessary labour has already been reduced (see 'Absolute and relative surplus value' above). In contrast, there is in principle no limit to the increase of constant capital.

Like the other counteracting tendencies, therefore, an increasing rate of exploitation ultimately cannot halt or reverse the basic tendency of the rate of profit to fall. Indeed, a rising rate of exploitation, the increasing productivity of labour and the falling rate of profit are all bound up together: the falling rate of profit is a consequence of capital's own tendency to develop productive forces in order to increase relative surplus value. 'Beyond a certain point, the development of the powers of production becomes a barrier for capital; hence the capital relation a barrier for the development of the productive powers of labour'. The very development of the productive forces that capital impels becomes a limit on the expansion of capital itself. This contradiction produces crises which capital can try to contain or resolve but which ultimately it cannot overcome. If Marx's language here becomes increasingly apocalyptic – these are not merely spasms or even crises but explosions, cataclysms, catastrophes – it is because he anticipates that this central contradiction of capitalism is ultimately irresolvable and will lead to its 'violent overthrow' (749, 750).

In the *Grundrisse*, Marx arguably tends towards a teleological analysis in which the tendency of the rate of profit to fall leads inevitably to crises and these crises lead inevitably to the overthrow of capitalism. In later texts, there is more emphasis on the counteracting tendencies, and the economic crises that result from the falling rate of profit are not understood as automatically producing full-scale political crises that overturn the entire mode of production. As one commentator puts it, after the *Grundrisse* 'crisis ceases to be understood as an anteroom of the overthrow of capitalism'.[101] Marx even suggests that capitalism can benefit from the economic crises that do occur. As he puts it in *Capital III*: 'Crises are never more than momentary, violent solutions for the existing contradictions, violent eruptions that re-establish the disturbed balance for the time being' (*C3*: 357). The understanding of crisis that can be found in the *Grundrisse* can at least in part be explained by the context within which the notebooks were written: Marx was writing in the midst of a severe global economic crisis that he hoped and maybe even expected heralded the end of capitalism.[102]

Study Questions

1. What is the relation between surplus value and profit?
2. How does the organic composition of capital affect the rate of profit?
3. What is the general rate of profit?
4. Why is there a tendency for the rate of profit to fall and what are the consequences of this tendency?
5. On what basis does Marx criticize Ricardo's theory of profit?

Miscellaneous

If you have been reading the *Grundrisse* as part of a reading group, then it is quite likely that by this stage the group will have disintegrated. If so, you should not worry too much, as the section of the text titled 'Miscellaneous' has far less to offer than the preceding sections. In large part, it consists of quoted material, often with no or minimal commentary from Marx. He also returns to certain topics, for example revisiting the category of money but without adding very much (789–816, 862–82).

Partly because it contains relatively little of interest, and partly for reasons of space, we will end our commentary without looking at 'Miscellaneous'. That does not mean that it contains *nothing* of interest. There are some helpful formulations and clarifications (some of which I have already cited in the commentary above). There are also some brief but important comments on credit and interest (842–5, 851–5, 861–2).[103] Finally, the abbreviated essays on 'Value' and 'Bastiat and Carey' are well worth reading. The former ends Notebook VII and was 'to be brought forward', taking us back to the start of Notebook I (881).

CHAPTER FOUR

Reception and Influence

In this chapter we will look at the history of the publication of the *Grundrisse*, the ways in which it has been read and used, and the relevance that it has for us today.[1]

Publication of the text

The *Grundrisse* remained largely unknown for almost a century after it was written. Initially, it made an impact only insofar as its arguments found their way into Marx's published writings: the 'Chapter on Money' was substantially reworked and published in 1859 as *A Contribution to the Critique of Political Economy* and the arguments in *Capital* can, of course, be traced back to the *Grundrisse*.

Of the 1857–8 manuscripts themselves, the 'Introduction' and the essay on Bastiat and Carey were the first sections to be published (by Karl Kautsky in *Die Neue Zeit* – the journal of the German SPD – in 1903 and 1904 respectively). An English translation of the 'Introduction' was published almost immediately afterwards, in 1904. Although Kautsky presumably had knowledge of the other seven notebooks that make up the *Grundrisse*, their 'discovery' was not announced until 1923, in a speech by the director of the Marx–Engels Institute, David Ryazanov.[2] The manuscripts were published in Moscow in two parts in 1939 and 1941, but did not become widely available outside of the Soviet Union until a version was published in Berlin in 1953. This was followed by translations into other languages. In the 1960s and early 1970s, there were partial translations into English, notably a 1964 version of the section on 'Pre-Capitalist Economic Formations', edited and introduced by Hobsbawm (and subsequently translated into a number of languages), a 1972 version of the 'Fragment on Machines', and a wide selection of short extracts, edited and introduced by David McLellan, which appeared in 1971. Two years later, the entire text was translated into English for the first time, with an alternative translation appearing in the Marx–Engels *Collected Works* in 1986–7.

The posthumous publication of the *Grundrisse* does not in itself make it unusual. Many of Marx's most influential texts were not published until after his death. *Capital II* and *III* were edited and published by Engels in 1885 and 1894 and the writings known as the *1844 Manuscripts* and *The German Ideology* were not published until 1932. The complete edition of the works of Marx and Engels remains a work-in-progress and our understanding of Marx and his theoretical contribution continues to change as previously unknown manuscripts are published and translated.[3] Nonetheless, the *Grundrisse* holds a singular place: not widely read or discussed until the 1960s, it appeared much later than Marx's other major works, and was not read by any of the central figures of twentieth-century classical Marxism, such as Lenin, Trotsky and Luxemburg. Although there are other manuscripts of Marx yet to be published, it is highly unlikely that any of them will have as significant an impact as the *Grundrisse*, and the reception of the latter has been unique.

Interpretations and uses

The *Grundrisse* has inspired various debates, focused not only on its content but also on the place of the manuscripts within Marx's work as a whole. One of its first and still most insightful readers was Roman Rosdolsky, whose book *The Making of Marx's 'Capital'* (originally published in 1968) remains a classic. As its title suggests, Rosdolsky's book argues that we should read the *Grundrisse* as a rough draft for *Capital*. Accordingly, the primary importance of the former lies in what it can tell us about Marx's *method*, and in particular the relation of that method to Hegel: 'the *Rough Draft* must be designated as a massive reference to Hegel, in particular to his *Logic*'.[4]

As noted in Chapter 1, the nature of the relation between Hegel and Marx is closely linked to questions about the relation between the early and later writings of Marx. In the mid-twentieth century these questions took on a special political significance: the discovery of the *1844 Manuscripts* brought to light a Hegelian, humanist Marx whose focus on the alienation of man was contrasted with and used to combat the economistic and deterministic Marx of Stalinism. Others – notably Althusser – acknowledged that the young Marx was humanist but claimed that there was an 'epistemological break' around 1845, when Marx abandoned his pre-scientific humanism and developed historical materialism as the science of history.[5]

For some, Althusser's thesis is, in effect, disproved by the *Grundrisse*, which they argue bridges Marx's early and late works and is as Hegelian as the *1844 Manuscripts*. (It is certainly noticeable that Althusser almost never mentions the *Grundrisse*, with the exception of its 'Introduction': see below.) Thus, for example, McLellan claims that 'Marx's thought is best viewed as a continuing meditation on central themes broached in 1844', with the *Grundrisse* as the 'centrepiece' of Marx's project.[6] While Rosdolsky focuses on the Hegelianism of Marx's method, McLellan finds a continuity in Marx's use of Hegelian themes and concepts, arguing in particular that alienation is as central to the *Grundrisse* as it is to the early works (a claim which arguably disregards the very different uses of the notion of alienation in different texts).[7]

An alternative and highly influential interpretation has been offered by the Italian Marxist Antonio Negri in his book *Marx Beyond Marx*, based on seminars that Negri gave at the École Normale Supérieure in Paris in 1978, at the invitation of Althusser. Like McLellan, Negri argues that the *Grundrisse* is at the centre of Marx's *oeuvre*, representing 'the summit of Marx's revolutionary thought'. For Negri, however, this is not because the *Grundrisse* reveals the continuity of Marx's philosophical preoccupations, but because it 'present[s] Marx as a whole': while *Capital* too easily lends itself to a restrictive deterministic reading, the *Grundrisse* gives us the *political* Marx, focused on the development of revolutionary subjectivity in response to crisis. As such – and in explicit opposition to Rosdolsky – Negri argues that rather than viewing it merely as a draft of *Capital*, we must on the contrary 'reconquer a correct reading of *Capital*' by subjecting 'it to the critique of the *Grundrisse*'.[8]

Negri's reading of the text – with its emphasis on the subjective agency of labour – reflects the concerns of autonomist Marxism, a movement in which he has played a leading role. Though they have produced diverse analyses of contemporary capitalism, one thing that tends to connect autonomist Marxists is their citation of the *Grundrisse* as a key text. In particular, they have been drawn to the notion of living labour, as a capacity on which capital necessarily depends yet which is antagonistic to capital.

Also central to autonomist analyses is the concept, taken from the *Grundrisse*'s 'Fragment on machines', of the 'general intellect', which Negri and his co-author Michael Hardt define as 'a collective, social intelligence created by accumulated knowledges, techniques, and knowhow'.[9] We have seen that Marx used this concept to highlight the increasing dependence of production on scientific knowledge that is a product of collective labour but is incarnated in fixed capital. Autonomists such as Paolo Virno have taken Marx's analysis further by modifying it in a couple of ways. First, it is argued that Marx underestimated the extent to which the general intellect would develop within capitalism: in our post-Fordist era 'the tendency described by Marx is actually fully realised but surprisingly with no revolutionary or even conflictual repercussions'.[10] Increasing dependence on the general intellect has undermined the law of value, but without coinciding with the dissolution of capitalism (as Marx had anticipated). As such, exploitation can no longer be understood as the extraction of surplus value through surplus labour but instead as '*the expropriation of the common* [...] Exploitation is the private appropriation of part or all of the value that has been produced as common.'[11] The typical example here is of open source or peer-to-peer software that is created collectively by unwaged amateurs and then appropriated by capital and transformed into profitable applications. Second, Marx overstates the extent to which the general intellect is objectified in fixed capital and 'thus neglects the way in which the general intellect manifests itself as living labour'.[12] In other words, we should focus not just on machines and technology but on 'the human activity required to create, support and enable this technoscientific apparatus'.[13] Because (it is argued) there has been a blurring of the line between labour and non-labour, '[w]hat is learned, carried out and consumed in the time outside of labour is then utilised in the production of commodities, becomes a part of the use value of labour power and is computed as profitable resource'.[14] Thus, the labouring subject, rather than fixed capital, becomes the repository of the general intellect. That blurring of labour and non-labour is, in turn, partly a consequence of the increasing hegemony of so-called 'immaterial labour', i.e. labour that produces not material goods but rather immaterial goods such as knowledge, emotions, and affects. This concept of immaterial labour has become very important in recent years, generating numerous debates as to its coherence, validity and applicability; ultimately it can be traced back to the autonomists' innovative reading of the *Grundrisse*.

As can be seen, rather than simply reading the *Grundrisse*, Negri and others linked to autonomist Marxism have undertaken what we might call a performative interpretation, reworking and applying its concepts and arguments. They have justified this inventive approach by reference to the *Grundrisse* itself. Hardt and Negri, for example, argue that the 'Introduction' demonstrates that Marx rejects all 'transhistorical theoretical frameworks' and instead embraces the view 'that our mode of understanding must be fitted to the contemporary social world and thus change along with history: the method and the substance, the form and the content must correspond'. As such, we can only be faithful to Marx by going beyond Marx to 'develop on the basis of his method a new theoretical apparatus adequate to our own present situation': hence the need for new concepts such as immaterial labour.[15] A similar argument is made by Moishe Postone, whose work has much in common with that of autonomist Marxism, not least in its favouring of the *Grundrisse* over *Capital*. Postone argues that 'Marx's emphasis on the historical specificity of the object of investigation' entails a 'historical relativization of thought'.[16] As evidence, Postone cites Marx's claim that 'even the most abstract categories' are 'a product of historic relations, and possess their full validity only for and within these relations'. We should remember, however, that in making this claim Marx is asserting the validity of certain categories 'for all epochs' (see 'Method of political economy' in Chapter 3) (105). In addition, the danger of interpreting Marx in terms of a historical relativization of thought is that it becomes circular: granted that theory must change if the object of investigation changes, how can that object and its changes be defined and recognized in the first place except through theory?

Equally, of course, we can ask the converse question: from where can the categories of theory come except from the empirical study of history? This question has been put to Althusser, who has used the 'Introduction' precisely to resist the historical relativization of thought. According to Althusser, to claim that our theoretical categories must change because history itself changes is entirely to misunderstand the 'Introduction', whose central value is precisely its distinction between the real object and the object of knowledge, or the real concrete and the concrete in thought. 'The whole misunderstanding in this reasoning lies in fact in the fallacy which confuses the theoretical development of concepts with the genesis of real history'. Althusser's Marx is thus totally opposed to those forms of historicism which advocate 'the reduction of all knowledge to the historical social relations'.[17]

Althusser uses the 'Introduction' to reinforce his separation of the Marxist dialectic from the Hegelian dialectic, developing a Marx who is as much an enemy of Hegelian historicism as of the empiricism and 'eternalism' of political economy. Drawing on Marx's claim that the order of categories must be determined by their relation in bourgeois society rather than by their historical sequence, Althusser insists that the investigation of the structure of bourgeois society is 'absolutely distinct' from the historical investigation of the transition from one mode of production to the next: what Marx studies is 'the *contemporary structure of society*, without its genesis intervening in any way whatsoever'.[18]

Althusser has been criticized for his 'structuralist' bracketing of history. In a penetrating analysis of the 'Introduction', the cultural theorist Stuart Hall has suggested that while it is true that Marx carefully demarcates the logics of theory and history, rejecting the evolutionary historicism that sees thought and history progressing in tandem, nonetheless he 'clearly is sometimes unrepentantly concerned, precisely, with the most delicate reconstruction of the *genesis* of certain key categories and relations of bourgeois society'. Hence 'it cannot seriously be maintained for long that [...] Marx wholly relinquishes the "historical" method for an essentially synchronic, structuralist one'. Hall thus argues that Marx has a 'historical – not "historicist" – epistemology'.[19]

The 'Introduction' is one of the few places in which Marx explicitly discusses questions of method and has thus been central to Marxist debates concerning both epistemology and the study of history. The condensed nature of this section's arguments means that it is open to a variety of conflicting interpretations – as the French historian Pierre Vilar notes, 'everyone takes [from it] what suits him, unfortunately'.[20] The *Grundrisse* has also been of special interest to historians for its section on 'Forms which precede capitalist production': after the 'Fragment on machines' and the 'Introduction', this is probably the most influential and widely cited part of the manuscripts. Marx's discussion of pre-capitalist modes of production has also been taken up by anthropologists, especially those within the French tradition of Marxist anthropology represented by figures like Maurice Godelier.

Of particular interest to a range of scholars has been the notion of the Asiatic mode of production, which has proved a source of controversy for a number of reasons. On the one hand, it has been used to challenge unilinear and Eurocentric conceptions of history, helping to show that there is more than one path to capitalism (and beyond to communism). On the other hand, it has come under suspicion both for subsuming an enormously diverse range of societies under one concept and for its potentially Orientalist connotations, specifically the implication that non-Western societies are of relevance only insofar as they can help us understand the development of European capitalism. Marx's depiction of Asiatic societies as stationary, despotic and backward might also be used to justify imperialism, with the latter presented as a progressive force, undermining the Asiatic mode of production and facilitating social and economic development. This is an argument which Marx himself seems to have supported in some writings.[21] Challenged on both empirical and theoretical grounds, many commentators have concurred with Perry Anderson's conclusion that the category of the Asiatic mode of production 'be given the decent burial that it deserves'.[22]

Geographers have also found the *Grundrisse* a valuable resource, for two reasons in particular. First, we saw that Marx has much to say about space (and its annihilation by time). Marxist geography was more or less invented by David Harvey, whose detailed reconstruction of Marx's economic theory in *The Limits to Capital* draws heavily on the *Grundrisse*. Second, geographers have taken inspiration from the *Grundrisse*'s ruminations on nature. Alfred Schmidt's *The Concept of Nature in Marx*, published in 1962, was one of the first studies of Marx to make use of the *Grundrisse*, which Schmidt claims 'contain[s] without a doubt Marx's most philosophically significant statements', representing 'the connecting link between the Paris Manuscripts and the fully-formed materialist economics of the mature Marx'.[23]

The *Grundrisse* today

Some commentators have played down the significance of the *Grundrisse*. For example, the economic historian Keith Tribe has called it 'a transitional and incomplete work' and 'an *incoherent* text' whose 'principal feature [...] is its unrelenting repetition and tedium'.[24] There is some truth to these claims – as anyone who has read the *Grundrisse* will recognize – but they also diminish the excitement that certain passages of the *Grundrisse* can inspire and which have made it one of Marx's most influential texts. Even if it could be shown that Marx definitively refuted or revised every claim made in the *Grundrisse*, the very fact that so many key figures in late twentieth- and twenty-first-century Marxism and beyond have made use of the *Grundrisse* means that we must consider it a central text of Marx's thought.

What, though, can the *Grundrisse* tell us today? Beyond its methodological and Marxological interest, in my view, there are four areas in particular that have contemporary resonance:

1 The *Grundrisse*'s comments on the tendency of capital to create a world market, its overcoming of barriers and its civilizing influence provide fruitful resources for analysing what gets called 'globalization', as well as for challenging certain elements of the 'anti-globalization' movement: on the evidence of the *Grundrisse*, at least, Marx would have no time for those who protest that globalization sweeps away local customs and traditions. To the contrary, the danger of the *Grundrisse* is that it lends itself a bit too much to a Eurocentric celebration of capital's progressive nature.

2 The concept of globalization is necessarily tied up with analyses of advances in transportation and communications technology. Notwithstanding the genuine novelty of recent developments in digital technology, the *Grundrisse* – especially the section on circulation and the 'Fragment on machines' – reminds us that these developments cannot be understood outside of an analysis of capitalist relations of production.
3 The flipside of the techno-utopianism that sees new technology as a panacea for the world's ills is the ecological catastrophism that sees civilization threatened by the dangers of overpopulation and environmental degradation. The *Grundrisse* shows us to what extent these 'natural' threats are tied up with the valorization of capital.
4 There is no doubt that the nature and distribution of labour have changed in recent decades, with service sector work now dominating in North America and Western Europe. Marx's division between productive and unproductive labour gives us a way to understand and analyse these changes (and in a way that is not necessarily compatible with the concept of 'immaterial labour' advocated by some Marxists).

There is some irony in the fact that it is precisely these four developments – globalization, new technologies, environmental and population pressures, and the changing nature of labour – that are cited by some as reasons for declaring the obsolescence of Marxism. While all of these themes are examined elsewhere in Marx's work, the discussions of them in the *Grundrisse* are especially striking, revealing or accessible.

Finally, the *Grundrisse* also poses a challenge to us – and not merely a challenge of interpretation. Negri is surely correct when he argues that the *Grundrisse* is one long critique of socialism in the name of communism: it is a revolutionary text that calls on us not just to understand or even reform capitalism, but to overthrow it.[25] What, however, can we do with such a text, at a time when mainstream opinion recoils from even modest social-democratic reforms? Yet perhaps this is the first strength of the *Grundrisse*: to remind us that capital is not 'a general, eternal relation of nature' (86).

CHAPTER FIVE

Further Reading

The definitive version of the *Grundrisse* (in German, of course) is that published in the *MEGA* (Marx 1976–81), which is also available online on the website of the Berlin–Brandenburg Academy of Sciences and Humanities (http://mega.bbaw.de/megadigital). It is on this version that the English translation in the *Collected Works* is based (Marx 1986–7). The Penguin edition, translated by Martin Nicolaus (Marx 1973), is based on the 1953 Berlin edition (Marx 1953), and is available online at the Marxists Internet Archive. The 'Introduction' (Marx 1975) and 'Forms which precede capitalist production' (Marx 1964) have been published separately, with helpful commentaries by the editors; McLellan has also edited a selection of extracts, with a short introduction that places the work in its textual and biographical context (Marx 1971). Christopher Arthur (2006) has written a useful guide to the different versions of the *Grundrisse* in English and their relative merits. For criticisms of the 'Foreword' to the Penguin edition (Nicolaus 1973), see Postone and Reinicke (1974–5) and Marquit (1977).

As background reading, Fine and Saad-Filho (2012), Eatwell et al. (1990) and Bottomore (1991), which includes a short entry by McLellan on the *Grundrisse*, are useful reference works on Marx and Marxism.

For the personal, political and intellectual context of the writing of the *Grundrisse*, Musto (2010) is very helpful. The essays by Krätke in Musto (2008) look at Marx's response to the 1857 crisis, while Calomiris and Schweikart (1991) examine the crisis itself and its American origins. On the influence of Hegel on the *Grundrisse*, see Mann (2008), the books by Uchida (1988) and Meaney (2002), and (on the influence of Hegel on Marx's work more generally) the essays in Moseley and Smith (2014). As for Hegel himself, while I do not accept that reading the *Science of Logic* (Hegel 2010) is absolutely necessary for understanding the *Grundrisse*, it can nonetheless be illuminating. What is sometimes known as the *Minor Logic* (Hegel 1975) is slightly more accessible, if only because it is shorter than the *Science of Logic* (or the '*Major Logic*'). Houlgate (2006) is a reliable guide to Hegel.

Callinicos (2014) looks at the influence of both Hegel and Ricardo on Marx: his book is on *Capital* but also has much to say about the *Grundrisse*. Milonakis and Fine (2009) place Marx's work within the history of political economy; Vygodski (1974), Mandel (1971) and Oakley (1984–5) place the *Grundrisse* within the development of Marx's economic theory.

There are not many books in English specifically on the *Grundrisse*. The most important is Rosdolsky's (1977), which acts as both a commentary on the *Grundrisse* and an attempt to put it to work in a wider analysis of Marx's mature economic theory. An incomplete work, it relies heavily on quoted extracts, but it is nonetheless an exceptional work of scholarship and a major contribution to the study of Marx, and essential reading for anyone who wants seriously to study the *Grundrisse*. A critique of Rosdolsky's interpretation is given by Mepham (1978).

The other major interpretation of the *Grundrisse* is that offered by Negri (1991): innovative, insightful and influential, it is also almost unreadable in places, especially if you are not already familiar with Negri's work and its context. A good place to start is Murphy and Mustapha (2005), especially the essay by Dyer-Witheford. The works that Negri co-authored with Michael Hardt are more accessible: *Empire* (Hardt and Negri 2000) uses the concept of the 'general intellect'; *Multitude* (Hardt and Negri 2004) has a brief methodological excursus based on the *Grundrisse*'s 'Introduction'. The broader use of the concept of the general intellect in autonomist Marxism is discussed in Chapter 9 of Dyer-Witheford (1999), while important studies include Vercellone (2007) and Virno (2007). Mason (2015) gives a popularizing update of autonomist ideas that also acts as an accessible introduction to the 'Fragment on machines'. The essay by Smith in Bellofiore et al. (2013) offers a critique of the autonomist position; the essay by Heinrich in the same volume provides a sober assessment of the 'Fragment on machines'.

Bellofiore et al. (2013) is one of two edited collections of essays dedicated to the *Grundrisse*: of the two, it is probably the more advanced, though many of its contributions are reworked versions of essays published elsewhere. The other collection is edited by Musto (2008) and has sections on the major themes of the *Grundrisse*, the context in which it was written and its reception and dissemination around the world; it is an invaluable resource for any student of the text.

There is a symposium on the *Grundrisse* in a special edition of the Marxist journal *Science & Society*, with essays by Moseley (2011) on surplus value, Starosta (2011) on machines, and Reuten and Thomas (2011) on the falling rate of profit. The critical geography journal *Antipode* also dedicated an issue to the *Grundrisse*: the essay by Sayre (2008) looks at the influence of the text within the disciplines of geography and anthropology. Any overview of Marxist geography must start with David Harvey: in addition to his *Limits to Capital* (2006), his guide to *Capital II* (2013) often cites the *Grundrisse*. Also highly influential is Henri Lefebvre's (1991) *The Production of Space*, which has a methodology that the author claims is inspired by the *Grundrisse*. The most important discussions of Marx and nature are found in Schmidt (1971) and the more recent books by Foster (2000) and Burkett (2014); all three make use of the *Grundrisse*. Schmidt's (1981) methodological discussions in *History and Structure* also cite the *Grundrisse*, especially its 'Introduction'.

The impact of the *Grundrisse* within anthropology can be seen in the collection by Seddon (1978), especially in the essay by Godelier on the Asiatic mode of production. A classic but subsequently much criticized study of the Asiatic mode of production is by Wittfogel (1957). The genealogy and critique of the concept by Anderson (1974) is recommended; an overview of the relevant debates can be found in the comprehensive collection by Bailey and Llobera (1981); Krader (1975) and Lubasz (1984) are also instructive. For the different uses of the *Grundrisse* by historians, see Hobsbawm (1964) and the essay by Wood in Musto (2008), both of which focus on pre-capitalist economic formations. See also Anderson (2010) and the essay by Basso in Bellofiore et al. (2013). Deleuze and Guattari (1977) make highly inventive use of the *Grundrisse*, in particular the section on pre-capitalist economic formations: see especially Part 3 ('Savages, Barbarians, Civilized

Men') of *Anti-Oedipus*. Read (2003) offers a novel reading of Marx which draws on the *Grundrisse*, as well as on Deleuze, Negri and Althusser. Vilar's (1973) thoughtful essay on Marxist history both draws on the 'Introduction' and is critical of Althusser's reading of the same.

The best analysis of the 'Introduction' is by Hall (2003). The essay 'On the Materialist Dialectic' in Althusser (1969) is, in effect, a commentary on the 'Introduction'; much of Althusser's contribution to *Reading Capital* (Althusser and Balibar 1970) is a reading of the 'Introduction'. The readings of the 'Introduction' by Della Volpe (1978) and Colletti (1973, especially Chapter 8) differ from Althusser's interpretation but share its anti-historicist and anti-Hegelian perspective. For an anti-Althusserian reading of the 'Introduction', see Chapter 4 of Sayer (1983). Somewhat against the grain, Echeverria (1978) plays down the significance of the 'Introduction', arguing that it is flawed and should not be used as a guide to reading *Capital*.

There are numerous essays and books on specific Marxian concepts, including on their use in the *Grundrisse*. On the concept of capital in general, see Fineschi (2009), plus his essay in Bellofiore et al. (2013) and the two essays by Arthur in Campbell and Reuten (2002). My own understanding has been influenced by Heinrich (1989); see also the exchange between Heinrich (2013) and Moseley (2013) in *Monthly Review*. Murray, in Bellofiore et al. (2013), looks at the concept of value in the *Grundrisse*; Saad-Filho (2002) is a useful guide to the concept in Marx's work as a whole and the surrounding debates. For a critical but sympathetic and thorough overview of the concept of money in the *Grundrisse*, see Chapter 4 of Nelson (1999). See also Lapatsioras and Milios (2012), with a reply from Sandemose (2013), and the essay by Toporowski in Bellofiore et al. (2013). On the *Grundrisse*'s concept of capital, see Part 3 of Bellofiore et al. (2013). Though it is not focused on the *Grundrisse*, Murray's essay in Moseley and Smith (2014) is helpful for understanding Marx's theory of profit and its relation to Hegel. Hudis (2012) contains a wide-ranging discussion of the *Grundrisse*'s vision of communism. On the *Grundrisse*'s notion of the individual, see Gould (1978) and Chapter 3 of Basso (2012).

Further readings on the *Grundrisse* are listed in the Bibliography. Once you have read the *Grundrisse*, the next step should be to read the three volumes of *Capital*, plus what is perhaps the most important of the other 'rough drafts', the *1861–63 Manuscripts*, found in volumes 30–4 of the *Collected Works* (and from which *Theories of Surplus-Value* was compiled).

NOTES

Chapter 1: Context

1 Vygodski (1974: 44) writes: 'The "Grundrisse" takes us into Marx's "creative laboratory"'. Cf. Rosdolsky (1977: 570), who states that the publication of the *Grundrisse* 'introduced us, as it were, to Marx's economic laboratory'. The phrase is taken up in the title of Bellofiore et al. (2013).

2 Lenin (1967: 66).

3 See Althusser (1969), especially the 'Introduction' and the essay 'On the Young Marx'.

4 Hegel (2010: 81–2).

5 Hegel (2010: 35).

6 Smith (1976: 456).

7 While Marx himself rarely used the word 'capitalism', instead writing of 'bourgeois society' or 'the capitalist mode of production', I use these terms interchangeably (as is common practice today).

8 Marx's main notebooks of this period were first published in 1932 as the *Economic and Philosophic Manuscripts of 1844*, often known simply as the *1844 Manuscripts*.

9 *The German Ideology* is the name given to a lengthy and unfinished set of manuscripts written by Marx and Engels in 1845–6, first published in 1932.

10 Smith (1976: 438).

11 Smith (1976: 51).

12 See Chapter 6 of Smith (1976).

13 Ricardo (1951: 11).

14 Ricardo (1951: 28).

15 Ricardo (1951: 35).

16 Cf. the definition of political economy at the start of Ricardo's

On the Principles of Political Economy and Taxation (1817): 'To determine the laws which regulate this distribution [of rent, profit, and wages – SC], is the principal problem in Political Economy' (Ricardo 1951: 5).

17 See, for example, the mentions of Thomas Hodgskin and William Thompson (416–17, 543–4, 703). Marx's most sustained engagement with the Ricardian socialists is found in his *1861–63 Manuscripts* (*CW*32: 373–449). For the argument that the Ricardian socialists can be counted as forerunners of Marx, see King (1983).

18 See the essays by Krätke in Musto (2008) for a summary and short discussion of these articles and notebooks.

19 Carver (1975b: 27) points out that Marx had experienced or anticipated a crisis almost every year since 1850 (though this is perhaps to underplay the special severity and impact of the 1857 crisis). See also Musto (2010).

20 As we have seen, Marx's study of political economy began in earnest in 1844 and, in 1845, he signed a contract to publish a *Kritik der Politik und Nationalökonomie* (which never materialized) (*CW*4: 675). Hence we could trace the *Grundrisse*, and even *Capital*, all the way back to 1844 – but to see such an unbroken continuity in Marx's economic studies would be to disregard the transformations and breakthroughs in his work, and in particular to underplay the significance of the *Grundrisse* as the start of a new period in his work.

21 Rosdolsky (1977: 10–55) gives a useful account of the changing structure of Marx's critique of political economy. See also the first chapter of Callinicos (2014).

22 Something like this approach is recommended by Cohen (1972) and by Iñigo Carrera in his essay in Bellofiore et al. (2013).

Chapter 2: Overview of themes

1 Hobsbawm (1964: 18).

2 On the *Grundrisse* and gender, see the essay by Wendling in Bellofiore et al. (2013). There is a large literature on Marxism and feminism, which critically examines Marx's views on gender and women: see for example Vogel (2013).

3 Marx offers an extended and very interesting discussion of competition in Notebook VI (649–52, 657–8).

4 Furthermore, there is in the *Grundrisse* a lack of consistency in Marx's definitions of capital in general. For the debates and literature on capital in general, see Chapter 5 in this book.

5 For a defence of Marx's labour theory of value against common criticisms, see Ehrbar and Glick (1986).

6 See the 'Index to the 7 Notebooks', written in June 1858 and found in Notebook M, and the 'References to My Own Notebooks', written in 1861, both published in the *Collected Works* translation (*CW29*: 421–9, 518–32). Neither is published in the Penguin translation, but that edition draws upon them for its 'Analytical Contents List' and its in-text headings.

Chapter 3: Reading the text

1 It was first published in 1903: see Chapter 4.

2 See the useful discussion in Salter (1992).

3 Smith (1976: 25).

4 Cf. the chapter on 'The syllogism' in Hegel's *Science of Logic*: 'The concept, when partitioned into its abstract moments, has *singularity* and *universality* [or generality – SC] for its extremes, and itself appears as the *particularity* that stands between them' (Hegel 2010: 590).

5 Hegel (1975: 121).

6 Later in the *Gundrisse* we read: 'The greater the extent to which historic needs – needs created by production itself, social needs – needs which are themselves the offspring of social production and intercourse, are posited as *necessary*, the higher the level to which real wealth has become developed' (527).

7 For an overview of this type of criticism and a defence of Marx, see Cahan (1994).

8 Cf. Carver (1975a: 151).

9 See for example Baudrillard (1975: 49): 'There is *neither a mode of production nor production* in primitive societies [...] These concepts analyse only our own societies, which are ruled by political economy'.

10 Cf. Harvey (2013: 23).

11 Note that Marx does not claim that this way of thinking – the ascent from the abstract to the concrete – is the only way of

appropriating the world: he also mentions 'the artistic, religious, practical and mental appropriation of this world' as alternatives, though he does no more than mention them (101).

12 Hegel (2010: 384).

13 Althusser (1969: 196–7) goes as far as to state: 'The *Introduction* is no more than a long demonstration of the following thesis: the simple only ever exists within a complex structure; the universal existence of a simple category is never original, it only appears as the end-result of a long historical process, as the product of a highly differentiated social structure.'

14 Smith (1976: 47–51). See also the comparison of mercantilism, physiocracy and Smith in the 'Chapter on Capital' (326–31).

15 The term 'real abstraction' is most associated with the twentieth-century Marxist thinker Alfred Sohn-Rethel (1978), though for Sohn-Rethel the key real abstraction is that of commodity exchange rather than labour.

16 See Chapter 7 of Negri (1991) for one discussion of what might have been included in the Book on Wage Labour.

17 Badiou (2011: 23).

18 'Of course the method of presentation must differ in form from that of inquiry. The latter has to appropriate the material in detail, to analyse its different forms of development and to track down their inner connection. Only after this work has been done can the real movement be appropriately presented' (*C1*: 102).

19 Negri (1991: 23, 39) argues that there are specific theoretical and practical advantages of beginning with money: 'Money has the advantage of presenting me immediately the lurid face of the social relation of value; it shows me value right away as exchange, commanded and organized for exploitation.' In contrast, beginning with the commodity (as in *Capital I*) 'is a more idealist, Hegelian method', bringing only 'abstraction and confusion'.

20 Hence the claim that commodities are sold at their value is only an initial assumption. As Marx writes later in the *Grundrisse*: 'All of these fixed suppositions themselves become fluid in the further course of development. But only by holding them fast at the beginning is their development possible without confounding everything' (817).

21 For a critical discussion of the relationship between value and price in the *Grundrisse*, see Nelson (1999: 65–9).

22 See Rosdolsky (1977: 114–18) for a discussion of the relation between logic and history in the *Grundrisse*.

23 See especially Section 1 of Chapter 1 of *Capital I*.

24 As Marx explains in a letter of 1868: the aggregate labour of any society must be distributed in specific proportions to meet the needs of that society. 'And the form in which this proportional distribution of labour asserts itself in a state of society in which the interconnection of social labour expresses itself as the *private exchange* of the individual products of labour' – i.e. in a capitalist society, in which production is privately rather than communally organized – 'is precisely the *exchange value* of these products' (*CW43*: 68).

25 Marx's argument in this section is made more succinctly and clearly in *A Contribution to a Critique of Political Economy*, in a critique of the Ricardian socialist John Gray: 'Commodities are the direct products of isolated independent individual kinds of labour, and through their alienation in the course of individual exchange they must prove that they are general social labour, in other words, on the basis of commodity production, labour becomes social labour only as a result of the universal alienation of individual kinds of labour. But as Gray presupposes that the labour time contained in commodities is *immediately social* labour time, he presupposes that it is communal labour time or labour time of directly associated individuals. In that case, it would indeed be impossible for a specific commodity, such as gold or silver, to confront other commodities as the incarnation of universal labour and exchange value would not be turned into price; but neither would use value be turned into exchange value and the product into a commodity, and thus the very basis of bourgeois production would be abolished. But this is by no means what Gray had in mind – *goods are to be produced as commodities but not exchanged as commodities*' (*CW29*: 321–2). In *Capital I*, the labour money theorists are dismissed simply in a footnote (*C1*: 161 n.26).

26 RentAFriend.com offers friends for hire for as little as US $10 an hour.

27 Bhaskar (1991: 147).

28 In his interpretation of these passages, Negri (1991: 32) places the emphasis on rupture rather than progression: 'this development [towards communism – SC] is struggle, break, creation. In no sense a restoration of an original essence.'

29 In *Capital I*, this movement from the commodity to money is discussed in Section 3 of Chapter 1. Rather than the historical or semi-historical terms of the analysis found in the *Grundrisse*, in this section of *Capital I* we find a conceptual analysis of the four

forms of value, namely the simple, expanded, general and money forms of value (*C1*: 138–63). See also the alternative version at the Marxists Internet Archive (https://www.marxists.org/archive/marx/works/1867-c1/appendix.htm).

30 In *Capital I*, but not explicitly in the *Grundrisse*, Marx distinguishes between money as measure of value and money as standard of price: 'For the standard of price, a certain weight of gold must be fixed as the unit of measurement' (*C1*: 192). Because this unit has been fixed, changes in the value of gold will not alter its function as the standard of price.

31 Since 1971, when the Unites States abandoned the gold standard, money has not been tied to a particular commodity. This does not invalidate Marx's theory of money, but it does at least call for its modification. See the essay by Caffentzis in van der Linden and Roth (2014) for a discussion.

32 Later, in Notebook VII, Marx provides a lengthy critique of those economists who believed that money is purely an 'ideal measure' in the sense that it is an imaginary and arbitrary value that need not be materialized in a specific substance (789–805).

33 Or as Marx puts it in *Capital I*, there is a 'contradiction between the quantitative limitation and the qualitative lack of limitation of money' (231). Cf. the distinction between quantitative and qualitative limit in Hegel (1975: 136; 2010: 153).

34 Uchida (1988: 152–3 n.1) argues convincingly that the editors have wrongly included this section (pp. 239–50 in the Penguin edition) in the 'Chapter on Capital' when it should in fact go in the 'Chapter on Money'.

35 As Negri (1991: 83) puts it, 'there is no value without exploitation'.

36 Cf. Ricardo (1951: 95): 'Capital is that part of the wealth of a country which is employed in production, and consists of food, clothing, tools, raw materials, machinery, etc. necessary to give effect to labour.'

37 Ricardo (1951: 22–3) does indeed call 'capital' the weapon that a hunter uses to kill a beaver or a deer.

38 See also the discussion of merchant wealth in Notebook VII (856–61).

39 See the essay by Campbell in Bellofiore et al. (2013) for a discussion of this point.

40 See also: '[I]n simple exchange or barter [...] where exchange takes place only for the reciprocal use of the commodity, the use value, i.e.

the content, the natural particularity of the commodity has as such no standing as an economic form' (267). This is the case not only in barter, but also in the simple exchanges that take place in capitalist society, 'the petty commerce' whose aim is 'the satisfaction of individual needs': 'The *content* of these purchases, like their *extent*, here appears as completely irrelevant compared with the formal aspect' (251).

41 The use of labour-power within the capitalist production process is the most important, but not the only, case of use value as an economic category: see Chapter 3 of Rosdolsky (1977) for a helpful discussion.

42 See the essay on abstract labour by Arthur in Bellofiore et al. (2013) for a further discussion.

43 See also the later critique of Malthus' notion that the value of a commodity represents the labour put into it with the addition of profits: 'This can only affect the distribution of the total profit, for if everyone obtained for his commodity the labour worked up in it + profits, then where would these latter come from, Mr Malthus? If one person obtains the labour worked up in his commodity + profit, then the other has to obtain labour worked up – profit' (599).

44 See especially Chapter 1 of *Capital II*.

45 As Engels put it, writing in 1891: 'If labour is the measure of all values, then indeed we can express "the value of labour" only in labour. But we know absolutely nothing about the value of an hour of labour, if we only know that it is equal to an hour of labour' (*CW*27: 196).

46 As Marx puts it in *A Contribution to the Critique of Political Economy*: 'how does production on the basis of exchange value solely determined by labour time lead to the result that the exchange value of labour is less than the exchange value of its product?' (*CW*29: 302).

47 See *Capital I*, Chapter 10 'The Working Day'.

48 The distinction between *Grenze* (limit, boundary, frontier) and *Schranke* (limitation, barrier, restriction) is adopted from Hegel (2010: 98–108). See also Hegel (1975: 136–7) and the explanation by Houlgate (2006: 356–93).

49 Negri (1991: 101) emphasizes that 'the devaluation of labour power [...] not only is not indefinite, but is, on the contrary, limited and reversible'.

50 Smith (1976: 330).

51 Smith (1976: 330).

52 Discussions of productive and unproductive labour can also be found in *Capital I* (*C1*: 1038–49), *Capital II* (*C2*: 207–13), and the *1861–63 Manuscripts* (*CW31*: 7–130).

53 'Hence the worker preserves the values of the already consumed means of production or transfers them to the product as portions of its value, not by virtue of his additional labour as such, but by virtue of the particular useful character of that labour [...] If the specific productive labour of the worker were not spinning [for example – SC], he could not convert the cotton into yarn, and therefore he could not transfer the values of the cotton and spindle to the yarn' (*C1*: 308).

54 See also Chapter 8 of *Capital I* for a clear discussion of constant and variable capital and the preservation of value.

55 These concepts are explained in detail in Chapter 8 of *Capital III*.

56 In *Capital I* this is discussed in Section 2 of Chapter 25 'The General Law of Capitalist Accumulation'.

57 For Heinrich (1989), it is these two topics in particular that stretch the distinction between capital in general and competition to breaking point.

58 See the chapter on 'Accumulation by Dispossession' in Harvey (2003).

59 In addition, there are further reasons why the notion of primitive accumulation can be used for the analysis of present-day societies: there are some societies that are still making the transition to capitalism (hence, for example, the eviction of peasant farmers in China); even in advanced capitalist nations workers have through class struggles won access to the means of subsistence (e.g. free healthcare) from which they can still be separated; and we can adapt Marx's schema in order to analyse 'extra-economic accumulation', i.e. forms of accumulation which take place outside of the capital–labour exchange.

60 In the Preface to *Capital I* Marx writes of 'the passive survival of archaic and outmoded modes of production' within capitalism, 'with their accompanying train of anachronistic social and political relations' (*C1*: 91).

61 See for example Book I, Chapter 10, Part 2 of Smith (1976).

62 See for example Anderson (2010), especially Chapter 5.

63 See Hobsbawm (1964: 20–7) on Marx's sources. See also the essay by Wood in Musto (2008)

64 On the reception and interpretation of the controversial category of the Asiatic mode of production, see Chapters 4 and 5.

65 In our own time this same question has been anachronistically revived by republican and 'communitarian' thinkers: see e.g. Sandel (1996).

66 See for example Lyotard (1993: 127–54).

67 See for example the references to 'inorganic nature' in Hegel (1970).

68 See for example 'First Draft of the Letter to Vera Zasulich', written in 1881, in which Marx claims that the Russian rural commune 'may gradually detach itself from its primitive features and develop directly as an element of collective production on a nationwide scale', hence becoming 'a *direct point of departure* for the economic system toward which modern society tends', i.e. communism (*CW24*: 349, 354). This letter and its drafts are often used as evidence of Marx's commitment to a multilinear theory of history, though the final phrase quoted here nonetheless has teleological or inevitablist overtones.

69 For example, a law introduced under Henry VIII in the sixteenth century stipulated that for a second offence of vagabondage the offender was to be whipped and have half his ear cut off. A third offence would result in death. Marx comments: 'Thus were the agricultural folk first forcibly expropriated from the soil, driven from their homes, turned into vagabonds, and then whipped, branded and tortured by grotesquely terroristic laws into accepting the discipline necessary for the system of wage-labour' (*C1*: 899). The analysis in *Capital I* is anticipated in a brief passage in the *Grundrisse* in which Marx mentions the methods of expropriation – from 'dissolution of the monastic orders' to 'enclosures of commons' – and touches on the 'coercive measures employed to transform the mass of the population, after they had become propertyless and free, into free wage labourers' (769).

70 See also the insightful commentary in the essay by Wood in Musto (2008).

71 The distinction between formal and real subsumption is laid out clearly in *Capital I* (*C1*: 1019–38).

72 Manufacture and large-scale industry are discussed in detail in Part IV of *Capital I*.

73 Malthus (1996: 14).

74 The development of a relative surplus population is dealt with in more detail and in a slightly different way in Sections 3 and 4 of

Chapter 25 of *Capital I*, where the development of an ever greater 'industrial reserve army' in proportion to the development of capital is termed '*the absolute general law of capitalist accumulation*' (*C1*: 798).

75 Smith (1976: 47–51).

76 See Smith (1976: 50).

77 See also the essay by Fetscher in Musto (2008).

78 Commercial capital is discussed in Chapters 16–18 of *Capital III*.

79 Production time is discussed in detail in Chapter 13 of *Capital II*.

80 The clearest discussion of fixed and circulating capital is in Chapter 8 of *Capital II*, though see also Chapters 10 and 11.

81 In *Capital II*, this crude materialism is referred to as a form of 'fetishism [...] which transforms the social, economic character that things are stamped with in the process of social production into a natural character arising from the material nature of these things' (*C2*: 303).

82 In the *Grundrisse*, Marx states that houses 'are circulating capital for the building-trade', which is incorrect given that for the building trade the house is the finished product, not an element used within the production process (723).

83 Similarly, in *Capital II* Marx states: 'Assuming that all other circumstances remain the same, the degree of fixedness grows with the durability of the means of labour' (*C2*: 240).

84 See Chapter 8 of *Capital III*: 'As far as concerns the proportion in which the capital is composed of fixed and circulating elements, this does not in any way affect the profit rate, taken by itself. It can only affect it either if this differing composition coincides with a differing ratio between the variable and constant proportions, in which case the variation in the rate of profit is due to this difference and not to the different ratio between circulating and fixed; or alternatively if the varying ratio between fixed and circulating components involves a variation in the turnover time that it takes to realize a certain profit' (*C3*: 250–1).

85 Though as Marx points out, because fixed capital is necessarily confined within a specific use value, we can also say that it is not the most adequate form of capital, because capital as value is indifferent to all use value: from this perspective, 'it is *circulating capital* which appears as the adequate form of capital' (694).

86 The enigmatic concept of 'the general intellect' has been highly influential; we shall return to it in Chapter 4.

87 See the analysis by Heinrich in his chapter in Bellofiore et al. (2013), upon which the following draws.

88 For an accessible overview, see Lanchester (2015).

89 Cf. Tomba (2013: 361): 'For instance, computers have not freed up time but instead have broadened labour-time, so that it invades the private sphere too. Thus one must not look back romantically to a pre-capitalist past, nor defend the development of the means of production as representatives of liberation.'

90 See in particular *The Poverty of Philosophy*: 'In acquiring new productive forces men change their mode of production; and in changing their mode of production, in changing the way of earning their living, they change all their social relations. The hand-mill gives you society with the feudal lord; the steam-mill, society with the industrial capitalist' (*CW6*: 166). Probably the best-known defence of Marx as a technological determinist is Cohen (2000).

91 See in particular Chapter 9 of *Capital III*.

92 See instead *Capital III*, especially Parts IV–VI.

93 For alternative responses to the transformation problem, see Chapter 10 of Fine and Saad-Filho (2010) and Chapters 8 and 9 of Kliman (2007).

94 See also Marx's discussions of theories of surplus value earlier in the *Grundrisse* (549–602).

95 This exact phrase is not used in the *Grundrisse*, but the theory itself is present there.

96 Smith (1976: 105, 144–5, 352–3).

97 See Chapter XXI of Ricardo (1951).

98 See especially Chapter VI of Ricardo (1951). Marx himself had earlier accepted Ricardo's claim about the relation between wages and profits. In his 1847 lecture on 'Wage Labour and Capital' (first published in 1849), he states: '*The exchange value of capital, profit, rises in the same proportion as the exchange value of labour, wages, falls, and vice versa. Profit rises to the extent that wages fall; it falls to the extent that wages rise*' (*CW9*: 219).

99 Cf. *Capital III*: 'The tendency of the rate of profit to fall is linked with a tendency of the rate of surplus-value to rise, i.e. a tendency for the rate of exploitation to rise. Nothing is more absurd, then, than to explain the fall in the rate of profit in terms of a rise in wage rates [...] The profit rate does not fall because labour becomes less productive but rather because it becomes more productive. The rise in the rate of surplus-value and the fall in the rate of profit are

simply particular forms that express the growing productivity of labour in capitalist terms' (*C3*: 347, *tm*).

100 In Chapter 14 of *Capital III* the counteracting tendencies are identified as: more intense exploitation of labour; reduction of wages below their value; cheapening the elements of constant capital; relative overpopulation; and foreign trade.

101 Tomba (2013: 363).

102 See Reuten and Thomas (2011), who argue that there were also theoretical reasons for the change of emphasis.

103 See also Chapter 27 of Rosdolsky (1977).

Chapter 4: Reception and influence

1 Both in this chapter and the next, I have restricted myself to sources that are available in English. Part III of Musto (2008) offers an account of the global dissemination and reception of the *Grundrisse* which is far more comprehensive than the summary I am able to offer here and is highly recommended. For more detailed references to the authors and texts discussed in this chapter, see Chapter 5 and the Bibliography.

2 Reprinted in German as Ryazanov (1925).

3 The *Marx–Engels Gesamtausgabe* – known as *MEGA*[2] to differentiate it from an original, unfinished complete edition – is projected to contain 114 volumes, more than half of which have now been published.

4 Rosdolsky (1977: xiii).

5 See Althusser (1969), especially the 'Introduction'.

6 McLellan (1971: 12, 3).

7 For convincing critiques of McLellan's claims on alienation, see Cowling (2006) and Cohen (1972). For a similar argument to that of McLellan, see Gould (1978: xiv), who claims that 'the *Grundrisse* constitutes the working out of Marx's early theory of alienation as political economy'.

8 Negri (1991: 18, 8, 19).

9 Hardt and Negri (2000: 364).

10 Virno (2007: 4).

11 Hardt and Negri (2004: 150).

12 Virno (2007: 5).

13 Dyer-Witheford (1999: 222).

14 Virno (2007: 5).

15 Hardt and Negri (2004: 140, 141)

16 Postone (2008: 130). See also Postone (1993).

17 Althusser and Balibar (1970: 114, 139).

18 Althusser and Balibar (1970: 112, 65)

19 Hall (2003: 138, 137).

20 Vilar (1973: 75).

21 See, for example, Marx's 1853 articles on India for the *New York Tribune* (*CW12*: 125–33, 217–22). It is on the basis of these articles that Edward Said (1995: 153–7) condemns Marx for his Orientalism. For a defence of Marx, and a wider discussion of his writings on non-European societies, see Anderson (2010).

22 Anderson (1974: 548).

23 Schmidt (1971: 214 n.43)

24 Tribe (1974: 181).

25 E.g. 'The Marxism of the *Grundrisse* is in effect the contrary of socialism' (Negri 1991: 83).

BIBLIOGRAPHY

Versions of the *Grundrisse*

Marx, Karl (1903), 'Einleitung zu einer Kritik der politischen Ökonomie', *Die Neue Zeit* 21 (1): 710–18, 741–5, 772–81.

Marx, Karl (1904a), 'Carey und Bastiat. Ein Fragment aus dem Nachlass', *Die Neue Zeit* 22 (2): 5–16.

Marx, Karl (1904b), 'Introduction to the Critique of Political Economy', in *A Contribution to the Critique of Political Economy*, trans. N. I. Stone. New York: The International Library Publishing Co.

Marx, Karl (1939–41), *Grundrisse der Kritik der politischen Ökonomie (Rohentwurf), 1857–58*, 2 vols. Moscow: Verlag für fremdsprachige Literatur.

Marx, Karl (1953), *Grundrisse der Kritik der politischen Ökonomie (Rohentwurf), 1857–1858*. Berlin: Dietz Verlag.

Marx, Karl (1964), 'Pre-Capitalist Economic Formations', in *Pre-Capitalist Economic Formations*, ed. E. J. Hobsbawm, trans. Jack Cohen. London: Lawrence & Wishart.

Marx, Karl (1968), 'Introduction to the Critique of Political Economy', in David Horowitz, ed. *Marx and Modern Economics*. London: MacGibbon & Kee.

Marx, Karl (1971), *The Grundrisse*, ed. and trans. David McLellan. New York: Harper & Row.

Marx, Karl (1972), 'Notes on machines', trans. Ben Brewster, *Economy and Society* 1(3): 244–54.

Marx, Karl (1973), *Grundrisse: Foundations of the Critique of Political Economy (Rough Draft)* trans. Martin Nicolaus. London: Penguin.

Marx, Karl (1975), 'The *Introduction* (1857)', in *Texts on Method*, trans. and ed. Terrell Carver. Oxford: Basil Blackwell.

Marx, Karl (1976–81), *Ökonomische Manuskripte 1857/58* in Karl Marx and Friedrich Engels, *Gesamtausgabe (MEGA)*, II 1.1–1.2. Berlin: Dietz Verlag.

Marx, Karl (1986–87), *Economic Manuscripts of 1857–58*, in Karl Marx and Frederick Engels, *Collected Works*, vols. 28–9. London: Lawrence & Wishart.

Other sources

Althusser, Louis (1969), *For Marx*, trans. Ben Brewster. London: Allen Lane.
Althusser, Louis and Étienne Balibar (1970), *Reading Capital*, trans. Ben Brewster. London: NLB.
Anderson, Kevin B. (2010), *Marx at the Margins: On Nationalism, Ethnicity, and Non-Western Societies*. Chicago, IL: The University of Chicago Press.
Anderson, Perry (1974), *Lineages of the Absolutist State*. London: NLB.
Arthur, Christopher J. (2006), 'A Guide to Marx's *Grundrisse* in English', www.chrisarthur.net/grundrisse.doc (last accessed 6 September 2015).
Badiou, Alain (2011), *Second Manifesto for Philosophy*, trans. Louise Burchill. Cambridge: Polity.
Bailey, Anne M. and Josep R. Llobera (eds) (1981), *The Asiatic Mode of Production: Science and Politics*. London: Routledge & Kegan Paul.
Basso, Luca (2012), *Marx and Singularity: From the Early Writings to the* Grundrisse, trans. Arianna Bove. Leiden: Brill.
Baudrillard, Jean (1975), *The Mirror of Production*, trans. Mark Poster. St. Louis, MO: Telos Press.
Bellofiore, Riccardo, Guido Starosta, and Peter D. Thomas (eds) (2013), *In Marx's Laboratory: Critical Interpretations of the* Grundrisse. Leiden: Brill.
Bhaskar, Roy (1991), 'Dialectics', in Bottomore (1991).
Bottomore, Tom (ed.) (1991), *A Dictionary of Marxist Thought*. Oxford: Blackwell.
Brewster, Ben (1972), 'Introduction to Marx's "Notes on machines"', *Economy and Society* 1 (3): 235–43.
Burkett, Paul (2014), *Marx and Nature: A Red and Green Perspective*. Chicago, IL: Haymarket Books.
Cahan, Jean Axelrad (1994), 'The Concept of Property in Marx's Theory of History: A Defense of the Autonomy of the Socioeconomic Base', *Science & Society* 58 (4): 393–414.
Callinicos, Alex (2014), *Deciphering Capital: Marx's Capital and Its Destiny*. London: Bookmarks.
Calomiris, Charles W. and Larry Schweikart (1991), 'The Panic of 1857: Origins, Transmission, and Containment', *The Journal of Economic History* 51 (4): 807–34.

Campbell, Martha and Geert Reuten (eds) (2002), *The Culmination of Capital: Essays on Volume III of Marx's* Capital. Basingstoke: Palgrave.

Carver, Terrell (1975a), 'A Commentary on the Text', in Karl Marx *Texts on Method*, trans. and ed. Terrell Carver. Oxford: Basil Blackwell.

Carver, Terrell (1975b), 'Editor's Preface', in Karl Marx *Texts on Method*, trans. and ed. Terrell Carver. Oxford: Basil Blackwell.

Cohen, G. A. (1972), 'Thoughts on the *Grundrisse*', *Marxism Today* 16 (12): 372–4.

Cohen, G. A. (2000), *Karl Marx's Theory of History: A Defence*. Oxford: Clarendon Press.

Colletti, Lucio (1973), *Marxism and Hegel*. London: NLB.

Cowling, Mark (2006), 'Alienation in the Older Marx', *Contemporary Political Theory* 5: 319–39.

Deleuze, Gilles and Félix Guattari (1977), *Anti-Oedipus: Capitalism and Schizophrenia*, trans. Robert Hurley, Mark Seem and Helen R. Lane. New York: The Viking Press.

Della Volpe, Galvano (1978), *Rousseau and Marx*, trans. John Fraser. London: Lawrence & Wishart.

Dobb, Maurice (1973), 'Grundrisse', *Marxism Today* 17 (10): 303–6.

Dyer-Witheford, Nick (1999), *Cyber-Marx: Cycles and Circuits of Struggle in High Technology Capitalism*. Urbana, IL: University of Illinois Press.

Eatwell, John, Murray Milgate and Peter Newman (eds) (1990), *The New Palgrave Marxian Economics*. London: Macmillan.

Echeverria, Rafael (1978), 'Critique of Marx's *1857 Introduction*', *Economy and Society* 7 (4): 335–66.

Ehrbar, Hans and Mark Glick (1986), 'The Labor Theory of Value and Its Critics', *Science & Society* 50 (4): 464–78.

Fine, Ben and Alfredo Saad-Filho (2010), *Marx's 'Capital'*. London: Pluto Press.

Fine, Ben and Alfredo Saad-Filho (eds) (2012), *The Elgar Companion to Marxist Economics*. Cheltenham: Edward Elgar.

Fineschi, Roberto (2009), '"Capital in General" and "Competition" in the Making of *Capital*: The German Debate', *Science & Society* 73 (1): 54–76.

Foster, John Bellamy (2000), *Marx's Ecology: Materialism and Nature*. New York: Monthly Review Press.

Gould, Carol C. (1978), *Marx's Social Ontology: Individuality and Community in Marx's Theory of Social Reality*. Cambridge, MA: The MIT Press.

Hall, Stuart (2003), 'Marx's Notes on Method: A "Reading" of the "1857 Introduction"', *Cultural Studies* 17 (2): 113–49.

Hardt, Michael and Antonio Negri (2000), *Empire*. Cambridge, MA: Harvard University Press.

Hardt, Michael and Antonio Negri (2004), *Multitude: War and Democracy in the Age of Empire*. New York: Penguin.

Harvey, David (2003), *The New Imperialism*. Oxford: Oxford University Press.

Harvey, David (2006), *The Limits to Capital*. London: Verso.

Harvey, David (2013), *A Companion to Marx's* Capital *Volume Two*. London: Verso.

Hegel, G. W. F. (1970), *Philosophy of Nature Volume III*, ed. and trans. M. J. Petry. London: George Allen & Unwin Ltd.

Hegel, G. W. F. (1975), *Hegel's Logic, Being Part One of the Encyclopaedia of the Philosophical Sciences*, trans. William Wallace. Oxford: Oxford University Press.

Hegel, G. W. F. (2010), *The Science of Logic*, trans. and ed. George di Giovanni. Cambridge: Cambridge University Press.

Heinrich, Michael (1989), 'Capital in General and the Structure of Marx's *Capital*: New insights from Marx's *Economic Manuscripts of 1861–63*', *Science & Society* 38: 63–79.

Heinrich, Michael (2013), 'Heinrich Answers Critics', *Monthly Review* December 1 http://monthlyreview.org/commentary/heinrich-answers-critics/ (last accessed 27 September 2015).

Hobsbawm, E. J. (1964), 'Introduction', in Karl Marx, *Pre-Capitalist Economic Formations*, ed. E. J. Hobsbawm, trans. Jack Cohen. London: Lawrence & Wishart.

Hobsbawm, Eric (2008), 'The Current Importance of Marx, 150 years after the *Grundrisse*', *ZNet*, 16 September https://zcomm.org/znetarticle/the-current-importance-of-marx-150-years-after-the-grundrisse-by-eric-hobsbawm/ (last accessed 31 August 2015).

Houlgate, Stephen (2006), *The Opening of Hegel's* Logic: *From Being to Infinity*. West Lafayette, IN: Purdue University Press.

Hudis, Peter (2012), *Marx's Concept of the Alternative to Capitalism*. Leiden: Brill.

Kemple, Thomas M. (1995), *Reading Marx Writing: Melodrama, the Market, and the "Grundrisse"*. Stanford, CA: Stanford University Press.

King, J. E. (1983), 'Utopian or Scientific? A Reconsideration of the Ricardian Socialists', *History of Political Economy* 15(3): 345–73.

Kliman, Andrew (2007), *Reclaiming Marx's "Capital": A Refutation of the Myth of Inconsistency*. Lanham, MD: Lexington Books.

Krader, Lawrence (1975), *The Asiatic Mode of Production: Sources,*

Development and Critique in the Writings of Karl Marx. Assen: Van Gorcum & Comp., B.V.

Lanchester, John (2015), 'The Robots Are Coming', *London Review of Books* 37 (5): 3–8

Lapatsioras, Spyros and John Milios (2012), 'The Notion of Money from the *Grundrisse* to *Capital*', *Science & Society* 76 (4): 521–45.

Lefebvre, Henri (1991), *The Production of Space*, trans. Donald Nicholson-Smith. Oxford: Blackwell.

Lenin, V. I. (1967), *Selected Works*, vol. 1. Moscow: Progress Publishers.

Lubasz, Heinz (1984), 'Marx's Concept of the Asiatic Mode of Production: A Genetic Analysis', *Economy and Society* 13 (4): 456–83.

Lyotard, Jean-François (1993), *Libidinal Economy*, trans. Iain Hamilton Grant. London: The Athlone Press.

McLellan, David (1971), 'Introduction', to Marx (1971).

Malthus, Thomas Robert (1996 [1798]), *An Essay on the Principle of Population*, 1st edn London: Routledge.

Mandel, Ernest (1971), *The Formation of the Economic Thought of Karl Marx*, trans. Brian Pearce. New York: Monthly Review Press.

Mann, Geoff (2008), 'A Negative Geography of Necessity', *Antipode* 40 (5): 921–34.

Mann, Geoff and Joel Wainwright (2008), 'Marx Without Guardrails: Geographies of the *Grundrisse*', *Antipode* 40 (5): 848–56.

Marquit, Erwin (1977), 'Nicolaus and Marx's Method of Scientific Theory in the *Grundrisse*', *Science & Society* 41 (4): 465–76.

Mason, Paul (2015), *Postcapitalism: A Guide to Our Future*. London: Allen Lane.

Meaney, Mark E. (2002), *Capital as Organic Unity: The Role of Hegel's* Science of Logic *in Marx's* Grundrisse. Dordrecht: Kluwer Academic Publishers.

Mepham, John (1978), '*The Grundrisse*: Method or Metaphysics?', *Economy and Society* 7 (4): 430–44.

Milonakis, Dimitris and Ben Fine (2009), *From Political Economy to Economics: Method, the Social and the Historical in the Evolution of Economic Theory*. London: Routledge.

Moseley, Fred (2011), 'The Whole and the Parts: The Early Development of Marx's Theory of the Distribution of Surplus-Value in the *Grundrisse*', *Science & Society* 75 (1): 59–74.

Moseley, Fred (2013), 'Critique of Heinrich: Marx did *not* Abandon the Logical Structure', *Monthly Review* December 1 http://monthlyreview.org/commentary/critique-heinrich-marx-abandon-logical-structure/ (last accessed 27 September 2015).

Moseley, Fred (2014), 'The Universal and the Particulars in Hegel's *Logic* and Marx's *Capital*', in Moseley and Smith (2014).

Moseley, Fred and Tony Smith (eds) (2014), *Marx's* Capital *and Hegel's* Logic*: A Reexamination*. Leiden: Brill.

Murphy, Timothy S. and Abdul-Karim Mustapha (eds) (2005), *Resistance in Practice: The Philosophy of Antonio Negri*. London: Pluto.

Musto, Marcello (ed.) (2008), *Karl Marx's* Grundrisse*: Foundations of the Critique of Political Economy 150 Years Later*. London: Routledge.

Musto, Marcello (2010), 'The Formation of Marx's Critique of Political Economy: From the Studies of 1843 to the *Grundrisse*', *Socialism and Democracy* 24 (2): 66–100.

Negri, Antonio (1991), *Marx Beyond Marx: Lessons on the* Grundrisse, trans. Harry Cleaver, Michael Ryan and Maurizio Viano, ed. Jim Fleming. New York: Autonomedia.

Nelson, Anitra (1999), *Marx's Concept of Money: The God of Commodities*. London: Routledge.

Nicolaus, Martin (1968), 'The Unknown Marx', *New Left Review* I/48: 41–61.

Nicolaus, Martin (1973), 'Foreword', to Marx (1973).

Oakley, Allen (1984–85), *Marx's Critique of Political Economy: Intellectual Sources and Evolution*, 2 vols. London: Routledge & Kegan Paul.

Piccone, Paul (1975), 'Reading the Grundrisse: Beyond "Orthodox" Marxism', *Theory and Society* 2 (2): 235–55.

Postone, Moishe (1993), *Time, Labor, and Social Domination: A Reinterpretation of Marx's Critical Theory*. Cambridge: Cambridge University Press.

Postone, Moishe (2008), 'Rethinking *Capital* in the light of the *Grundrisse*', in Musto (2008).

Postone, Moishe and Helmut Reinicke (1974–5), 'On Nicolaus' "Introduction" to the *Grundrisse*', *Telos* 22: 130–48.

Read, Jason (2003), *The Micro-Politics of Capital: Marx and the Prehistory of the Present*. Albany, NY: State University of New York Press.

Reuten, Geert and Peter Thomas (2011), 'From the "Fall of the Rate of Profit" in the *Grundrisse* to the Cyclical Development of the Profit Rate in *Capital*', *Science & Society* 75 (1): 74–90.

Ricardo, David (1951), *On the Principles of Political Economy and Taxation*, ed. Piero Sraffa. Cambridge: Cambridge University Press.

Rosdolsky, Roman (1977), *The Making of Marx's 'Capital'*, trans. Pete Burgess. London: Pluto Press.

Rovatti, Pier Aldo (1973), 'The Critique of Fetishism in Marx's *Grundrisse*', *Telos* 17: 56–69.

Ryazanov, David (1925), 'Neueste Mitteilungen über den literarischen

Nachlaß von Karl Marx und Friedrich Engels', *Archiv für die Geschichte des Sozialismus und der Arbeiterbewegung* 11: 385–400.
Saad-Filho, Alfredo (2002), *The Value of Marx: Political Economy for Contemporary Capitalism*. London: Routledge.
Said, Edward (1995), *Orientalism*. London: Penguin.
Salter, John (1992), 'Adam Smith on Feudalism, Commerce and Slavery', *History of Political Thought* 13 (2): 219–41.
Sandel, Michael J. (1996), *Democracy's Discontent*. Cambridge, MA: Harvard University Press.
Sandemose, Jørgen (2013), '*Grundrisse*, *Capital*, and Marxist Scholarship', *Science & Society* 77 (4): 561–8.
Sayer, Derek (1983), *Marx's Method: Ideology, Science and Critique in* Capital. Brighton: The Harvester Press.
Sayre, Nathan F. (2008), 'Assessing the Effects of the *Grundrisse* in Anglophone Geography and Anthropology', *Antipode* 40 (5): 898–920.
Schmidt, Alfred (1971), *The Concept of Nature in Marx*. London: NLB.
Schmidt, Alfred (1981), *History and Structure: An Essay on Hegelian–Marxist and Structuralist Theories of History*, trans. Jeffrey Herf. Cambridge, MA: The MIT Press.
Seddon, David (ed.) (1978), *Relations of Production: Marxist Approaches to Economic Anthropology*. London: Frank Cass.
Smith, Adam (1976), *An Inquiry into the Nature and Causes of the Wealth of Nations*, 2 vols. Oxford: Clarendon Press.
Sohn-Rethel, Alfred (1978), *Intellectual and Manual Labour: A Critique of Philosophical Epistemology*. London: MacMillan.
Starosta, Guido (2011), 'Machinery, Productive Subjectivity and the Limits to Capitalism in *Capital* and the *Grundrisse*', *Science & Society* 75 (1): 42–58.
Tomba, Massimiliano (2013), 'Accumulation and Time: Marx's historiography from the *Grundrisse* to *Capital*', *Capital & Class* 37 (3): 355–72.
Tribe, Keith (1974), 'Remarks on the theoretical significance of Marx's *Grundrisse*', *Economy and Society* 3 (2): 180–210.
Uchida, Hiroshi (1988), *Marx's* Grundrisse *and Hegel's* Logic. London: Routledge.
Van der Linden, Marcel and Karl Heinz Roth (eds) (2014), *Beyond Marx: Theorising the Global Labour Relations of the Twenty-First Century*. Leiden: Brill.
Vasilyeva, Tatyana (1986–7), 'Preface', to Karl Marx and Frederick Engels, *Collected Works*, vols. 28–9. London: Lawrence & Wishart.
Vercellone, Carlo (2007), 'From Formal Subsumption to General Intellect: Elements for Marxist Reading of the Thesis of Cognitive Capitalism', *Historical Materialism* 15 (1): 13–36

Vilar, Pierre (1973), 'Marxist History, a History in the Making: Towards a Dialogue with Althusser', *New Left Review* I/80: 65–106.
Virno, Paolo (2007), 'General Intellect', *Historical Materialism* 15 (3): 3–8.
Vogel, Lise (2013), *Marxism and the Oppression of Women: Toward a Unitary Theory*. Leiden: Brill.
Vygodski, V. S. (1974), *The Story of a Great Discovery: How Karl Marx Wrote "Capital"*, trans. Christopher S. V. Salt. Tunbridge Wells: Abacus Press.
Wainwright, Joel (2008), 'Uneven Developments: from the *Grundrisse* to *Capital*', *Antipode* 40 (5): 879–97.
Wittfogel, Karl A. (1957), *Oriental Despotism: A Comparative Study of Total Power*. New Haven, CT: Yale University Press.

Online resources

The Berlin–Brandenburg Academy of Sciences and Humanities *MEGA*^{2} Digital Edition.
http://mega.bbaw.de

The International Institute of Social History *MEGA*^{2}
https://socialhistory.org/en/projects/marx-engels-gesamtausgabe

Marxists Internet Archive
https://www.marxists.org

INDEX

www.ingramcontent.com/pod-product-compliance
Lightning Source LLC
Chambersburg PA
CBHW062020270326
41929CB00014B/2265

* 9 7 8 1 4 7 2 5 2 6 7 4 8 *